SNIPER

Random House
New York

SNIPER

Inside the Hunt for the Killers
Who Terrorized the Nation

Sari Horwitz and Michael E. Ruane

With exclusive reporting from the metropolitan staff of
The Washington Post

To those whose lives were lost and to those who were wounded
or terrorized by the events of October 2002

"What a loss; a life taken by an evil or deranged person with access to a deadly rifle. He didn't know the people he shot, but every one of them left behind shattered lives and broken hearts. . . .

"May your memory always be for a blessing, and may your memory inspire us to be a blessing to our own families, to those who love us, and to the whole world."

Rabbi David Saperstein at the funeral
for sniper victim Lori Lewis Rivera

CAST OF CHARACTERS

Suspects

John Allen Muhammad   Lee Boyd Malvo

State and Local Police

MONTGOMERY COUNTY, MARYLAND, POLICE DEPARTMENT

Chief Charles A. Moose, Montgomery County Police Chief
Captain Bernard (Barney) J. Forsythe, Director of the Major Crimes
    Division
Captain Nancy Demme, Police Spokesperson
Commander Drew Tracy, Third District Station
Lieutenant Philip C. Raum, Deputy Director of the Major Crimes Division
Sergeant Nick DeCarlo, Major Crimes Division, Homicide/Sex Section
Sergeant Roger Thomson, Major Crimes Division, Homicide/Sex Section
Corporal Gene Curtis, Major Crimes Division, Homicide/Sex Section
Detective Patrick McNerney, Major Crimes Division, Homicide/Sex
    Section
Detective Terry Ryan, Major Crimes Division, Homicide/Sex Section
Detective Jim Drewry, Major Crimes Division, Homicide/Sex Section
David McGill, Forensic Specialist, Tactical Operations Division, Tactical
    Division
Officer Jeff Nyce, Tactical Operations Division, Tactical Division
Officer Derek Baliles, Public Information Officer
Officer Alan Felsen, Fourth District Station

BALTIMORE CITY POLICE

Officer James Snyder   Officer Deborah Kirk

PRINCE GEORGE'S COUNTY, MARYLAND, POLICE

Chief Gerald M. Wilson
Dr. William Vosburgh, Director of Forensics Lab
Detective Joseph Bergstrom, Criminal Investigation, Homicide Unit

MARYLAND STATE POLICE

Major Thomas Bowers
First Sergeant Keith Runk
Trooper First Class Chris Paschal

Lieutenant David Reichenbaugh
Trooper First Class Rob
Draskovich

METROPOLITAN POLICE DEPARTMENT, WASHINGTON, D.C.

Chief Charles H. Ramsey

Detective Tony Patterson, Major
Crimes Section

FAIRFAX COUNTY, VIRGINIA, POLICE

Chief J. Thomas Manger

Detective June Boyle, Homicide
Division

HANOVER COUNTY, VIRGINIA, POLICE

Sheriff V. Stuart Cook

HENRICO COUNTY, VIRGINIA, POLICE

Chief Henry W. Stanley

PRINCE WILLIAM COUNTY, VIRGINIA, POLICE

Chief Charlie T. Deane

SPOTSYLVANIA COUNTY, VIRGINIA, POLICE

Major Howard Smith

Virginia State Police

Lieutenant Tom Martin

Montgomery, Alabama, Police

Chief John H. Wilson   Sergeant Scott Martino

Federal Agencies

Bureau of Alcohol, Tobacco and Firearms

Michael Bouchard, Special Agent in Charge, Baltimore Field Division
Jim Cavanaugh, Special Agent in Charge, Nashville Field Division
Jeffrey R. Roehm, Special Agent in Charge, Washington Field Division
Joseph M. Riehl, Assistant Special Agent in Charge, Baltimore Field
   Division
Walter A. Dandridge Jr., Chief Ballistics Examiner

Federal Bureau of Investigation

Gary M. Bald, Special Agent in Charge, Baltimore Field Office
Van A. Harp, Assistant Director in Charge, Washington Field Office
Gary Noesner, Unit Chief, Crisis Negotiation Unit
Kevin Lewis, Assistant Special Agent in Charge, Baltimore Field Office
Toni M. Fogle, Assistant Special Agent in Charge, Washington Field
   Office
Vincent Montagnino, Technical Supervisor, Washington Field Office
Brad Garrett, Special Agent, Washington Field Office
Charles B. Pierce, Special Agent, Hostage Rescue Team

U.S. Marshals Service

Johnny L. Hughes, U.S. Marshal for the District of Maryland
Lenny DePaul, Supervisory Inspector, N.Y./N.J. Regional Fugitive Task
   Force

William J. Sorukas Jr., Senior Inspector, Technical Operations Group
Michael P. Moran, Senior Inspector, Technical Operations Group
Tim Hein, Inspector, Technical Operations Group
Kevin Engel, Inspector, N.Y./N.J. Regional Fugitive Task Force

U.S. CAPITOL POLICE

Chief Terrance W. Gainer

Prosecutors

JUSTICE DEPARTMENT

Attorney General John Ashcroft
Deputy Attorney General Larry D. Thompson

U.S. ATTORNEY, DISTRICT OF MARYLAND

Thomas M. DiBiagio, U.S. Attorney
A. David Copperthite, Assistant U.S. Attorney

MONTGOMERY COUNTY STATE'S ATTORNEY'S OFFICE

Douglas F. Gansler, State's Attorney
Katherine Winfree, Deputy State's Attorney
John J. McCarthy, Deputy State's Attorney

COMMONWEALTH ATTORNEY FOR FAIRFAX COUNTY

Robert F. Horan Jr., Commonwealth Attorney

COMMONWEALTH ATTORNEY FOR PRINCE WILLIAM COUNTY

Paul B. Ebert, Commonwealth Attorney
Richard A. Conway, Assistant Commonwealth Attorney
James A. Willett, Assistant Commonwealth Attorney

PREFACE

For three weeks in the fall of 2002, the prospect of sudden death haunted millions of Americans across a stretch of the mid-Atlantic and upper South, from Pennsylvania to the Carolinas. With good reason. Between October 2 and October 22, thirteen people were selected and shot, investigators believe, by two drifters with an old car and a military-style rifle. Ten people died—three of ghastly head wounds, seven from wounds of the back, chest, or stomach. The victims were chosen at random as they were going about the daily chores of life.

During one of the first interviews for this book, an accomplished Maryland prosecutor began to cry when she recalled the terror of just going to work for much of that month. She described the seconds ticking by as she waited for a traffic light to change, the walk from her car to her building, the relief she felt upon reaching the sanctuary of her office each morning. We too were deeply affected by the killings. We lived and worked in the threatened communities. Our children attended schools in the area, in one case within a mile of two of the Maryland shootings. We felt the same fear.

Washington, like New York, was a target of the terrorist attacks of September 11, 2001. In the months that followed, the armed guards, security checks, and fighter jets flying round-the-clock over-

head were constant reminders that the nation's capital and its sur-
rounding suburbs were still under threat. The sniper attacks, less
than thirteen months later, were terrorist acts of another shocking
kind, and no less instructive in revealing the vulnerabilities of a free
society.

In response to the shootings, one of the largest investigations in
the history of American law enforcement was concentrated in the
Washington area. It involved thousands of local and state police; sheriff's deputies; federal agents, marshals, and technicians; state and federal prosecutors; and police departments across the country. This is
the story of that investigation.

By tradition in this country, law enforcement is a local and state
responsibility. But crimes on the scale of the sniper killings demand
a response by every resource at a community's disposal and thus present huge challenges in organization and leadership. The task force
formed to stop the snipers tried to blend local, state, and federal authorities, with the mixed results that perhaps are inevitable in a complex effort made under life-or-death pressure. There were errors in
judgment, missed opportunities, examples of institutional rivalry,
and, at times, chaos. There was also extraordinary camaraderie and
ultimately successful policing based on twenty-first-century technology and old-fashioned hard work and intuition.

In other words, it was an investigation that should serve as both
a model and a warning for dealing with whatever threats the future
may hold.

As reporters for *The Washington Post*, we covered many of the
events as they unfolded in October 2002, reporting on the progress
of the investigation and talking to the devastated families and
friends of some of the victims. Then in December we began our research for this book on what went on behind the scenes. We interviewed investigators and eyewitnesses who had never spoken
publicly and who described their roles in painful and heroic detail.
We examined court transcripts, copies of crucial pieces of evidence,
autopsy reports, and photographs. We interviewed top officials in

the FBI, the Bureau of Alcohol, Tobacco and Firearms, and the Justice Department, as well as detectives and police officers in Maryland, Virginia, and the District of Columbia.

We were provided copies of secret investigative reports and confidential photographs describing the lives and travels of John Muhammad and Lee Boyd Malvo, including the contents of their car and computer. We obtained a revealing summary of a critical part of the six-and-a-half-hour conversation Malvo had with investigators in Virginia after his arrest. We surveyed shooting scenes and visited the suspects' haunts in Washington State. We test-fired the type of rifle believed to have been used in the shootings to prove to ourselves the relative ease with which it is possible to kill someone from a great distance.

We have told the saga of Malvo and Muhammad and their capture as investigators, witnesses, and key participants believe it happened. Those who helped us have done so with a sense of public spirit, a desire for accuracy, and compassion for those whose lives were lost.

Sari Horwitz
Michael E. Ruane
Washington, D.C.
July 2003

CONTENTS

Trail of the Sniper

*The crimes—and victims—that have been linked
to John Muhammad and Lee Boyd Malvo*

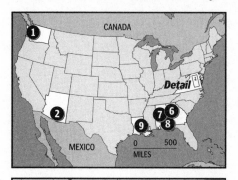

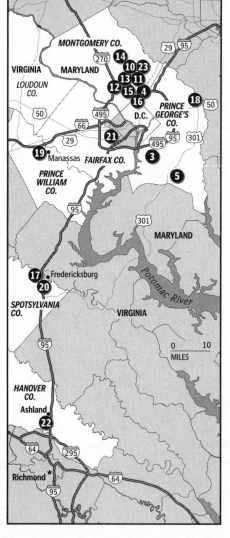

	DATE	TIME	LOCATION
1	Feb. 16	7 p.m.	Tacoma, WA
2	Mar. 19	Unknown	Tucson, AZ
3	Sept. 5	10:30 p.m.	Clinton, MD
4	Sept. 14	10:10 p.m.	Silver Spring, MD
5	Sept. 15	10:00 p.m.	Brandywine, MD
6	Sept. 21	12:16 a.m.	Atlanta, GA
7	Sept. 21	7:20 p.m.	Montgomery, AL
8	Sept. 21	7:20 p.m.	Montgomery, AL
9	Sept. 23	6:40 p.m.	Baton Rouge, LA
10	Oct. 2	5:20 p.m.	Aspen Hill, MD
11	Oct. 2	6:02 p.m.	Wheaton, MD
12	Oct. 3	7:41 a.m.	White Flint, MD
13	Oct. 3	8:12 a.m.	Aspen Hill, MD
14	Oct. 3	8:37 a.m.	Silver Spring, MD
15	Oct. 3	9:58 a.m.	Kensington, MD
16	Oct. 3	9:20 p.m.	Washington, DC
17	Oct. 4	2:27 p.m.	Fredericksburg, VA
18	Oct. 7	8:09 a.m.	Bowie, MD
19	Oct. 9	8:10 p.m.	Manassas, VA
20	Oct. 11	9:28 a.m.	Massaponax, VA
21	Oct. 14	9:15 p.m.	Falls Church, VA
22	Oct. 19	7:59 p.m.	Ashland, VA
23	Oct. 22	5:55 a.m.	Aspen Hill, MD

VICTIM	AGE	CONDITION	CIRCUMSTANCES
Keenya Cook	21	Killed	Shot in home of aunt, Isa Nichols
Jerry Ray Taylor	60	Killed	Shot on golf course. No conclusive link
Paul J. La Ruffa	55	Wounded	Shot in parking lot of restaurant
Rupinder "Benny" Oberoi	22	Wounded	Shot outside a beer and wine store
Muhammad Rashid	32	Wounded	Shot in front of liquor store
Million A. Woldemariam	41	Killed	Shot in front of liquor store
Claudine Lee Parker	52	Killed	Shot at a liquor store
Kellie Adams	24	Wounded	Shot at a liquor store
Hong Im Ballenger	45	Killed	Shot in parking lot of Beauty Depot
None		No injuries	Michaels craft store window shot
James D. Martin	55	Killed	Shot in grocery store parking lot
James L. "Sonny" Buchanan	39	Killed	Shot while mowing lawn at auto dealer
Premkumar A. Walekar	54	Killed	Shot while pumping gas
Sarah Ramos	34	Killed	Shot while sitting on bench in front of a restaurant
Lori Lewis Rivera	25	Killed	Shot while vacuuming minivan
Pascal Charlot	72	Killed	Shot while about to cross street
Caroline Seawell	43	Wounded	Shot while loading goods into car
Iran Brown	13	Wounded	Shot after being dropped off for school
Dean Harold Meyers	53	Killed	Shot while pumping gas
Kenneth Harold Bridges	53	Killed	Shot while pumping gas
Linda Franklin	47	Killed	Shot in lower-level parking lot of Home Depot
Jeffrey Hopper	37	Wounded	Shot in Ponderosa Steakhouse parking lot
Conrad E. Johnson	35	Killed	Driver shot inside his bus

SNIPER

1

An October Evening

The bullet was the color of a new penny. It was less than an inch long and weighed about as much as a wedding ring. It left the muzzle of the rifle at a velocity of around three thousand feet per second, stabilized on its brief journey across the parking lot by six rifling grooves inside the barrel that gave it a clockwise spin.

A relatively lightweight bullet, .223 inches in diameter, it was undisturbed in its flight by wind, precipitation, or obstruction. In its wake, though, it left an unusually loud boom, in part the product of the weapon's short, sixteen-inch barrel. In hindsight, it was clearly the sound of a gunshot, though slightly muffled and missing the telltale whip snap of a rifle.

It was 6:02 P.M. on Wednesday, October 2, 2002, about an hour before sunset on another warm, dry day in Montgomery County, Maryland, the prosperous suburb just northwest of Washington, D.C. The temperature had peaked near ninety degrees at 2:00 P.M., and the area was still parched by a drought that stretched back a year.

At the Shoppers Food Warehouse in Wheaton, about ten miles from the D.C. line, a surveillance camera perched like a big gray bird over the store facade caught the bustle of evening rush hour. In silent, jerky, black-and-white video, the camera captured cars pulling into the supermarket parking lot and a steady stream of people walking to the entrance—commuters breaking from the outbound river of traffic to slip in a midweek market run or to grab a gallon of milk on the way home. But the camera was not the only thing scanning the parking lot that evening.

Somewhere, probably less than fifty yards away, someone peered through the tiny glass screen of a battery-powered Bushnell holographic gun sight. The sight, which looked like the screen of a tiny video game, was mounted atop a Bushmaster XM15 E2S rifle, which had been stolen from a gun shop in Tacoma, Washington, several months earlier. The shop did not yet know it had been taken.

The Bushmaster, called a "flat top" because it lacked the rifle's characteristic carrying handle, also had a bipod, a two-legged stand that could be folded under the barrel. It was the kind of setup the military's special ops people might use. Good for quick "target acquisition"—as the task of a sniper is euphemistically described. A commercial model of the military's M-16, the Bushmaster was a version of the classic American infantry rifle that has been carried from Vietnam to the Persian Gulf. But at this moment the rifle, with the logo of a coiled snake etched on the magazine well pointed from inside a beat-up Chevrolet Caprice that was stopped nearby. The car had tinted windows and a hole cut in the trunk just over its New Jersey license plate.

As the store video and the shooter focused on the lot from opposite directions, a gray 1990 Mazda pickup with a camper top and an American flag on its antenna pulled in. It waited for another vehicle to move, then turned into a parking place. A balding man in a business suit, dress shirt, and tie, with a grocery list in his pocket, got out and walked toward the supermarket. He was fifty-five, stood five feet eleven, and weighed 194 pounds. He wore glasses and carried a white handkerchief, a black pen, and a blue cell phone in a leather case. His lunch container was in the truck on the front seat. His name was James D. Martin. He worked for the federal government's National Oceanic and Atmospheric Administration (NOAA), the parent agency of the National Weather Service, and liked to stop at the market on the way home from work to get something for dinner.

Martin was a churchgoing man, a member of the PTA, and a mentor to children at an inner-city school. He was on his way from his office at NOAA headquarters in Silver Spring, about five miles south, to his home in a development, about five miles north. There was a supermarket much closer to his home. But he also had to pick up some things for his church youth group, and this store, on the corner of Georgia Avenue and Randolph Road, had great prices.

Martin had grown up poor in southeastern Missouri. He had been in the service during the Vietnam War and had worked his way through college. He had come to Washington as a young man over thirty years ago. Now he had a split-level in the suburbs with a two-car garage, a remodeled rec room decorated with Civil War memorabilia, and a dog. His eleven-year-old son, Ben, was a Boy Scout. His wife's name was Billie. She was a Scout leader and a Sunday school teacher.

On the videocamera Martin moved stiffly, as if in an old-time movie. On the little screen of the Bushnell optical gun sight, a colored target designator fixed him from behind as he walked toward the entrance to the supermarket. He strode past one parking space, then another, an easy mark walking a straight line. From the old car, the black rifle jumped, and boomed, and sent its shiny bullet across the lot. Just a whiff of burned gunpowder may have lingered in the air.

The bullet struck Martin square in the back, slicing through his suit jacket and dress shirt and leaving a tiny hole in his skin one-eighth of an inch wide, smaller than the head of a plastic push pin. It cut through vertebra T7, below his shoulder blades, and severed his spinal cord, instantly paralyzing his lower body. Slowing down, it tore a slightly upward path, perforating his aorta, the main trunk of his cardiovascular system; the pulmonary artery to his lungs; and the pericardium, the membrane surrounding his heart. There was little deflection en route and almost no fragmentation as the bullet burst through his sternum, making a hole three-quarters of an inch by one-half inch shaped like a piece of broken glass. Later, at the autopsy, the medical examiners would find on his neck a tiny shard of gray metal that looked like lead.

Martin began to fall as soon as his spinal cord was cut. The catastrophic drop in blood pressure caused by his other wounds would have then led to swift unconsciousness. The brain carries only about a ten-second reserve of oxygen. A witness heard him moan and saw him crumple onto his left side, losing his glasses. He struck his face on the blacktop, gashing his nose and forehead. No one noticed the Caprice with the New Jersey license plate slip back into the evening rush and disappear.

A few parking places away, Kimberly Sadelson, a title clerk at a local car dealership, was loading groceries into her Honda when she heard the boom and saw Martin go down. She had her five-year-old son, Joseph, with her and hesitated to go near. She heard a woman scream and a man yell for someone to dial 911. From her cell phone Sadelson made the call.

"I'm at Shoppers Food Warehouse on Randolph Road," she said when a dispatcher answered. "And a man just fell in the parking lot. There was a loud noise. But we're not sure if he was shot."

"Okay, is he bleeding?" the dispatcher asked.

"Yes," she said.

"Where's he bleeding from?"

"I don't know," she said, her voice fearful and a little irritated. "I'm like half an aisle away from him."

"Is it inside?" the dispatcher asked.

"No," she said. "It's outside in a parking lot."

Across a busy road from the supermarket, Alan Felsen, a Montgomery County police officer, had also heard the boom. He had spent most of the day on bicycle patrol in a nearby business district but had been assigned to spend the last hour of his shift patrolling in one of the county's Impala cruisers.

Still dressed in his summer uniform—black shorts and light brown polo shirt with POLICE on the back—Felsen had just pulled out of the parking lot of the Fourth District police headquarters, across the street from the supermarket. He had cut through an apartment complex and was waiting to pull into traffic when he heard the noise. He had his windows down, but the sound didn't register right away as a gunshot. It was missing the edge, the crack, of a firearm. It had clearly come from the supermarket parking lot.

For several seconds Felsen looked across the street toward the source of the sound, but he saw nothing. No commotion. No running. No screaming. He wondered if someone had dropped something large, a loaded pallet, maybe, at the gardening store beside the supermarket.

Then he pulled into the traffic, flicked on his emergency dome lights, and made a U-turn into the parking lot. He found people there frozen, standing, as if in a weird painting. He pulled up to the nearest bystander and called out the window: "What happened?" No response. "What's going on here?" Then, out of the corner of his eye, he spotted a figure prone in the parking lot. He realized what he had heard. He grabbed his radio and yelled, "Break, break, break!" to get through the other transmissions. "Six-King-thirteen!" he said, using his call sign. "I'm at Shoppers Food Warehouse on Randolph. I've got the sound of a shot. One down."

After getting out of his cruiser, he paused for a split second to look around, then jogged to the victim. "Did anyone see anything?" he yelled over his shoulder. People were still frozen. "Anyone who heard the shot needs to stay here," he shouted. Felsen wondered for a moment if this might be a suicide. He needed witnesses.

About an hour earlier, a call had gone over the radio about a shooting in another shopping center a few miles away in Aspen Hill. A bullet had gone through the window of an arts and crafts store called Michaels. It had struck one of the store's illuminated checkout numbers, the number 5. But the holes were almost seven feet up, and no one had been hit. Felsen thought it probably wasn't related.

Felsen called to the man on the ground to see if he was conscious. There was no reply. He knelt beside him. Martin's chest, shirt, and suit coat were soaked with blood, and pressing Martin's neck for a pulse, he felt nothing. Martin wasn't breathing, either. Though he had never seen a gunshot wound this bad, Felsen was a former volunteer firefighter and had witnessed some bad accidents. He pulled on a pair of latex gloves and began CPR chest compressions. It quickly became a bloody business.

From the crowd of bystanders, a woman asked: "Can I help?"

Felsen looked up. By chance, it was a friend, Marjorie Fiske, a local volunteer EMT Felsen had known when they were both county police dispatchers. Fiske had been a few yards away, loading her car outside the store, when she noticed the commotion.

"Margie," Felsen called, "go get my first-aid bag."

Fiske ran to Felsen's cruiser but couldn't find his kit. So she went to her car and got the first-aid bag she always carried with her. Together, they worked on Martin, trying to get a pulse back. As Felsen did the compressions, Fiske placed two pieces of gauze over Martin's mouth. She pinched his nose shut and began blowing air into his lungs. She could hear gurgling inside. A nurse stepped out of the crowd and joined the effort.

The nurse pulled Fiske's big trauma scissors from her bag and cut open Martin's shirt. Underneath was a huge clot of blood and a hole in his chest. The trio used more gauze on his chest to try to stem the blood. Already his shirt, tie, and coat were soaked, and blood was streaming across the parking lot.

More police arrived from the district headquarters across the street. Paramedics from the fire station next door to it also arrived and took over from Felsen. Felsen peeled off his gloves, washed his arms with gauze and disinfectant, and watched as they worked on Martin.

It was almost sunset. Minutes passed, and after a while, the paramedics gave up. They placed a sheet over Martin, who lay on his back in the soft light of the evening, his feet and hands sticking out.

Fiske, too, had stepped back. "Can I get out of here?" she said, shaken and worried about getting to a function at her son's high school down the road.

Felsen wondered what could have happened. Guy walking across a parking lot. A gunshot. Guy goes down with a through-and-through wound. No robbery. No carjacking. Nobody sees anything. Probably some kind of rifle involved. Felsen thought it was an accident. Somebody popped off in a neighborhood nearby, and the high-powered bullet found this poor man. What else could it have been?

Across the sprawling county, the usual calls were going out to the people who were notified when there was a homicide. One of the first was to Detective Patrick McNerney of the department's Major Crimes Division, Homicide/Sex Section. McNerney was working the 2:00-to-11:00 shift out of Montgomery County police headquarters, a nondescript redbrick office building set among scores of other nondescript office buildings in the bland office park landscape just west of the county seat of Rockville.

McNerney, a seventeen-year veteran of the department and the son of a retired federal judge, took the phone call from the department's communications center. There had been an "0100," a homicide, at a Wheaton supermarket. The victim had been shot. McNerney, an imposing blond-haired man who often wore a blue tie with shamrocks on it, was light on cases. This one was his: He would put it on like a jacket and wear it until it was over, for as long as it took. He alerted an evidence collection team, and they headed for the scene.

As they maneuvered through the traffic with lights and sirens, they crossed a county that epitomized the vast changes that had overtaken the once serene postagricultural life of the Washington suburbs. The rural enclave where Confederate general J. E. B. Stuart passed through on the way to Gettysburg began its transformation after World War II. More than a half century later, there were still farms, but much of Montgomery County was highly developed and affluent, with growing communities of Asian, Hispanic, and African immigrants. Its population had grown to over 870,000— substantially more, it boasted, than Baltimore's. Its citizens were generally safe and content. Traffic congestion was the chief worry. The county had seen only twenty murders so far in 2002, not counting Martin's. There had been forty-seven traffic fatalities.

Arriving at the supermarket parking lot, McNerney found the typical crime scene circus. Martin was on his back under a sheet. He had what to the medics looked like a nasty chest wound. Customers were going in and out of the Shoppers Warehouse, but a crowd of bystanders—"looky-loos," McNerney called them—had gathered, drawn by the TV trucks. McNerney's job was to slow the scene down, "stop time," if you will. Nobody in, nobody out. Then take it frame by frame. Nail down who was where, who saw what, who heard what. He had an investigator with a camera start taking pictures of everybody around. You never knew who might turn up.

The next step was to look for surveillance cameras, ubiquitous now at stores and ATM machines. One was spotted outside the supermarket, and McNerney went to find store security to rewind the video and play it for him. The camera captured the murder clearly. But it didn't show much. Martin pulled in, got out of his truck, walked a few parking spaces, and fell down. Nobody was around him. He must have been shot from longer range and, judging by the cannonlike ka-*boom* that witnesses reported, probably with a rifle. Occasionally rifles were used in suicides in the county, or in domestic homicides, where the killer grabs the handiest weapon. But outdoor rifle homicides like this were almost unheard of.

McNerney started people searching for clues. It looked as though Martin had been shot from the front, so police began searching the area between his body and the front and side of the store for the shell casing that might have been left behind. They were very thorough. Later, they checked the soles of witnesses' shoes and the tire treads of cars in the lot. By now, McNerney's supervisor, Sergeant Nick DeCarlo, had arrived. DeCarlo, fifty-two, had been with the county police twenty-eight years. He was a no-bull type of detective. Often, when he spoke, he sounded as if he were on the witness stand. McNerney liked him. He was a good boss.

It was time to take a look at the body. The formal autopsy would be done the next day at the Maryland State Office of the Chief Medical Examiner, in Baltimore. But DeCarlo wanted to do a preliminary body check for clues. The victim was well dressed, DeCarlo thought, but not flashy. He had an NOAA ID badge. DeCarlo examined the chest wound. It wasn't huge, but it was jagged. Then he rolled the body over, pushed up Martin's shirt and suit coat, and found the much smaller wound in the back. This, the detectives realized, was an entrance wound. The front wound was an exit wound. Martin had been shot in the back, not the chest. The searchers were concentrating on the wrong part of the parking lot.

"Wow, we're looking the wrong way, guys," McNerney said. "We've got to look the other way." The detectives now guessed the shot had come from near some parked truck trailers directly across the lot from the supermarket entrance. A search turned up no evidence there, either. But all this reinforced the idea that Martin had been shot with a rifle. Tiny entrance wound, larger exit. Long-range. DeCarlo figured Martin had been hit by a common rifle bullet, something like a .223.

But even in broad daylight, no one had seen much. A woman in an adjacent lot claimed to have seen a white Toyota speeding off. But that wasn't much help. The shooter couldn't have been that far away. There were too many obstructions. But how could he have done it? Randolph Road and Georgia Avenue were packed with traffic. The parking lot was busy, and there was a police station right across the street. Officer Felsen was there within seconds. It had to have been someone from out of the area. No local would have chanced it. And why this victim? Why not the woman loading groceries with her child, or the volunteer medic, or another woman, who was putting diapers in her car ten feet away? Why him?

As the detectives worked, a uniformed officer approached McNerney and told him a friend of Martin's had come to the supermarket looking for him. The friend had been sent by Martin's wife, Billie, who had heard about the shooting on the news and was worried that her husband had not come home from work. McNerney questioned the friend and then acknowledged that it was Martin who had been killed. McNerney asked the friend if he would come with him while he broke the news to Martin's wife: "We're going to change her life 180 degrees when we talk to her."

McNerney hated this part of the job. He had a son about the same age as Martin's. The friend agreed to escort him and, along with McNerney and another detective, Mike Brent, drove to Martin's home. Billie Martin greeted them on the front porch, as if she knew they were coming. McNerney and Brent introduced themselves, and McNerney delivered the dreadful news.

"I'm sorry that what you've been watching on TV is in fact your husband," McNerney said. "He is deceased. We're working to figure out what happened. We'll do everything we can to do that."

Billie Martin began to cry. What should I do now? she kept asking. What am I going to do? They talked on the porch for an hour while her little boy stayed inside. She did not invite the detectives in.

––––––––––

Earlier in the evening, before leaving for the murder scene, DeCarlo had called his boss, Lieutenant Philip C. Raum, the deputy director of the department's Major Crimes Division, who was at his home in Clarksburg, in the rural northwestern part of the county. Raum, in turn, telephoned his superior, Captain Bernard J. Forsythe, the division director, who was also off duty and lived near Raum.

What do we have? Robbery? Domestic? Carjacking? asked Forsythe.

Nope, Raum replied, nothing like that. It wasn't a "smoker," as they called crimes with a smoking gun and a clear motive.

Okay, said Forsythe, what?

"We really aren't sure," Raum said. He told Forsythe about the surveillance tape but added that it showed little. Forsythe said they ought to go have a look.

The men were friends as well as neighbors. Forsythe was fifty-five and about to retire after thirty-one years in the department. He had already entered an early retirement program, and his last day was in three months. He had hoped to take the following week off to help settle his elderly parents, who had just moved to an assisted living community in Maryland from North Carolina's Outer Banks. But whatever happened in the supermarket parking lot would ultimately be his responsibility. He'd direct the investigation, and success or failure would come to roost in his first-floor corner office, just below that of the county police chief, Charles A. Moose.

Forsythe's widely used nickname was Barney, which wrongly suggested a hayseed. Though he was about to be overwhelmed by one of the biggest crime cases in law enforcement history, he was not unsophisticated. He headed the main detective unit of a capable, medium-size suburban police force. But his detectives were accustomed to handling one murder at a time. Forsythe's nickname, and first name, had been given him in honor of a revered Catholic chaplain who had gone ashore with his father, Jim, an army lieutenant, at the landing on Guam in 1944. Although Jim Forsythe later became a sales rep for Pfizer, his father had been a homicide detective in Newark, New Jersey, and the family could trace its law enforcement roots back to the 1880s. Born in Newark, Barney Forsythe had been raised in Prince George's County, Maryland, one of eight children. He had been an MP in the army, then joined the Montgomery County Police Department in 1971. His younger brother, Kevin, also became a police officer, in Phoenix, but was killed in 1984 when he was run over by a truck while directing traffic after an accident.

Barney Forsythe was an old-fashioned cop. He came to work at 6:00 A.M. At crime scenes he often wore a faded baseball cap to cover his thinning hair and a hand-me-down department trench coat with his heavy gold badge clipped to the lapel. He was notorious for being unable to send an electronic page accurately. His co-workers chuckled whenever they received an incomplete callback number on their pagers: "I bet it's Barney." But he was also a seasoned and disciplined investigator. A bad turn in a case would just bring a sigh of resignation.

Some detectives found him too disciplined, complaining that he never talked to them. He had, it was said, adopted the methodical, maddening pace of the detective he had been for many years. He preferred the staff meeting to the car chase and often disdained the use of his cruiser's emergency lights and siren. He was humble almost to the point of seeming insecure and had taught himself over the years to resist emotion. He would not allow himself to get up or down as a case unfolded. Others might feel joy, frustration, anger, or satisfaction during the roller coaster of an investigation. He could not. He had to be steady. Somebody had to be able to pick the crew up off the floor if things fell apart, which in police work they often did. And somebody had to resist the euphoria when something looked so good they could taste it. Used well, such discipline could be a vital quality in a commander. Forsythe's would be severely tested over the next few weeks.

He would be lucky, though. He would shortly be paired on his monumental task with a man of similar background and thinking, a larger and more colorful figure who saw Forsythe's knowledge of the county and its ways as the necessary complement to his own broad experience in investigating sensational national crimes. His name was Jim Cavanaugh. He was the special agent in charge of the Nashville office of the federal Bureau of Alcohol, Tobacco and Firearms (ATF). As Forsythe hurried to the supermarket that night, Cavanaugh was in Tennessee.

Forsythe and Lieutenant Raum arrived at the parking lot together at about 8:30 P.M. Raum looked more like a high school literature teacher than a detective. But he was emotional about his job, and more creatively profane, than Forsythe. Both men were religious. Raum was a Catholic. He had a brother who was a priest. Forsythe had been raised Catholic but now attended a small rural Methodist church, where he was an usher.

Forsythe knew the area well, having twice been assigned to the station across the street. He and Raum conferred with DeCarlo and helped search the area for evidence. There still seemed to be no likely motive, which was puzzling and unsettling. Who is out there just shooting someone for no apparent reason right across from the police station in broad daylight at rush hour? Raum thought, figuring that if he were going to whack somebody, it wouldn't be here.

They wondered about the other shooting, the one at the Michaels store a few miles north at Georgia Avenue and Aspen Hill Road. It was the same sort of deal, although no one had been hurt. A single shot from a rifle. No witnesses. No evidence. It had to be related. Forsythe and Raum decided to take a look there, too.

A cashier, Ann Chapman, said that inside the store she had heard a huge bang and felt something whizzing over her head. She looked up at her register number, a big illuminated plastic box bearing the number 5. It had a hole in it, and it was quivering and smoking. Outside no one had seen much. The Michaels parking lot would have been a tough place to get off a shot and not be spotted. There were better and more secluded sight lines across Aspen Hill Road on the grounds of St. Mary Magdalene Episcopal Church and also in a pet cemetery next door.

But the best spot might have been a clump of trees just south of the church. Raum had searched the same spot a day or two earlier as part of a robbery investigation. He'd found a homeless man sleeping there. But he didn't think they were looking for a homeless man now. He and Forsythe began to muse about the worst scenarios. What if there was no motive? What if somebody was just out shooting at people?

There was one potential clue. A pizza deliveryman named Steve Cribbin thought he had seen something. Cribbin had been waiting to go on duty, relaxing in his car outside the Papa John's pizzeria three doors down from Michaels, when he'd been startled by a loud boom. An army veteran, he had recognized what sounded like a rifle. He sat up and looked around. About thirty seconds later, he saw a blue car drive across the parking lot. It caught his attention because it was the only thing moving. He saw two African American men inside. They were laughing. He thought the car was a Thunderbird or a Malibu or a Taurus or an Escort. It appeared to be blue, he thought, maybe light blue.

Cribbin was rattled. He didn't want his story spread around. Suppose these guys came after him next? But the police were perplexed. It didn't look as if the shot had come from where Cribbin saw the car. His story was thin, like the phantom Toyota in the Shoppers Warehouse parking lot. The police discounted it.

Forsythe and Raum soon gave up for the night and headed home. It would be important the next day to get a bunch of officers back to the murder scene about the same time Martin had been shot. They could talk to people in the lot, maybe stop some motorists. Witnesses didn't always come forward right away. Maybe somebody had seen something. They also needed to examine Martin's background. Perhaps there was something in that. Maybe somebody was out for him, though McNerney didn't think so based on what he had learned about Martin that night. Before the group broke up for the evening, McNerney voiced his fear. "We got a problem," he said. "I think there's a sniper out there."

It was almost dark. Martin's body had been taken to the medical examiner's. The parking lot was cleaned up and the police tape taken down. Felsen had talked to a police counselor, which was pretty standard procedure, and had gone home. So had Marjorie Fiske, and Kimberly Sadelson and her little boy.

———————

At 7:47 P.M., Sean Thielke, a plainclothes county police officer, was on a stolen car watch in the Wheaton Plaza shopping complex on Georgia Avenue, a mile or so south of the murder scene. Thielke, who worked out of the police station across the street from where Martin was killed, had gone over to see if they needed help. The scene was under control, so he went on his stakeout. He was parked near the south end of the complex, where he could watch cars rolling north on Georgia Avenue from downtown Silver Spring and from Washington. It was a good place to check for stolen vehicles, which Thielke did by running license plate numbers through a laptop computer in his unmarked cruiser. As he watched, he spotted an old dark Caprice with tinted windows and New Jersey tags. The car looked like hell. The tinting was so dark that he could not see inside.

It was what police call a "felony car," potentially stolen, potentially trouble. Plus it looked like a former police car, which many criminals are known to love.

When the Caprice stopped at a light, Thielke pulled out and began following. He entered the car's license number, NDA-21Z, into his laptop. He still couldn't tell how many people were inside. It looked like one. Thielke didn't know that the car's tag had been run by another county officer about eight hours earlier in the same general area. The computer couldn't tell him that. He didn't know that the other officer had then run the owner's name. That time the only suspicious data the computer retrieved was that the owner, one John Muhammad, had a spousal protection order against him. Such orders were commonplace. The Caprice was not stopped. Now, after a few blocks and another query, Thielke's computer gave him the same answer. The car was clean. He peeled off and returned to his stakeout. The Caprice continued on its way.

Two hours later, Portia Burch, a private security guard at the White Flint Mall, approached a barefoot African American man in an isolated section of the mall parking lot, behind the Lord & Taylor department store. The mall, about a mile north of the Capital Beltway, was about four miles southwest of where Martin was killed. Burch was in a red Jeep Liberty with flashing lights. The man was courteous, soft-spoken, almost effeminate, she thought. It was John Muhammad. The Caprice, with its New Jersey tags, was parked about twenty yards away.

Muhammad told Burch he was traveling through Maryland from New Jersey with his son. He was just trying to get some rest. Burch could faintly see that someone else was in the car. She told him the lot gates would be locked by 1:00 A.M. As long as he was gone by then. Don't worry, he said, he'd be gone by then. The car was still there when she came by at 11:00. But when she went off duty at 12:15 A.M., it had left.

2

Roots of Rage

On the last day of August 2001, Mildred Muhammad received the phone call she had been awaiting for a year and a half. The call was from an investigator in Bellingham, Washington, and his news made her shriek with joy. "I have your children," said Whatcom County sheriff's detective Tom McCarthy.

Muhammad lived across the country, in a town house in Clinton, Maryland, just southeast of Washington, D.C. Her three children—John junior, Salena, and Taalibah—were at the center of a domestic war that had been going on between her and her estranged husband since before the couple parted ways the year before in Tacoma, Washington, where they lived. John Muhammad had threatened to kill Millie, as she was known to her friends, and at one point, as their marriage dissolved, she had gotten an order of protection against him. Her husband had then vanished and taken the children with him. So fearful had she been that she had, at times, gone around in disguise and had painted her car a different color to avoid detection. Finally, she moved as far away from Tacoma as she could.

Muhammad was a mysterious man. Some people called him "the chameleon" because he seemed to have so many different personas. He could be charming or menacing with those he met. He was both gentle and harsh with his children. He was obsessed with military discipline and physical fitness, and he had a fascination with firearms. He had been in the army and the National Guard for seventeen years, serving in the Persian Gulf War and becoming involved in controversy. Once he was accused of purposely igniting a thermite grenade in a tent full of soldiers in Saudi Arabia. Though he was cleared in the case, he told his wife he had been brutalized after he was taken into custody. When he left the service, Mildred had found him changed, bitter toward his country, the army, and later his family.

A convert to Islam and a member of the Nation of Islam, he had been born John A. Williams on New Year's Eve 1960 in New Orleans. His father, a railroad porter, was mostly absent. When his mother, Myrtis, got sick with breast cancer, she moved with her five children to Baton Rouge to be near her family. She died when Muhammad was three, and he was raised by his aunts in an African American enclave called Scotlandtown. Growing up, he had fathered a son, Travis, with a girlfriend and had another son, Lindbergh, with his first wife, Carol, whom he married in Baton Rouge in 1981. They lived in a trailer. She would later say he was a militaristic control nut. He would say she was bulimic. He divorced Carol in 1987 and married Mildred the next year. In 1994, they settled in Tacoma with their children after his discharge from the army.

The couple had then lived in a small rented house with a one-car garage on South Ainsworth Street in a multiethnic development called Wapato Estates. It was just off Interstate 5 and two blocks from a large city park that had its own spring-fed lake. The family made "a model family picture," a neighbor wrote later. Mildred loved the house.

With $10,000 borrowed from some neighbors, Muhammad and his wife started a car repair business—Express Car/Truck Mechanic, Inc. The idea was that they would make car repair house calls. Their motto was "The Future Is Here Now." Mildred was the president. Her husband was the chief mechanic. Repairs would be quick and on the spot. Plus, "The customer has the opportunity to establish a working relationship with the mechanic," they wrote in a pitch for a new loan in 1997.

The couple soon found that some repairs couldn't be done on-site. Muhammad had to bring them home, and their yard became cluttered with broken-down cars, bumpers, and engine parts. But the fledgling business seemed to be going well, and one day, in need of an accountant, Mildred saw a sign in a window, stopped her car, and walked in. She and Isa Nichols hit it off so well that Nichols eventually became a business adviser, friend, and confidant.

Nichols helped the Muhammads land contracts to service fleets of cars. One was with a small local police department. But Muhammad had problems with details. He would forget to replace the caps on a car's oil pan after draining the oil. When that happened with some police cars, the contract was terminated. But he got along well with customers—a little too well, Mildred's relatives would claim later. Her brother would say that John sometimes accepted sex as pay for fixing a woman's car. And at least one of his female customers, a nurse, fell in love with him and began a long-term romantic relationship.

Everything that was going wrong Muhammad blamed on Mildred. The business went into a decline because she was failing as office manager. She was also slipping in her duties to the local mosque they attended. And in 1996, he became enraged when she sided with his first wife, Carol, in a dispute over their son, Lindbergh. The boy, then thirteen, was visiting Tacoma, and Muhammad sought to avoid a court order requiring him to return the child to his mother. Muhammad planned to leave town with Lindbergh. Mildred convinced him to send the boy home. She believes he never forgave her.

They separated on September 9, 1999, according to court papers, and Mildred filed for divorce in December. Their marriage was "irretrievably broken," her filing stated. He wanted to act like a single man, she told friends, so let him be a single man. That same month, Muhammad went to a Tacoma gun shop and bought a Bushmaster XM15 E2S rifle, a civilian version of the military rifle he knew so well in the army. It cost him $871.69.

On February 11, 2000, Mildred asked the Pierce County Superior
Court for an order of protection against Muhammad. In her filing
she wrote that three days earlier he had come to their South
Ainsworth Street home, threatened her, and told her he had tapped
her phone. He came back the next day, saying he wanted to visit their
little boy, who was sick. When Mildred said the boy was asleep, John
pushed her out of the way. She called the police, who came and told
her they could do little without a restraining order. John came back
the next day, again threatening her. "You are not going to raise my
children," she later said he warned her. "You have become my
enemy, and as my enemy, I will kill you." Then she said she retorted:
"I've been sleeping with the enemy." The order was served March 8.

Still, Mildred allowed Muhammad to see the children whenever
he wanted and did not speak ill of him to them. She even allowed
Muhammad to begin taking the children on weekends. By then, she
was no longer working. Her ailing mother, Olevia B. Green, was living with her, and she was behind on the rent. John had told the landlord he was no longer responsible for it.

On Monday, March 27, Muhammad took the children to school
after they had spent the weekend with him. But "Lil John," as they
called John junior, got sick and went home to his mother's. Salena
also became ill at school, and Mildred told her husband he had to
pick up Salena because she didn't want to leave her son alone. Instead, Muhammad picked up both girls and then stopped by around
3:30 to get his son, telling Mildred they were going clothes shopping. Mildred agreed but said she wanted the kids back in two hours
for their grandmother's seventy-third birthday party. They never
showed.

At 7:30, Muhammad called to say that they were still shopping
at Kmart and would be home shortly. At 11:25 P.M., Muhammad
called his wife one last time. Now they were in Seattle, he told her,
but they were starting back. They probably were at the airport, but

there was little Mildred could do. Muhammad had borrowed $1,100 from a friend, emptied the $521 from the children's bank accounts, and bought airplane tickets to the Caribbean island of Antigua. Mildred Muhammad would not see her children again for seventeen months.

Without a job and behind in the rent, Mildred was told she had to be out of the South Ainsworth Street house by the end of May. She finally found a job, but two weeks later, she collapsed at home from stress and exhaustion and was taken to Tacoma General Hospital. Two days later, Muhammad called her in the hospital. She didn't know where he was, and after she asked about the children, he hung up. Her mother then called and said Muhammad had just telephoned her to say he was going to kill his estranged wife. Mildred was placed under tight hospital security, then moved to Phoebe House, a shelter for abused, homeless, and troubled women in Tacoma. She got in with the help of her accountant friend, Isa Nichols, the shelter's bookkeeper and a friend of its founder, Mary East.

For the next year, the shelter was Mildred's home. She searched for her children as best she could, setting up a Web site, prodding the courts, and engaging private investigators. But she had no success, and in June of 2001, she left Phoebe House to join her mother, who was living with a sister in Clinton, a suburb of Washington. She got a job in a local hospital and began a new life.

––––––––––

Muhammad and his children arrived in Antigua on March 28, 2000, aboard American Airlines flight 5502. They were met at the airport by a local travel agent, Janet Kellman, the cousin of a Tacoma man, Randolph Simon, whose car Muhammad repaired. Simon told Kellman his friend wanted his children to see Antigua.

Muhammad and the children were all traveling under false names. He had fake Wyoming identification, saying he was Thomas Allen Lee. The children were passed off as Fred Allen Lee, Teresa Lee, and Lisa Lee. The children each carried small suitcases. Muhammad carried a large green duffel bag. They introduced themselves to Kellman as the Muhammads and said they were on vacation. She allowed them to stay with her family in St. John's, the capital. They all slept together in one room: the children in the lone bed, Muhammad on the floor.

After four weeks of freeloading, Muhammad said he was running low on money and had to return to the States. Kellman agreed to watch the children, but while Muhammad was away, she became suspicious and started asking them questions. Kellman guessed they had been abducted and telephoned Muhammad in Tacoma to tell him to come get them. He returned with what he said was a notarized letter from his wife giving him permission to have the three kids with him. Kellman didn't believe it and ordered them to leave.

Muhammad and the children then moved into the home of a Charles and Euphernia Douglas, a white wooden house directly behind the Greensville Primary School. Muhammad enrolled his children and struck up a friendship with the principal, Janet Harris. Authorities believe Muhammad persuaded Harris to lie about how long she had known him when he applied for an Antiguan passport. An "honest and trustworthy young man," she called him, endorsing a job application on June 22. "He adheres to high moral and religious principles." He charmed Muriel Bennett, one of the teachers at the school, into telling him her mother's name, Eva Ferris. He then altered his birth certificate to list Ferris as his mother and cited her Antiguan birth on a passport application. He was issued an Antiguan passport that July and traveled constantly between the Caribbean and the United States the rest of the year, using the alias Thomas Lee.

Muhammad was plying a shadowy trade in forged identity documents that he sold to would-be immigrants, and clearly it was an area in which he had extensive personal experience. Since his conversion to Islam in the mid-1990s, he had used as last names both Williams and Muhammad, and eventually he had over a dozen aliases, an altered birth certificate, an illicit passport, numerous driver's licenses and identity cards, and scores of tales about who he was. He was a soldier, a spy, a teacher, a welder, a businessman, a musician, a promoter, a stockbroker, a mechanic. At heart he was a con man, handsome and smooth. In hindsight, he sounded almost delusional.

While at home in Tacoma, he continued fixing cars and staying with friends. At Phoebe House, staffers thought they spotted him lurking outside. On May 23, 2000, he regretfully sold his Bushmaster back to the gun shop where he had bought it, at a $200 loss. Records indicate he was in Antigua seven days later. He was back in Tacoma a month after that, and in Antigua a month later. In September, he helped Charles Douglas enter the United States illegally, traveling with him from Puerto Rico to Portland, and he moved between the States and Antigua in October and November.

In laid-back Antigua, Muhammad seemed possessed. He was always moving—jogging, hurrying with his dark backpack over his shoulder, talking endlessly on the pay phone outside BJ's Superette, a convenience store near the elementary school.

Trying to get a job on the island, he applied to be a school track coach, filing an application with the Antiguan government that included a forged recommendation he claimed was from the famous 1968 Olympic gold medalist Willie Davenport. The letter said that Davenport was the track coach at Southern University in Baton Rouge and that Muhammad had been his "exceptional" assistant for two years.

Davenport, a beloved figure at Southern, lived in Baton Rouge until his death in 2002. He had started the women's track program in the 1970s and had taught in the ROTC program. But he was never the school's track coach, and the letter was written on obviously forged university stationery. Muhammad also included an endorsement from a fictitious track coach at Louisiana State University and badly faked master's and bachelor's diplomas from LSU and Southern. The forged signature of Kweku K. Bentil, Southern's dean of graduate studies, looked like a child's. Finally, he included a fanciful army document indicating that he had been in the 82nd and

101st Airborne Divisions, two special forces groups, had attended sniper school, and had taught urban warfare. "A job well done!" he quoted an officer saying of him.

The Antiguan authorities noted that the papers all looked forged and rejected his application. Muhammad resorted to fixing cars and painting houses. But then he would be gone again, off to the United States on business. Antiguan authorities estimate he earned over $60,000 from his immigration scams.

Muhammad had indeed been in the military, though not in the illustrious units he cited. Yet his army experience had probably been among the most formative of his life, in ways good and bad. Poor and with no prospects, he had enlisted in the Louisiana Army National Guard in August of 1978, for a six-year hitch. He was seventeen. That October he was ordered to active duty and was released the following February. He remained in the guard for five years, then enlisted in the regular army in November of 1985 and stayed until 1994.

Muhammad joined the combat engineers, who were experts in everything from mine clearing to bridge building. He studied metalworking and reached the midrange grade of "sharpshooter" with the M-16 rifle. His ex-wife told people he was a demolition expert and could make a weapon out of anything. But his military record was sprinkled with trouble. In 1982, while still in the National Guard, he was court-martialed for disobeying orders, slugging a sergeant, taking someone else's tape measure, and briefly going AWOL. The AWOL and tape measure charges were later dropped. He was fined $100 and received a suspended sentence of seven days in jail.

More serious accusations were leveled against him during the Gulf War, though the story and its outcome were murky. While serving with an armored cavalry regiment's engineering company in the Saudi Arabian desert, Muhammad, by then a seasoned veteran, became embroiled in a series of racial conflicts with other soldiers. Former members of his unit remember him as intelligent, smooth, and fit, with a crushing handshake, but also as difficult. Again, most of the tension was over petty stuff, like his wearing of an unauthorized head scarf. At one point, a higher-ranking white sergeant, Kip Berentson, chastised him for sleeping in another soldier's sleeping bag. Berentson would recall that Muhammad was livid and gave him "the stare of death." They almost came to blows in that incident, and they clashed repeatedly. He thought Muhammad got away with things because he was black. Berentson was accused of picking on him.

The worst incident happened with the thermite grenade. It was in the middle of the night, and the grenade, designed to burn fiercely rather than fragment, was ignited inside a tent where a dozen soldiers were asleep. The heat started igniting ammunition, and there was a mad scramble before everyone got out safely. Berentson didn't think it was an accident, and was immediately suspicious of Muhammad, who had had an argument with a corporal earlier in the day. The MPs and army criminal investigators were summoned, and Muhammad was taken away in handcuffs.

The upshot of the case was never clear. There was no record of any disciplinary action in Muhammad's file, and he was apparently exonerated. But Berentson wrote down his name—which was then John Williams—and serial number on a piece of paper and put it in his wallet. Convinced that their paths would someday cross violently, he wanted police to have a lead if anything ever happened to him. He was still carrying the piece of paper eleven years later.

————

One of the people Muhammad helped spirit to America from the Caribbean in the fall of 2000 was a Jamaican seamstress named Una Sceon James. She was a single mother in her thirties with a teenage son who had wandered from Jamaica to St. Martin to Antigua, working menial jobs and trying to figure a way to get into the United States. After landing in Antigua on January 15, 1999, she worked twelve hours a day selling chicken and drinks at a roadside grill. She dreamed of moving to Florida, which she and her son briefly visited that summer after he joined her from Jamaica.

James and her teenage boy lived in a rented two-bedroom house.

He attended a local Seventh-day Adventist high school, where he excelled at cricket, science, art, and geography. He was fifteen. His father, Leslie, a brick mason, who had three other children by two other women, was back in Jamaica. The boy's name was Lee Boyd Malvo.

Ever since he could remember, Lee Malvo had been hauled around by his mother like a forlorn puppy. She'd dump him with friends or relatives while she went off in search of work or fortune. He'd get comfortable, then she'd suddenly appear, uproot him, and drop him someplace else. Jamaica to St. Martin. Back to Jamaica. He lived with her sister for several years, then with a cousin, then in a boarding home, then with other relatives, then with a kindly teacher. His mother loved him, doted on him, and did all this, she said, so she could make a future for him. He was worth it.

"The zeal with which you work will assure you maximum success in your course of studies," English teacher Patricia Deacon wrote in his report card in 1998. "Continue to be the pleasant, caring, and loving child you are."

In a green exercise book, Malvo drew animals and cartoon figures, along with his arithmetic and compositions. Though he was bright, his elders thought he seemed needy and insecure. He was a slight boy and craved the companionship of adult men. What he needed, his relatives said, was a father. In 1999, he told friends at his high school in northern Jamaica that he was leaving for good. He was going to Antigua to be with his mother. Maybe now he'd at least have some stability.

But a little over a year after he arrived in Antigua, his mother announced she was leaving again. He would have to stay alone for a while, but she'd send for him. She told their landlord that she was going back to Jamaica to visit her sick mother. But she was really headed to the land of her desires: Florida. She had agreed to pay Muhammad to arrange illegal passage and documents to the United States for herself and her son. Lee would have to wait his turn, but soon they would be reunited and start their new life in America.

Back in Antigua, weeks passed. No rent was paid on the house.

James sent her son some money through Muhammad. But it wasn't much, and she did it only once. The landlord shut off the utilities. Malvo angrily punched holes in the walls. Finally, one day near the end of the year, John Muhammad drove up to the white-and-peach wood-frame house and began loading up the few furnishings: a bed, plastic dining room table and chairs, a freezer. Malvo was moving in with him.

Here was a man for the boy. Muhammad had been to war, walked like a drill sergeant, and talked about how well he could shoot. He was tall, good-looking, dashing, and slightly mysterious. And he was willing to take under his wing a Jamaican boy with no father and barely a mother, who read the Bible, played cricket, and didn't have an eastern Caribbean cent to his name.

Malvo quickly fell under his influence. In the household crowded with children where he now lived, he clashed jealously with the other kids, especially with Muhammad's son, John junior. By March 2001, Malvo had converted to Islam, bringing a copy of the Koran to the Seventh-day Adventist school and reciting the sayings of the Prophet during morning prayers. His grades began to slip, and one day Muhammad appeared at the school in a new guise. He announced that he was Malvo's uncle and henceforth his guardian in Antigua. By the end of the month, Malvo had stopped coming to school. He was now calling Muhammad "Dad."

March was a dicey month for Muhammad. His con scheme almost came to an unpleasant end at the Antigua airport, where Muhammad—or Norman, as he was known—often bought tickets, sometimes thousands of dollars' worth, and had aroused the suspicions of an American Airlines check-in clerk. One time he booked a flight the clerk happened to be on. When he wasn't on the plane, she realized he had given the ticket to someone else. On March 11, when Muhammad tried to buy a ticket under the name of Dwight Russel, with an address in Tacoma, the police were called. Police later learned that an illegal immigrant who had paid Muhammad $2,500 was waiting in an airport men's room for his ticket to America.

Muhammad told police his name was James Edwards and he was from Texas. A search of his luggage produced a forged Washington State driver's license and a Florida birth certificate. Muhammad was arrested and jailed at police headquarters in St. John's. Two days later, he escaped. An Antiguan government report later said that he "walked out" of the police station in "a suspicious sequence of events" that resulted from "an obvious gross lack of security."

It was a close call, and on April 14 he tried again, flying this time under his still legal name, Williams, to St. Martin and then to Miami with two Jamaican women and a little girl. They were stopped at the Miami airport. The women, carrying obviously forged documents, were turned away, but Muhammad was not prosecuted because of lack of evidence.

That same month, he legally changed his name to Muhammad. When he appeared in Tacoma's Pierce County District Court to petition for the name change, Judge Molly Davis asked why he wanted to do it.

"For religion purposes," he replied.

"Are you changing your name to defraud or mislead any person or creditor?" she asked.

"No, ma'am," he replied.

"I'll go ahead and grant your name change, then," she said.

"So I don't need to come up there?" he asked.

"No, you don't," the judge said.

"I don't need to show you no paperwork? I don't need to bring no witnesses up or anything like that?" he asked.

"Yours is pretty simple," the judge said.

"I feel cheated," Muhammad said, his high-pitched laugh audible on the tape of the hearing.

The next day, he was issued a Washington State driver's license under the name John Allen Muhammad. On May 20, he returned to Antigua, using his new driver's license as identification, and stayed at the luxurious Grand Pineapple Beach resort.

But his Antigua adventure was coming to an end. On May 31, Muhammad, his three children, and Malvo left Antigua for good on American Airlines flight 5527 bound for Puerto Rico. Malvo traveled as Lindbergh Williams, Muhammad's son by his first marriage.

They went to Florida, where Una James was waiting. She had gotten a job in a Red Lobster restaurant in Fort Myers, where she had agreed to pay $2,500 to a co-worker, Jeremiah Neal, to marry her so she could legitimize her status in the United States. They were married April 20 but were rarely together. Malvo was turned over to his mother and new stepfather. He got his school immunizations in July and the next month registered for classes at Cypress Lake High School, where before long he was earning As and Bs and taking advanced placement classes.

Muhammad and the children apparently did not stay long in Fort Myers. In June, Muhammad was seen in Tacoma. In August, the four showed up on the doorstep of the Lighthouse Mission, in the remote and picturesque port town of Bellingham, Washington. The mission, a Christian homeless shelter, could trace its roots back to the 1920s. About fifteen miles from the Canadian border, it was a way station for transient souls trying, and mostly failing, to get into Canada or waiting to grab the ferry to distant Alaskan towns like Sitka, Juneau, or Skagway. These were people trying to leave something behind, people seeking "the geographical cure," as the mission counselors called it: trying to change their lives by changing location.

Muhammad and the children, who signed in under the last name of Thomas, immediately caught the attention of the mission's director, Reverend Al Archer, a Baptist minister and former navy pilot who had headed the mission for thirty years. Archer, who still wore a bomber jacket bearing the emblem of his squadron, had been called to the ministry while in the navy. Finding himself in Bellingham after his discharge, he had taken to mission work and helping people no one else would help. Over the years, he had seen all kinds at the Lighthouse. Rarely had he seen anyone like Muhammad.

It was very unusual for a father to show up with children. Most of the mission's clients were unaccompanied men. Archer saw some women with children, who were housed in a women's shelter outside town. But a man with his kids? Archer, who as mission director did not often have time to interact with residents, made a point of seeing the four when they arrived.

He found them in the mission chapel, a spartan room with an altar, green plastic chairs, and wooden shelves filled with Bibles and hymnals. They looked a little the worse for their travels. But the children seemed happy, and their father seemed devoted to them. Muhammad told Archer he had been through a divorce, had custody of the children, and was trying to get his life back together. He was smart, courteous, and well-spoken. Archer thought he was a bit smooth. But he seemed to be a man genuinely trying to rebuild a comfortable world for his children. Among the clients Archer mostly saw, disordered men tortured by drugs, alcohol, and mental illness, Muhammad was impressive. Archer told Muhammad he would do anything he could to help.

Shortly after they arrived, Archer helped sign the children up for the local schools and drove Muhammad the two miles to the local office of the state Department of Social and Health Services, where he could apply for public assistance. While Muhammad was filling out the paperwork, Archer took the children with him on his daily walk at a local mall and then treated them to hot chocolate. Afterward, he drove them all back to the mission.

With his friendly manner, Muhammad could easily get the day jobs that most of the mission residents landed. The children were in school and would soon get some state help. Archer thought it was all working out great.

But Muhammad's story already was starting to unravel. His application for state assistance that day contained enough irregularities that it was flagged and sent to the Division of Fraud Investigations. There an investigator, Lowell Bieber, noticed that Muhammad and the children sounded a lot like the man who had vanished with his children from Tacoma the previous year in a custody case. On August 30, Muhammad's name was run through a court database, which revealed the order of protection against him. Bieber alerted the court where Muhammad's divorce case was heard, and it sent a writ of habeas corpus, an order to pick up the children, to the Whatcom County sheriff in Bellingham. It landed on Detective Tom McCarthy's desk.

McCarthy, who liked to say his job often involved "writs of habeas grabis," verified the order with Pierce County and telephoned Mildred for details. He started looking for the children by going to the Bellingham School District headquarters but was told the district had no children that fit the description. He then went to an elementary school near the shelter. The school secretary told him the children had been brought there originally but were now enrolled in other schools in the district: the girls, Salena and Taalibah, at Parkview Elementary; John junior, at Whatcom Middle School.

McCarthy went to Parkview and had the girls summoned. He told them they were not in any trouble, but their mother missed them. "She sent me here," McCarthy told them. "She loves you very much.

"Which one of you is Salena?" he asked.

"Don't say anything," she responded.

"I'm Taalibah," her sister blurted.

The girls were upset and frightened but admitted who they were. They wanted to know what was going to happen to their father.

"I'm not going to take your dad to jail," McCarthy said. But, he said, "Your dad did get the judge kind of angry."

McCarthy gathered the children and their backpacks, dropped them at his office, and then went to the middle school to pick up John junior. His reaction was the same: "What's going to happen to my dad?" McCarthy brought the boy back to his office and gave the children pizza and soda for lunch. While they watched cartoons on TV and told another detective they had been living in Antigua, McCarthy telephoned Mildred and told her the good news.

"They found my babies! They found my babies!" she screamed.

McCarthy put each of them on the line to talk to her. When he got back on the phone, she said, "God bless you. God bless you."

McCarthy said she had made his day. "Now," he said, "you've got to get out here and get to court."

Finding Muhammad was not difficult. McCarthy telephoned the mission, told the receptionist that he had the children, and left orders for Muhammad to call him back at the sheriff's office. At 4:30, Muhammad appeared in the foyer of the police station, and McCarthy invited him in.

"No," Muhammad said. "We can talk here."

McCarthy explained what had happened and showed Muhammad the court order. Muhammad said his wife had allowed him to have the children.

"Well, Mildred says you took the children," McCarthy replied. "Why were they in school registered under another name?"

Muhammad didn't answer.

The children had been taken, McCarthy said, and there would be a court hearing in Tacoma to review the case. Muhammad could tell his side then. He told Muhammad they were lovely kids. "We had to do this," he said.

"That's it?" Muhammad asked. "How come I'm not getting arrested? Isn't this a crime?"

McCarthy said he had no arrest warrant for him.

Muhammad was well groomed and well dressed, in clean jeans, a polo shirt, and tennis shoes. McCarthy noticed how physically fit he looked, with not an ounce of fat on him, and guessed he'd be tough to tangle with. Muhammad didn't smile, and his face was tense—McCarthy could see his jaw muscles working. McCarthy wrote the address of the juvenile facility on a yellow sticky pad so Muhammad could drop off the duffel bag he was carrying that was filled with the children's clothes. Muhammad thanked him and left.

That was easy, McCarthy thought to himself.

On Tuesday, September 4, 2001, Muhammad appeared in Pierce County Superior Court in the eleven-story County-City Building in

Tacoma, a few blocks from the harbor. Deputy Sheriff Curtis Wright served him with the court papers when he arrived at the front desk. Wright noted that Muhammad was wearing wrinkled clothes and looked dirty and disheveled. When he reached Commissioner Mark Gelman's second-floor courtroom, Mildred Muhammad was already there, accompanied by a lawyer. Six years earlier, in this same building, she and John together had fought a bitter battle with his first wife, Carol, over custody of Lindbergh. Now they were enemies, fighting over their children.

"Your Honor, could I say something?" Muhammad asked. He did not have a lawyer.

"Just a moment, sir," Gelman said. The only reason for the proceeding was to implement a court order Mildred had received in January awarding custody and control of the children to her. Muhammad didn't seem to understand, or pretended that he didn't.

"Your Honor, can you please tell me what's going on?"

Gelman tried to explain, but Muhammad still didn't seem to grasp what was happening.

The judge explained that the court orders stipulated he could not see his children. He had abducted them illegally. Now they would be exclusively with his ex-wife. He couldn't see them or visit them, and according to the earlier court order, she could legally take them away and hide them from him forever. Muhammad tried to interrupt: "The children was never missing."

Gelman said that was an issue for a later time. "Right now the children shall be returned to mother. . . . That's the order of the court." Did Muhammad understand now?

"Yes," he replied, his voice tinged with anger. "I am not able to see my children."

Afterward, Muhammad bumped into Wright, the deputy sheriff, in the hallway.

"How do I get my kids back?" he asked.

"You just left court, and the judge gave them to your wife," Wright answered.

"Well, how do I get them back?" Muhammad repeated.

Wright thought Muhammad was somehow not connecting to reality and that he looked lost and defeated. "You need an attorney," he said.

The next day, the state's Child Protective Services turned the children over to their mother. Mildred Muhammad took them and vanished, never to see her husband again. Muhammad, despondent, remained in Tacoma for a few days, staying with friends. Among them was his old army buddy Robert Holmes, who lived in a ranch-style duplex in a run-down Tacoma neighborhood called Oakland. Muhammad had moved in temporarily with Holmes, an auto mechanic and strapping former boxer with a shaved head, after he and Mildred split up. Holmes would later recall how angry and depressed Muhammad seemed after the hearing.

Muhammad went to see a Tacoma lawyer, John Mills, who handled custody cases. Muhammad was broke, but Mills agreed to help anyway. Mills agreed to try to set up a new court hearing and suggested that Muhammad get friends to write the court letters vouching for his integrity. He helped Muhammad file motions asking that the children be found and returned to him. But Mills told Muhammad that it was all meaningless unless he found his ex-wife.

Muhammad did not return to the Lighthouse Mission until October 3. He stayed for a week, left, and then returned a few weeks later. But the terrorist attacks on New York and Washington on September 11 had made Archer suspicious. Muhammad had lied about the children. He was gone for weeks at a time, got calls at the mission from travel agencies, and seemed to travel constantly. Now, amazingly, Muhammad wanted him to write a recommendation to the court.

Archer, conscious of his calling, decided to write a carefully worded endorsement. He finished the letter on October 17, while visiting relatives in Kentucky, and e-mailed it to the mission. The letter concerned only the period of August 16 to 31. Archer praised Muhammad as a father. He said the children seemed to love him. He described Muhammad as a gentleman and a friend. But when Archer called the mission to see if the e-mail had arrived, one of his staffers said: "Al, I don't think you want to send that letter." Muhammad, he said, was slippery and up to something.

Archer never sent the letter. Instead, from Kentucky, he called the FBI office in Seattle. It was the first time in thirty years that he had ever called the authorities about a mission resident. He told the FBI he thought Muhammad might be a terrorist. They listened but had little reaction: He was probably just into drugs. Before Archer left Kentucky, he told his relatives about Muhammad: "Someday," he said, "you're going to read about this guy in the newspapers."

3

The Road to Mayhem

On October 20, when Al Archer returned to Bellingham from Kentucky, he found John Muhammad sitting in the chapel of the Lighthouse Mission with a teenage boy. He was slight, about five feet five, 125 pounds, with what sounded like a trace of a Caribbean accent. Muhammad introduced him as Lee and said he was the second son he had often spoken about. Archer was dubious. What do you want to do with your life? he asked the boy. I want to go to school, he answered. What kind of school? Archer asked. The response, six weeks after 9/11, gave him chills: Flight school, the teenager said. Archer did not probe much further. He was still hoping the FBI would respond to his call, and he was afraid that if he started asking a lot of questions, Muhammad and his new sidekick would disappear. Better to sit tight and watch.

Malvo's time at Cypress Lake High School in Fort Myers had been brief. Although he was a good student, the abrupt change to settled apartment living with his mother did not suit him. Una James was known to be strict, and he still had no father in his life. His mother's six-month "marriage" to Neal, who hadn't been around much anyway, had ended. No doubt Malvo missed the excitement of being with Muhammad. He was strict, too. It was "Yes, sir" and "No, sir" with him. But he had a code and a mission—however vague. Malvo told his mother he wanted to be with Muhammad.

Twelve days before turning up at the mission, Malvo had failed to show up for school. His mother telephoned a friend, a Haitian immigrant named Antoine Eveque, in tears. "I can't find my son," she cried. "I can't find my son. I've been looking everywhere. . . . I don't know what to do." She was afraid to call the police. After years of Una leaving him, her son had now left her.

Malvo boarded a Greyhound bus for the long, cross-country journey to join his "dad." Muhammad seemed to be expecting him. As early as August 24, before losing his children in court, he had listed Malvo as one of his sons when he registered the family at Bellingham's Interfaith Community Health Center, and the day before Malvo disappeared, Muhammad took out a membership at the YMCA in Bellingham for himself and four children—John junior, Salena, Taalibah, and Lee Malvo.

Malvo almost certainly had help from Muhammad in getting to Washington. Una told a friend that Malvo had called her about a week after he vanished. She later told police he had called twice: Her caller ID had indicated that one call came from the mission and another came from Tacoma. She jotted down the Tacoma number and thought it was Muhammad's sister's. It was actually the home of his girlfriend. On October 16, Malvo was formally withdrawn from Cypress Lake High School. Someone purporting to be a Malvo relative told the school the family was moving to Alabama.

To Archer and the mission staff, the relationship between Muhammad and Malvo seemed unusually close. They went everywhere together, and it was impossible ever to talk to Malvo by himself. In a group, Malvo hardly spoke. One time, during dinner, Malvo arrived at a table ahead of Muhammad and began chatting with a staff member and some other residents. When Muhammad arrived a few seconds later, he glared at the boy as if to say: "Keep your mouth shut." The two often left the shelter on weekends, and when they returned they would have to sleep on thin, vinyl-covered mattresses on the mission's dining room floor, where the overflow residents stayed. They often pulled their mattresses together away from the others.

Malvo enrolled at Bellingham High School, not far from the mission. Again he was a good student. He befriended a cheerleader and struck his fellow students in a history class as surprisingly knowledgeable about military weaponry. But he kept to himself and spent most of his time reading or on the computers in the library. Muhammad would sign up for day jobs or go to the Y to work out.

Archer kept a close watch on the two, but outside his hearing, Muhammad was talking about some strange things. One mission resident would later tell authorities that Muhammad put out the word that he wanted to kill his wife in Tacoma. He talked about how he'd like to do it, perhaps by shooting her from a car and using a silencer. He wanted it to be secret and anonymous and wondered about making a gun port in the car and a silencer out of a Coke bottle or something else.

And he obviously knew all about rifles from the army. He'd been trained with the M-16, reached the grade of sharpshooter, and had to requalify with the rifle every year he was in the service. He'd also had a Bushmaster, until he'd had to sell it. That was a fine weapon. With a good scope, that thing was deadly at well over a hundred yards, even in the hands of a fool. But it would be nice if it were more compact, with a shortened barrel and a collapsible stock. It would be much more discreet and portable that way.

On November 28, Muhammad persuaded a female acquaintance, Kristine Sagor, to drive him to Ferndale, fifteen miles north of Bellingham, where he paid a visit to Glen Chapman, a firearms connoisseur who ran a gunsmith shop out of his garage. Muhammad told Chapman he wanted to alter a rifle so it could be carried in a small case. It was for his son, Muhammad said, so the boy could take his rifle on the bus when he went target shooting. He wondered if Chapman could take his son's model 70 Winchester, a popular bolt-action rifle, cut the twenty-two-inch barrel in half, and thread it so it could be reassembled. He also wanted the stock altered so it would fold up.

Chapman was wary. First, if you cut a twenty-two-inch barrel and threaded it at the two meeting points, the barrel would be too weak. It would probably blow up when the weapon was fired.

Second, even if it didn't blow up, you could never get the barrel's rifling grooves lined up so the bullet went straight. Third, this was all
illegal. Rifles with a barrel shorter than sixteen inches were against
the law. Finally, there was Muhammad himself—nicely dressed and
well-spoken, but probably a federal agent.

Chapman told them he wouldn't do it, and said no gunsmith in
the area would do it either. Plus, he told Muhammad, if his son ever
got caught with an altered rifle like that, he'd be thrown in jail for a
good while. Muhammad thanked him and left. Chapman didn't
think he really owned a 70 Winchester, and he told his wife, Anita,
that he thought he'd just been set up by the ATF. He told all his gun
friends: Look out. The feds were on the prowl.

Muhammad had met Sagor at an apartment complex in Sumas,
a town outside Bellingham, where he sometimes worked and where
she was the property manager. He was known around the complex as
a model employee, the kind of guy you'd want to have home for dinner. He was such a hard worker and was so articulate that one day the
complex's owner, Greg Grant, asked him what he was doing at the
mission. Muhammad said he was going through a divorce and was
trying to get custody of his children. He was really a teacher, he said.

Another time Muhammad told Grant he had to take a trip to the
Caribbean to sell a house he owned on one of the islands. It made
Grant wonder how Muhammad, living at the mission and paid $6 an
hour, could afford such a trip. And once, Muhammad asked Donald
Haaland, a maintenance man at the complex, where he could find a
silencer for a gun.

Sagor thought Muhammad was an operator and that there was
something frightening about him. Muhammad told her he had been
in army special forces for twenty years and the commodities business
for fifteen. He said he often fasted for days. None of it added up.
After the Chapman visit, she called the Bellingham police, the FBI,
the U.S. Border Patrol, the ATF, and Bellingham High School to
warn them about Muhammad. But there was nothing anyone could
do. It was all just talk.

Every morning, Muhammad would walk Malvo partway to Bellingham High School, then go to work, the Y, or a local bar to drink a beer and watch TV. The two were often seen walking around town, conspicuous because there were so few African Americans in Bellingham. Evenings they would show up at Stuart's Coffee House, a cozy place at Bay and Prospect Streets that sold banana shakes, carrot cake, and lemon bars. Stuart's felt like somebody's living room, with carpets on the floors, lamps on the tables, and chessboards scattered around. Muhammad and Malvo would sit near the door and spend hours talking and playing chess. They seldom spoke to anyone else. It was the same at the Y. Sometimes they went together, sometimes alone. They worked out hard and kept to themselves. Occasionally, someone overheard comments that sounded militant and anti-American.

At the mission, Archer was still leery of Muhammad, though he liked Malvo. Sooner or later, he figured, there would be some clue as to what was going on. Until then, Archer decided, he'd keep his mouth shut. About 2:00 P.M. on December 14, the receptionist transferred a phone call to his office from a young woman with a Jamaican accent. She was calling from the bus station in south Bellingham, where she had just gotten off the bus from Seattle. She said her name was Una James, Lee Malvo's mother, and she had come to get him away from John Muhammad. Finally, Archer thought, we're getting somewhere.

Archer drove to the bus station in his Chevy van and found James surrounded by most of her worldly belongings: a small TV set and five or six boxes of clothes, pots, and cooking utensils. There was more coming that was still on a bus in Chicago. A month earlier, James had quit her job at the Red Lobster in Fort Myers, broken the lease on her apartment, and moved out. On December 8, she had left for Bellingham to search for her son.

Archer helped get her stuff in his van, and they drove around town for about a half hour, talking about the best way to get Lee away from Muhammad. Archer suggested two or three options, one of which was to go to the Bellingham police and say she was his mother and he was a runaway. Archer got her a room in a motel, and they made the call.

At 7:00 P.M., two Bellingham officers went to the mission and bumped into Malvo and Muhammad on their way out. Malvo told one of the officers, Kent Poortinga, that he had left Fort Myers to get away from his mother and Bellingham was as far west as he could go. He said he also thought it was a place where he could get a better education. He told Poortinga he had just met Muhammad at the mission and that Muhammad had agreed to pretend he was his father so he could get into Bellingham High School.

The officers drove Malvo to the police station, where Archer had already brought his mother. Their reunion produced mixed emotions. Malvo was glad to see her, though upset that she had come to take him away from Muhammad. But the police wouldn't hand Malvo over to his mother because all her identification was still on the bus in Chicago. Instead they turned him over to the state's Child Protective Services, which placed him in a shelter for the night. Archer took James to dinner and then back to the motel.

The next day, he helped James collect the rest of her things from the bus station. She dug out her papers and showed them to the police, who fetched Malvo from the youth shelter. Then Archer took mother and son to breakfast. The reunion seemed complete. Muhammad had vanished, scared off, Archer believed, by the police. Everything would be better without him. Archer set up Malvo and James at the Lighthouse and its women's shelter, and soon they would go back to Florida.

But the Bellingham police had become suspicious. They had found out about Muhammad's custody battle and that he had once been detained by immigration officials. Malvo's records at the high school were practically nonexistent. The day he went back to school, December 18, two police officers, Allan Jensen and Jeffrey Hinds, went to question Malvo and he spun a new story. Now he told them he had moved to Bellingham with his mother's permission after coming to the United States on a Jamaican passport, which he had since lost. She had moved here to be with him, he said, but didn't like the area and now planned to move to New York, while he stayed in Bellingham. That was not what his mother had told them, Jensen and Hines replied. Besides, he was pretty young to be living alone in a homeless mission. Nothing that Malvo said seemed to quite make sense, so they decided to alert the U.S. Border Patrol.

The next day, border patrol supervisory agent Keith M. Olson began trying to locate Malvo and his mother. He first went to the women's shelter, where he found James loading her belongings into a taxi. When she could not supply any immigration documents, he arrested her.

Malvo had skipped school that day, but someone at the school told Olson he often hung out at the city library and the YMCA. He wasn't at the library, but when Olson checked at the Y front desk, he saw Malvo's membership card. Olson found Malvo, with Muhammad, in the locker room. They had just come out of the showers. He told Malvo he was being taken into custody.

Was Malvo with Muhammad? he asked.

"Yes," Malvo replied.

"No," Muhammad said.

Malvo looked at Muhammad in disbelief.

Olson asked Muhammad if he wanted to go with Malvo or if he had anything he wanted to give him.

"No," said Muhammad, who was facing the locker, his head turned from Olson.

Alarmed that Muhammad might have a weapon, Olson ordered him to move. When he refused, Olson pushed him aside and examined the locker. He did not see a gun, but Olson was worried enough to grab Malvo, now dressed, and back out of the locker room. Outside, he dialed 911 for backup. But by the time police arrived and went back to the locker room, Muhammad was gone.

When Olson interviewed James back at the Bellingham border patrol office, she told him that she and Malvo had entered the country by stowing away on a container ship bound for Miami. Olson took her fingerprints and picture as well as those of her son, which was standard procedure. One of his agents, Raymond R. Ruiz, typed up a brief report that included what would later prove to be a crucial piece of information. The four-paragraph arrest narrative mentioned that an individual, unrelated to Malvo, was involved in a custody dispute over the boy with James. That individual was a John "Mohammad."

Malvo and James were placed in Immigration and Naturalization Service (INS) custody. She was taken to Seattle; he was taken to a juvenile facility outside Spokane. They were fingerprinted and held for about a month, and on January 23 they were released on bond, pending a later hearing. The border patrol and the INS would later blame each other for the release. A few days later, James telephoned Archer. She and Malvo were in Bellingham, she said, and she wondered if Archer could help her cash a check. He said he would try and drove them to a bank. But James didn't have enough identification, so she couldn't get any money. Archer drove them back to the bus station. They wouldn't say where they were staying.

A few weeks later, James called one last time, asking about some belongings she had left behind, not saying where she was. They were safe in storage, Archer said.

"By the way," he asked, "is Lee still with you?"

"No, he's not," she answered.

Archer didn't inquire further. He was sure he knew where Malvo was: back with John Muhammad.

———

Muhammad had reappeared at the Lighthouse shortly after Malvo and his mother were arrested. He said little about Malvo to anyone and stayed through most of December and January. It was the second time he had lost a "son" to the authorities in Bellingham, and he was once again a family of one. But Muhammad continued to show up at the Y early in the morning to work out. He could be heard occasionally fuming that 9/11 had begun the fitting downfall of America. He also continued to work on his rifle problem. He showed up at a dealer in Fife, Washington, near Tacoma, and, as in the Chapman visit, said he wanted to buy a hunting rifle that could be broken down into three parts. The dealership told him it was possible, but it would be very expensive.

After they were released, Malvo and James split up. James appears to have stayed in the area; Malvo probably rejoined Muhammad briefly in Bellingham. They knew Archer had helped James, so they had to be careful. On January 27, four days after Malvo's release from detention, Muhammad checked out of the mission for good. Bellingham would continue to be one of their rest stops for several more months, but they would be mostly on the road. Muhammad had good friends in Tacoma as well as someone with whom he wanted to settle a score.

In February, Muhammad and Malvo moved in with Earl Lee Dancy Jr., an acquaintance who had an apartment near a golf course in Tacoma. Muhammad had known Dancy for about two years. Dancy worked at the Seattle-Tacoma International Airport, and Muhammad was there a lot. Dancy also had things Muhammad was interested in—guns.

He had an MAK-90, a Chinese version of the AK-47 assault rifle. He had a model 70 Winchester rifle with a scope—perhaps Muhammad's inspiration for the Chapman visit. He had a Phoenix Arms .22 pistol, a compact SIG-Sauer .45 pistol, and a Smith & Wesson .44 Magnum revolver. He also had a Remington model 700 .308 hunting rifle.

Dancy also had a computer, and Muhammad eagerly bought software and a new printer to try to manufacture fake documents. He scanned onto a floppy disk birth certificates from Florida and Texas, a Connecticut driver's license, and a blank Texas driver's license, all bogus. Dancy thought Muhammad's missing children were in Antigua and Muhammad was going to use the documents to get them back. To Dancy, Muhammad seemed filled with anger at as well as hatred for the United States and all authority. The country, he said, got what it deserved on September 11.

Most of his anger was directed at his ex-wife and one of her friends. They had conspired to take his children, and he would get them for it. He had Dancy track his wife on an Internet Web site to the Washington, D.C., area. He told Dancy that he had once had a Bushmaster and that it killed him to have to sell it. All he had now was a lousy scope. He'd love to have that Bushmaster back and maybe a silencer. He told Dancy he had qualified as a sniper in the army. Dancy thought this was odd because Muhammad was not a good shot.

Still, he and Malvo often went shooting together at the Tacoma Sportsmen's Club, where Muhammad seemed obsessed with Malvo's marksmanship. Muhammad coached him and bragged about how well he was coming along. If Malvo made any mistakes, Muhammad made him run laps and do push-ups. Malvo always obeyed.

Dancy gave Muhammad and Malvo free use of the firearms and the run of the apartment. They played video games, especially the Xbox game *Halo,* a so-called first-person shooter game in which bold cybersoldiers battle alien forces of evil. The sound effects were fabulous. Malvo loved the game's sniper mode. Muhammad, who had a navy SEALs sniper video, coached him in that, too. One of his favorite movies was *Savior,* in which Dennis Quaid plays an American whose family is killed in a Muslim terrorist bombing in Paris. He avenges them by slaughtering people in a local mosque, then winds up as a mercenary and a sniper in Bosnia. But, in the end, he is redeemed by nurturing an infant born to a raped Serbian refugee.

Muhammad had the movie practically memorized. It was his story, in a mixed-up way: the wronged soldier hero redeemed by a child.

————

On the drizzly evening of February 16, 2002, shortly after Muhammad and Malvo moved in with Dancy, authorities believe they borrowed his trim little .45 SIG-Sauer and carried it across town to the Roosevelt Heights neighborhood on Tacoma's east side. On the corner of East 34th Street and East Roosevelt Avenue sat a pale yellow house overlooking the city's dockyards, the Puyallup River, and foggy Commencement Bay in the distance. It was a nice house, with a stone wall and a porch that faced 34th Street and the city below. There was an attached two-car garage with electric doors and a sign beside the front door that said PLEASE REMOVE SHOES. It was the home of a U.S. Army soldier named Joseph Nichols and his wife, Isa—the same Isa who had been the Muhammads' bookkeeper years before and, more recently, Mildred Muhammad's staunch ally.

Isa didn't like Muhammad. She called him "the chameleon" because he could adapt to any environment. But she thought he was really more like a snake. "You could be sitting in front of him and not know you were in danger," she would say. He had called Isa the previous June, right after he got back from Antigua, trying to find out where Mildred was. Isa, in turn, wanted to find out where the children were, so she invited Muhammad over for a cookout. But he was cagey and didn't give up anything. Neither did Isa. When he drove away, her husband jotted down his license number.

Isa wasn't home that night in February. She was out picking up her thirteen-year-old daughter, Tamara, from a sleepover. Her husband wasn't home, either. The only people in the house were the Nicholses' twenty-one-year-old niece, Keenya Cook, who lived with her aunt and uncle, and Keenya's six-month-old daughter, Angeleah. Keenya was upstairs, about to bathe the baby, who lay on a towel on a bed. There was some food simmering on the stove in the kitchen. Isa and Tammy would be back momentarily.

At about 7:00 P.M., the doorbell rang. Keenya went downstairs in her shirt, jeans, and socks to see who was there. The outdoor porch light, to her right, illuminated the front steps beneath the overhang that protected the caller from the drizzle. But it was dark out and hard to see through the long, narrow cut-glass window in the front door. Cook was a cautious person who wouldn't have opened the door to a stranger, but maybe this was her estranged boyfriend, who had visited earlier in the day. Or maybe it was someone who looked like a kid from the neighborhood. The diminutive Malvo would later say he was the one standing on the doorstep with a pistol. Cook opened the door and looked out onto Roosevelt Avenue. As she did, a single bullet crashed through the thin bone just below her left eye and lodged at the base of her skull. She collapsed in the foyer, beside the ejected brass shell casing and a growing pool of blood.

Moments later, Isa and Tammy pulled into the driveway. Isa waited in the car while Tammy walked around to go in the front door, which was oddly ajar, and open the garage. But in a second the teenager came running back to the car. "Mommy! Mommy!" she cried. "Hurry!"

Initially, police suspected that Keenya's boyfriend, with whom she'd had some rough times, might be responsible for her murder. They took him in and questioned him. But after a while, the case went cold. Isa had the blood cleaned out of the foyer, and Joe installed a camera outside the front door. Nobody had any idea who had killed Keenya. As the months passed, Isa Nichols never dreamed that the .45 slug from the SIG-Sauer might have been meant for her.

———

Dancy's apartment wasn't the only place Muhammad and Malvo stayed during the winter of 2002. Sometimes they would sleep in his car in the apartment complex parking lot. Sometimes they'd visit with other friends in Tacoma: his old army pal Holmes, who thought Muhammad was a little nutty; and Muhammad's girlfriend, whom he had met when he was fixing her sister's car in 1996. Her car had needed repairs, too. He came to her house, and a relationship began.

She was a nurse, and divorced with several children. A carpenter's daughter, she had been raised in Tacoma and had been there almost all her life. Muhammad was honest, gentle, and respectful with her. He opened doors for her, carried her packages, and fixed her daughter's car for free. He became a family friend. She heard about his battle with his wife and his anguish over his missing children. He told her he had been devastated when his wife accused him of threatening her with violence. That was the lowest blow, he said. "You know me," he told her. "I would never, never raise my hand to a woman." His wife knew, he said, that the way to hurt him the most was to keep the children away from him. The children were his world. He lived for them, and the nurse knew that. From a drugstore in Tacoma, she had wired him money when he had them in Antigua. Losing the children "broke" him.

This woman, who wishes to remain unnamed to protect her family, trusted Muhammad. They would work out together at a gym in nearby Lakewood, and he became her guru, trainer, and cheerleader, urging her to take better care of herself, pushing her to work out harder. He was inspiring and positive and fascinating. He seemed to care about everyone and rarely got angry. Sometimes he would stay with her for a while, a few days or a week. Then he'd leave. She fell in love with him and dreamed that someday they might have a life together.

But Muhammad had no interest in a settled life. He was gone much of the time, but he would give the woman's name and phone number as a way to contact him. He would call in, and she would tell him who was trying to reach him. She was like a secretary. He wrote down her name as an emergency contact for Malvo when he registered Malvo at the mission in Bellingham. Malvo called his mother from her home in Tacoma, and his mother later called several times to check on her son's whereabouts.

Muhammad had introduced Malvo as a teenager he was mentoring. He told her that Malvo was intelligent beyond his age and that he was trying to further the boy's education. His mother was a struggling single parent. His father was not around. Muhammad said he was trying to fill Malvo's need for a male role model. When she saw them together, they were like a caring teacher and his student.

But by 2002, Muhammad's lifestyle had gotten to her. She wanted a stable relationship, and she was tired of wondering when he'd be around, tired of his comings and goings. Her house felt as if it had a revolving door, she told him. His life was so frantic, so desperate, and her house was a haven, a place to rest. He would arrive looking haggard. "You need a good meal," she would say. "You need some sleep." In her home, he could find peace and rejuvenation. But after a week or so, he'd be gone again. She wanted a steady partner, and she knew he would never change. Sometimes he would shake his head and wonder how they had ever met. They were so different. So what, she'd say, they still might have been soul mates. She had prayed that things with them would work out. But they didn't.

She had moved away to Colorado for a year, and when she came back to Tacoma, she tried to keep some distance between them. Then she moved again, within Tacoma, in April of 2002, and she didn't tell him her new address. Later she would worry that she might have been a reason for what happened. What if she had still been his refuge, his place of peace?

———————

Muhammad and Malvo lingered in the area but could not escape trouble. They were arrested for shoplifting tea and vegetarian burgers from a supermarket in Tacoma and released on their own recognizance. The Cook murder was in the headlines. And in March, they accidentally bumped into Malvo's mother on a bus in Seattle. There was a ruckus as James tried in vain to wrest her son free. They needed to get out of town. Packing up Muhammad's big duffel bag, they headed south to Los Angeles. From there, on March 13, Muhammad, in the company of a "Lee Muhammad," took a Greyhound bus to Arizona.

Muhammad's older sister, Odessa Newell, had just retired from the air force and lived in Tucson. Their relationship was a difficult one. In the mid-1990s, she had lent him her car while she was stationed in Korea. After she retrieved it from him in Tacoma in 1995, they had not spoken for five years.

Newell picked them up at the bus station. They had dinner and drove around Tucson sightseeing. Then she dropped them off at an

Econo Lodge. Newell took them back to the bus terminal on March 16, but they didn't board an outbound bus for nine days.

Three days after Muhammad and Malvo were dropped off, Jerry Ray Taylor, a sixty-year-old salesman for a frozen foods distributor, was practicing his game at the Fred Enke Golf Course about a mile from Newell's home. A little after lunch, he suddenly collapsed, shot in the back, apparently with a rifle. His attacker dragged his body into some underbrush and took out his wallet but left his cash and credit cards. Witnesses later said they saw a black man carrying a bedroll emerge from an adjacent bird sanctuary, where it was thought the shot came from. Two other golfers found Taylor's body in the brush and called police. Some suspicious DNA was recovered from Taylor's pants. But the killer was never found.

On March 25, Muhammad and Malvo boarded a northbound Greyhound out of Tucson under the names Edward Williams—the name of Muhammad's brother in Baton Rouge—and Edward Williams Jr. A woman named Jill Farrell was driving the bus that day. It was a 337-mile haul that originated at noon in Nogales, on the Mexican border, and wound up in Flagstaff at 10:00 P.M. Behind her seat she put a backpack containing a black zipper pouch with her credit cards. She left the backpack open between Tucson and Phoenix, where she took it out during a two-hour layover.

When Farrell arrived in Flagstaff, she discovered her credit cards were gone. She canceled two of them immediately but forgot about her Bank of America Platinum Visa card. But the bank canceled the card almost immediately because someone had already used it to buy $12.01 worth of gasoline at a service station in Tacoma.

Throughout April and May, Muhammad and Malvo moved back and forth between Bellingham and Tacoma. They were seen frequently at the Bellingham Y, now as Wayne and John Weekly. They could no longer go to the mission and at one point were spotted sleeping on a bench near the bus depot. Two college-age men offered them a place to stay, and they accepted. Once more they switched personas.

Now they were John and Lee Williams, residents of Jamaica who were touring the United States before Lee started college. They'd just come from the Southwest, and seemed ragged but respectable, inviting their hosts to come visit them in Jamaica someday. Father and son were into hygiene and nutrition, sticking to an unusual diet of fruit, vegetables, bread, crackers, and honey. The elder "Williams" said he had once been a U.S. Army Ranger. And one of the few articles of clothing that his "son" wore was a black T-shirt from the British Columbia Rifle Association. The shirt said SNIPER on it.

Muhammad was still on his mission. One day he pored through the phone book looking for a metal shop that could sell him an eighteen-inch piece of tubular titanium. It was for a friend, he said. He made similar inquiries of another Bellingham acquaintance, Harjeet Singh, an immigrant from India with whom he had trained at the Y. Did he know of any machine shops in British Columbia that could make a silencer? He had a book about silencers, and over tea at the local Community Co-op he showed Singh drawings of how they worked.

About a week later, Muhammad showed up at the co-op again. He pulled from his backpack a hollow, eight-inch-long piece of pipe that was threaded at one end and looked as though it had rifling through its core. Muhammad told Singh it was a silencer, and this frightened him. But Singh had heard Muhammad say outrageous stuff before. Once he said he wanted to shoot up a tanker truck and wreak havoc on the interstate. He'd hide in the woods and then sneak away. Another time he said he'd like to kill some cops and then plant a bomb at the funeral home and kill some more.

Muhammad always seemed to have money, often from Caribbean countries, according to Singh, and he was involved in some kind of dispute with an ex-wife who was in Philadelphia or someplace. Sometimes when Muhammad traveled, he would leave Malvo with Singh, and the teenager would talk more freely. Once Malvo told what sounded like a tall tale: When they were in Arizona in March, they had killed two golfers on a golf course, robbed them, and hidden their bodies. Singh thought he had made it up. Months later Malvo would tell a prison guard in Baltimore that he had shot a "senator" on a golf course.

After a few weeks in Bellingham, Muhammad and Malvo returned briefly to Tacoma, hitching a ride to Holmes's garage with one of the college kids. Again they wound up at Dancy's. In early May, police suspect, they borrowed Dancy's big .44 Magnum revolver and went to Temple Beth El, a modern-looking Reform synagogue less than a mile from Dancy's, for some target practice. On a Sabbath morning in early May, Rabbi Mark S. Glickman found a tiny hole in the back wall of the synagogue's ark, where the Torah scrolls are kept. Mice, he thought.

But a few days later, he noticed another small hole in the ark. He called the police, who found two more holes, in the fence outside and in the synagogue wall itself. They dug two bullets out of the synagogue wall and the ark. Six months later, after the snipers were linked to Tacoma and a horrified Dancy turned in his weapons for examination, authorities, at the rabbi's prompting, matched the slugs from Temple Beth El to Dancy's long-barrel revolver.

———

Muhammad and Malvo liked to go to a gun store called Bull's Eye Shooter Supply. The store, located around the corner from a city arena on Tacoma's gritty Puyallap Avenue, has a huge mural of an African safari scene on one of its outside walls. The scene depicts lions, elephants, giraffes, and a huge water buffalo with crosshairs painted over its left eye. Inside the store, scores of rifles are stacked in close quarters in first-floor wall displays. On the second floor, there is a twelve-lane indoor pistol range. Muffled bangs could be heard from the range.

In early July 2002, Bull's Eye received a Bushmaster XM15 E2S, serial number L284–320, with a sixteen-inch barrel. It had been manufactured at the Bushmaster factory in Windham, Maine. A day or two after the Bushmaster arrived, a store armorer began upgrading the rifle for sale, much as a car dealer would add extras to a new car from the factory. The armorer added a Hogue rubber hand grip, a Harris bipod, a high-tech light-laser system, and a Bushnell holographic gun sight. The rifle, propped on its bipod, was displayed on the front counter.

Most ex-soldiers are familiar with a Bushmaster, but some purists dismissed it. It wasn't a heavy-duty hunting rifle. It fired a tiny .223-caliber bullet that some states banned for use against large game. While it was okay for small game like foxes, groundhogs, and prairie dogs, and hence was called a "varmint" round, the bullet was too small to humanely stop a big deer, for example. But its size appealed to the military because more .223 rounds could be carried by a soldier, and on the battlefield it didn't matter whether an enemy was killed or wounded. The Bushmaster was also very easy to use.

Muhammad would linger for hours in the part of the store where the Bushmasters were sold. At the end of one weekend, shortly after it arrived, someone noticed that the rifle that had been displayed so prominently was missing. The assumption was that it had been sold, and it was not until three months later, when it turned up in Muhammad's car, that Bull's Eye Shooter Supply realized the rifle had been stolen.

————

One day that July, John Muhammad and "John Muhammad Jr." boarded another Greyhound and headed southeast for Muhammad's hometown of Baton Rouge. From Tacoma, they headed to Denver, and Albuquerque, and El Paso. There, on July 20, a gun collector and retired insurance salesman named Gary Roger Buchanan had come to a gun show at El Maida, a Shriners auditorium, with several items to sell. One of the guns was a five-shot .22 Magnum revolver his brother had given him as a birthday present several years before. He was asking $169 for it.

Buchanan kept his guns in a display case, which he opened only when someone wanted to see one of them. He'd open the case and then lock it again afterward. But things were so busy that he sometimes forgot to relock the case. At one point that day, when he was distracted talking to someone, he turned his back, and when he looked in the display case again, his .22 was gone.

———————

Around 10:00 one night that month, Muhammad turned up at the home of his first cousin Charlene Anderson in Baton Rouge, in a car driven by an old girlfriend. Anderson, a campus police officer at nearby Southern University, invited him to stay. Muhammad said he first had to go get his "son," who was with one of his aunts. When they returned, Muhammad ordered Malvo out of the room and told Anderson a wild story.

He and the boy were on a secret undercover military mission to track down five hundred pounds of stolen C-4 military explosives. There were other teams searching other cities; his assignment was to search Baton Rouge. Malvo, he said, wasn't really his son but a well-trained secret operative, and part of the team. Five hundred pounds of C-4 was a lot, he told Anderson, removing from his duffel bag a rifle in a case and two boxes of bullets as if to underscore the seriousness of his mission. Anderson thought it was all a little too crazy. The next night she lied, saying she had a friend coming to stay, and kicked her visitors out.

The two secret operatives spent the next week staying with relatives and friends of Muhammad—his sister Aurolyn, whom he hadn't seen in twelve years; his brother, Edward; his ex-wife, Carol. He telephoned an old high school classmate, Janet M. Scott, and told her he and Mildred and the kids were living in the Virgin Islands, where he had a prosperous export business. God had blessed him, he said. He touched base with his son Travis Warren, now twenty-two, whose mother he had never married, and he told stories that nobody believed. He and Malvo were unkempt and hungry, and at one point, Muhammad had but a few grubby $5 bills in his pockets. But they did have guns. In addition to the rifle Anderson saw, they had a small revolver they fired in the woods across the street from his brother's house until his sister-in-law sent her son over to ask them to stop.

By early August, they were back on a Greyhound—now as Lee Williams and Lee Williams Jr.—headed west: Shreveport, Dallas, Amarillo, Denver, Portland, and finally Tacoma, where they stopped in to see Robert Holmes again. They had been to see Holmes several times now in the last few months. Holmes was a big guy, a former boxer who still hung out at a boxing gym in Tacoma's rough Hilltop neighborhood. The forty-six-year-old son of a steelworker in Youngstown, Ohio, Holmes had entered the army late, after being laid off at a grocery chain warehouse. He'd done a four-year hitch and left the service in Fort Lewis, Washington. He thought about going home to Youngstown but was told there was no work there and not to bother coming back. He settled in Tacoma, thirteen miles away, like a lot of Fort Lewis retirees, and eventually opened a garage.

Holmes had known Muhammad since they'd been in the army together in the late 1980s. After they got out and Muhammad started his repair business, he would often bring cars to Holmes's shop to work on them. When Muhammad closed his repair business, he gave Holmes his customer list. Holmes felt sorry for his old friend. Muhammad had not been the best husband, but he'd really been devastated by losing his children in the divorce. Holmes knew the Jamaican kid wasn't his son—that was typical John crap. Muhammad would say crazy stuff sometimes. He kept calling Malvo his "little sniper." Holmes believed his friend had kind of lost it. But Malvo got something out of the deal, too. Holmes saw that he was basically a needy kid. Malvo loved being around Muhammad, was "enchanted" by him. "If you saw them interact," Holmes said, "it was a father-son deal."

Muhammad was strict. But to Holmes it was just old-fashioned African American parenting. The boy would stay in line or else. Muhammad had been the same with his own children.

Malvo, speaking with his jailers later, would refer to Muhammad as his father and would vehemently deny it when he was asked if the relationship had ever included sex. "Hell no," he said. "We Jamaicans don't play that."

Before his divorce, according to Holmes, Muhammad was not a gun person. But afterward Muhammad was always bringing guns around to show him. First was his old Bushmaster, which he once left at Holmes's house for a month. Then he had some kind of deer rifle. "Why do you have that?" Holmes asked him. "Why don't you get an M-16? That's what we were trained on. That's what you're used to. You know how to disassemble it, clean it, everything." Holmes grew increasingly worried about his friend. One time after a gun visit, Holmes was concerned enough to ask Muhammad if he was going after Mildred. "Nope, nope," Muhammad said. "I'm not going to do anything to Mildred." But then he and Malvo showed up with the homemade silencer, the rifle in an aluminum case, and some kind of book that showed how silencers were made.

"Can you imagine the damage you could do if you could shoot with a silencer?" Holmes remembers his friend saying. He showed Holmes a metal tube, coated in rubber, with an outer metal sleeve, but said he didn't know how effective a silencer it really was. Holmes had an old tree stump in his small backyard, so he said: "Fire it in the stump and see if it works."

Muhammad walked outside with his rifle for the test. Holmes was watching TV; Malvo was in the kitchen eating Ritz crackers—they were always eating his Ritz crackers. Holmes could hear the results. The first shot was pretty quiet, the second less so. The third sounded like a normal loud gunshot. The silencer didn't really work. Holmes was relieved. Muhammad left the parts behind when he and Malvo left.

This time, the stay in Washington was brief. They shopped

around for a car and found an ancient white Lincoln that a friend had in his auto garage. It was massive, and Muhammad particularly liked the size of the trunk. But it cost $3,500, and Muhammad didn't have anything like that kind of money.

Near the end of August, a customer of Muhammad's wanted him to fix her car at Holmes's garage. Muhammad told her he could do the job, but she better hurry because he was about to leave town. By now, he and Malvo did not have many places left to stay. There'd been a falling-out with Dancy back in May. He had called home from a trip and was upset to find Muhammad and Malvo there with his wife. He'd asked them to leave, which they had done, but they continued to visit. On August 17, Dancy drove to Sportco, a sporting goods warehouse in Fife, just outside Tacoma, and left his Remington 700 .308 rifle in the car. When he came back to the car, the rifle was gone. An angry Dancy suspected it was his final contact with his two former houseguests.

At about 10:30 P.M. on Thursday, September 5, Paul J. La Ruffa, the proprietor of Margellina's Italian restaurant, in Clinton, Maryland, had just closed for the night. He was walking with an employee and a customer across the parking lot of the Clinton Center, a small strip mall where his restaurant is located, just off busy Route 5, which runs south from Washington, D.C. He was carrying a black leather briefcase, filled with about $3,500 in cash, and a $1,400 Sony VAIO laptop computer he had owned for about nine months. The money would finance a killing spree; the computer would be a crucial tool in keeping it going.

La Ruffa was married and had a son and two grandchildren. He had operated his restaurant for sixteen years. It was named after a district in Naples. He'd never been there but had heard it was nice. He opened the back door of his sleek green Chrysler 300M, put his laptop and briefcase on the backseat, and then got in. Just as he did, he saw a shadow at the driver's-side window, and he sensed a smallish figure. Almost instantly, there were several flashes of gunfire. The window shattered and bullets plowed into his left arm, chest, and side. As La Ruffa leaned to his right, trying to duck, someone yanked open the back door and grabbed his briefcase and laptop. La Ruffa opened his door, staggered into the parking lot, and hollered for somebody to call 911, vowing to himself that he was not going to die in that lousy parking lot. His attacker, who had been hiding behind a church van parked at one end of the lot, escaped into a wooded area bordering the shopping center.

Just down the road a few blocks was a development of modern houses, with streets like Black Willow, Mayapple, and Button Bush. One street was called Quiet Brook Lane. Living there at the moment was a forty-one-year-old divorcée with three children. She had recently moved from Tacoma, Washington, to escape an abusive husband. Her name was Mildred Muhammad.

La Ruffa guessed he had been shot five or six times, although one bullet appeared to have made several holes in him: two in his left arm and one in his side. Both of his lungs collapsed. He was rushed to a local hospital, spent several hours in surgery and several days in intensive care. But he survived. In the operating room, doctors left behind some of the shattered bullet fragments but were able to remove one "good" slug and turn it over to police. It appeared to be from a small-caliber pistol, like a .22.

The next day, from the bus terminal in Camden, New Jersey, John Muhammad and Lee Malvo telephoned Nathaniel O. Osbourne, the brother of Walford Osbourne, someone Muhammad knew from Antigua. They were just passing through town, had a little money, and were wondering if Osbourne, who lived in Camden, could help them buy a car. Osbourne felt sorry for them. They looked dirty and hungry, although they did have a nice laptop computer. Osbourne fed them, gave them some clothes, and took them to look at cars.

They passed on a Honda Accord and a Honda Prelude. Too small. Then they went to Sure Shot Auto Sales in Trenton, where

Muhammad's eye was caught by a big blue 1990 Chevrolet Caprice. It was a former Bordentown, New Jersey, police cruiser. Though it was originally white, the police had painted it blue and used it as an unmarked detective's car. It had a little front-end damage, but otherwise was okay. It had 146,975 miles on it, but the car was for his son, Muhammad told the dealer, or he might use it as a taxi. For $250, Muhammad and Malvo now had a car and the freedom to go where they liked. They headed back south.

On September 12, they were in Alexandria, Virginia, making a purchase from a health food store in the afternoon and placing a calling card call to Antigua from a Shoppers Food Warehouse that night. They made another call from an Alexandria video store early the next morning.

On September 14, across the Potomac River, in the Hillandale section of Silver Spring, Maryland, Arnie Zelkovitz and his employee Rupinder (Benny) Oberoi were just closing Zelkovitz's Hillandale Beer and Wine store for the evening. It was around 10:00 on a Saturday night. They were outside, and Zelkovitz was showing Oberoi how to lock up. Suddenly there was a boom. Oberoi thought it was a firecracker. Zelkovitz thought it was a backfire. In a second Oberoi was on the ground, pain filling the left side of his body, a tiny hole in his lower back. Zelkovitz looked at the wound and said: "You've been shot."

In the parking lot of a nearby Safeway supermarket, an employee noticed an old dark car that might have been a Chevy Caprice pull out of a parking space and drive away. He told the police about it, but the feeling was that it was probably just a customer. Oberoi was taken to the hospital, where he was found to be very lucky. The bullet had bruised a kidney and his liver and had lacerated his diaphragm and colon. There was nothing more serious. But there was not enough of the bullet left for the police to make any comparisons. Zelkovitz was baffled. There was no robbery. Nobody had said anything to them. It could be that he had pissed someone off someplace. But Benny? He was a nice young guy. Why would someone want to shoot him?

The next night, September 15, at almost the same time, Muhammad Rashid, a Pakistani immigrant, was closing up Three Road Liquor, a drive-through liquor store with a tiny bar and poolroom in Brandywine, Maryland. Three Road was set back off the highway, at the bleak intersection of Route 5 and Brandywine Road, across the street from a tattoo parlor. It was only about four miles from where La Ruffa had been shot ten days before and about three miles from Mildred Muhammad's address.

It was raining. Rashid had just sent the bartender home. He glanced out the window before he left and spotted an old dark car parked beside the store with its hood up. He went outside and had just started turning the lock in the door when he heard two loud sounds. Two holes appeared in the door, one in the frame inches from his head, another in the glass right in front of him. He realized he was being robbed. He turned and saw a slight, dark-skinned man with a pistol. There was a flash and another bang, and Rashid felt a stab in his abdomen. He dropped down and played dead.

The attacker rolled him over, searched his pockets, found his wallet, and then patted him, as if in satisfaction. Rashid had the sensation that someone else was present, too. He waited until well after he heard his attacker walk away, then he sat up and called 911 from his cell phone. Rashid was helicoptered to a Washington trauma center, where his injuries were found to be serious but non-life-threatening. This time, doctors were able to retrieve the bullet and give it to police, who discovered an interesting thing: It matched the ones that had been fired at Paul La Ruffa.

Muhammad and Malvo were mobile now. On September 16, they made a calling card call from a Pep Boys in Temple Hills, Maryland, about twelve miles north of Brandywine. The next day, they made a call from the YMCA in Silver Spring; the day after that, from a restaurant called the Ponderosa Steakhouse, in Ashland, Virginia, just north of Richmond. They had gone into a nearby dollar store and asked where there was a good place to eat. An employee recommended the Ponderosa. They came back a little while later and thanked her. It was indeed a good restaurant. They'd be back. On September 19, at 4:27 A.M., they were found sleeping in the car in the parking lot of a Ramada Inn in Petersburg, Virginia, on the other side of Richmond. They seemed to be headed south.

Two days later, and five hundred miles to the southwest, Mimi Taddesse and her friend Million A. Woldemariam were about to close up her business, Sammy's Package Store, a liquor outlet on Martin Luther King Jr. Drive SW, in Atlanta. It was 12:16 A.M. and raining. Woldemariam, an Ethiopian immigrant, had gone outside to warm up his car and spotted another car idling in the lot. Sammy's was in an isolated spot west of downtown. Sprawling Westview Cemetery was across the street, and Interstate 20 was a block or two north.

When her friend came back inside, Taddesse, also an Ethiopian, told him not to go out again. She was worried about that other car. No one else was supposed to be out there. But Woldemariam went back out anyhow, to stand guard. He had been gone a few seconds when Taddesse heard gunshots. She looked out the door and saw him collapsed in the rain. She saw nothing else. Woldemariam died eleven hours later at the Atlanta Medical Center. He had been shot twice in the upper back, just below the neck, and once in the back of the head. His wallet was missing. It looked as though someone had sneaked up on him, just as with La Ruffa and Rashid. And just as in their shootings, the bullet pieces picked from his wounds were small and probably from a .22 pistol.

Later that afternoon, Joey Matthews, a part-time gun dealer from Dothan, Alabama, was manning his display at a gun show at the Montgomery, Alabama, Civic Center. At about 2:30, a black teenager, who was with an older black adult, approached Matthews and began asking about a Bushmaster XM15 E2S that he had on display. The boy handled the rifle and asked about its range, accuracy, scope mountings, reliability, and magazine capacity. The boy, who had some kind of foreign accent, said he'd like to buy the rifle, but he was only seventeen. The adult never spoke.

September 21 was a Saturday, and that meant football in Montgomery. The Hornets of Alabama State University were playing the
University of Arkansas–Pine Bluff that night in the city's Cramton
Bowl. The stadium would be filled with ASU black and gold. As the
evening kickoff neared, Claudine Parker, an ASU graduate, was
anxious to close up the state liquor store she managed a few blocks
away. Parker, fifty-two, had season tickets and planned to join her
friends at the game right after work. Parker loved sports.

That evening, she was working with a twenty-four-year-old
cashier named Kellie Adams, who had been robbed at gunpoint in a
liquor store the previous December. Adams had thought about quit-
ting, but state jobs were hard to come by, and she guessed she would
never be robbed twice. They had just locked up. Adams had to go pick
up her eighteen-month-old daughter from a relative who was baby-
sitting. Parker was heading for her car and the game. Then came two
gunshots. Adams thought she had been struck by lightning. A bullet
went through the back of her neck, broke her left jawbone, and
sheared off the tops of two upper teeth before coming out her cheek.

Parker was struck in the back by a bullet that severed her spinal
cord, paralyzing her instantly and wreaking fatal internal injuries.
She had no heartbeat when paramedics arrived minutes later. They
managed to revive her, but she died in Montgomery's Jackson Hospital about three hours later. Adams, too, was rushed to Jackson,
where she underwent surgery and recovered. Montgomery police
officers, who were close enough to hear the shots, arrived in seconds
and saw a man with a handgun standing over the women, going
through their purses. They chased him, but the gunman vanished.
They did get three puzzling clues.

At the scene, investigators found a gun collector's magazine that
the killer apparently dropped. There were fingerprints on it, but
they didn't match anything in the local database. Doctors also recovered pieces of the bullet that killed Parker. It was later found to be a
.223 rifle round, from something like an M-16. And many days after
the attack, a passerby found a pistol in some underbrush along the

route that Parker's killer had taken to escape. It was a small North American Arms five-shot .22-caliber Magnum revolver. Police didn't know it yet, but it was Gary Roger Buchanan's stolen birthday gun from El Paso.

By September 22, Muhammad and Malvo were back in Baton Rouge. They made two calling card phone calls that evening and bought $2.26 worth of lettuce and bell peppers from a Piggly Wiggly store the next morning. The night of the twenty-third, at about 6:40, Hong Im Ballenger had just locked up the Baton Rouge Beauty Depot business where she worked on Florida Boulevard. Ballenger, forty-five, was a native of Korea who had married an American GI, James Ballenger. She and another employee were headed for their cars. Ballenger had reached her SUV and had her car keys and purse in her hands. Suddenly there was a loud boom and Ballenger was down on the pavement, killed almost instantly by a bullet in the head.

The employee spotted a large dark car, driven by a black man, pull out of a vacant field about seventy-five yards away and then stop about a block to the east. There, it picked up another black man, who was holding Ballenger's purse. The car sped away. Police called out the bloodhounds, but they found nothing. Doctors removed pieces of the bullet from Ballenger's body. Police saved them as evidence. They appeared to be from a .223 rifle round.

The day after the Ballenger murder, Muhammad and Malvo were in Our Daily Bread, a health food market a few miles down Florida Boulevard from the beauty store. The two had been in the same store over the summer, and some of the people who worked there suspected they'd been shoplifting. This time, the staff watched them carefully until they left. And on September 27, the two purchased a $1.99 container of grape juice at a Save-A-Lot store that was also on Florida Boulevard about a mile from the Ballenger killing.

They seemed to knock around Baton Rouge to no purpose. They again visited Muhammad's son Travis, who would remember the old car with the New Jersey plates and a rifle his father kept in a duffel bag. Muhammad exercised at a local branch of the YMCA, telling people he was a doctor who could heal people with herbs.

At 2:58 P.M. on September 28, in Gulfport, Mississippi, city police officer Scott Courrege became suspicious of a beat-up blue Caprice with New Jersey tags parked at 28th Street and 25th Avenue. He ran the license number through a crime computer and found no problems.

Muhammad and Malvo were on the road again. Gulfport was 134 miles due east of Baton Rouge, via the big east-west Gulf Coast Interstates 12 and 10. They had paused there to buy some produce and pick up a few DVDs from a video store. Two days later, they were five hundred miles north, in Anderson, South Carolina, probably having passed back through Montgomery, Alabama, and Atlanta. They made a calling card call at 11:38 A.M. from a rest stop on Interstate 85, which cuts northeast across North Carolina and hits Interstate 95 just below Richmond. At 1:24 A.M. on October 1, a police officer in the Washington suburb of Fairfax County, Virginia, ran the Caprice's license number through a crime computer to see if it was legit. The owner was identified as John Muhammad. The officer then ran the name through the computer. The only thing found in the database was an order of protection that had once been granted to his wife.

In twenty-one days, Muhammad and Malvo had traveled over 2,600 miles in their Caprice. In the next few weeks, they would be staying in a more confined geographic area.

4

A Rifle at Rush Hour

At 7:41 A.M. on October 3, 2002, the Washington morning commuter rush was reaching its height. The major highways that connect to the city like spokes to a hub, and the sixty-four-mile Beltway that rings the capital, were swollen with some of the heaviest traffic in the nation. From the Maryland suburbs north and west of town, the rush cascaded downhill along four roughly parallel roadways: Georgia Avenue, Connecticut Avenue, Rockville Pike, and Interstate 270. All were pretty much clogged, as usual.

The blazing heat of the Washington summer was gone. There was a breeze out of the west, and the sun had burned off some morning fog. Two blocks off the traffic crush on Rockville Pike, in a largely commercial area called White Flint, James L. Buchanan Jr., a thirty-nine-year-old landscaper, was mowing grass behind a car dealership.

His nickname was Sonny. He was the son of a retired Montgomery County policeman and had grown up in Gaithersburg, about fifteen miles north. He had a fiancée and had recently moved his work to Virginia, but he continued to help the folks at the Fitzgerald Auto Mall, who had been longtime customers. Pushing a green Lawn-Boy with a cloth grass catcher, he was mowing a small, bland patch of lawn along Huff Court, an isolated street that ran behind the dealership and ended at the parking lot of the sprawling White Flint Mall. He was probably less than a hundred yards from where the security guard, Portia Burch, had seen John Muhammad the night before.

Over the din of the Lawn-Boy and the traffic, there was suddenly a loud crack. Buchanan had his back turned. A block away, Rick Tyner was driving to work with his wife. Tyner was a Vietnam veteran and had seen combat with the 101st Airborne Division. He couldn't believe what he heard: "That was a rifle shot," he told his wife. In the parking lot of the car dealership, the mechanics saw Buchanan, in his shorts, T-shirt, and baseball cap, staggering toward them. He had left his lawn mower, which kept on rolling, and was clutching his chest and gasping. Malvo would laugh later when he told investigators how the mower kept going. Buchanan got about two hundred feet inside the fence and collapsed on his face. One of the mechanics ran to him and yelled for someone to call 911. Jim King, a parts manager, got on the line to emergency dispatch.

"This guy's lawn mower did something, man," King told the dispatcher. "It chopped him up. He's bleeding real bad. He's down and out. . . . He's bleeding out the mouth. His lawn mower caught the curb or something."

But when Tyner went to examine the mower, nothing seemed wrong with it. He had gone to look after rushing to Buchanan's side just before the paramedics arrived. He had watched as they turned Buchanan on his back, revealing a hole in his chest the size of a coffee mug. With all the blood, it only looked that big. The wound was actually about an inch and a half by an inch and a quarter, and there was a smaller hole right beside it. Closer inspection would have also revealed a tiny hole in Buchanan's back about an eighth of an inch wide, very similar to the hole found in James Martin's back the night before.

When the medics cut off Buchanan's shirt, they detected a faint heartbeat. They didn't notice the fine grains of lead stuck to the shirt fabric. Police would find them weeks later in the blood drying room at headquarters.

Buchanan was rushed to the trauma unit of Suburban Hospital, in Bethesda. The on-duty trauma surgeon, Dr. Jim Robey, was waiting in the trauma bay with an emergency team. Buchanan was in cardiopulmonary arrest on arrival, so they had to be quick and aggressive. Robey took a large "ten-blade" scalpel and made a fast sixteen-inch lateral incision across Buchanan's left chest. He used scissors to cut through the muscle. He inserted a rib spreader between two of Buchanan's ribs and cranked it open. He wanted to see if he could fix the damage and if there was any motion at all in Buchanan's heart. But not only was Buchanan's heart still, it was empty of blood. His chest cavity largely was, too. "Doc," one of the medics remarked, "he bled more than anyone I've ever seen."

There was nothing to do but sew him back up. Robey was still thinking Buchanan had suffered some kind of freak lawn mower injury, as he had been told. In fact, a .223 rifle bullet had struck Buchanan almost in the same spot as James Martin and torn through his left lung. Tumbling like an errant rocket, and coming apart, the bullet had perforated his left pulmonary vein, sent fragments into the left ventricle of his heart, and broken a rib when it exited his chest.

As Robey was finishing, Ann Kuzas, a supervisory trauma nurse who had been standing by, spoke up. "Jim, you think this could be a gunshot wound?" she asked.

"You know, it very well could be," he said. If the chest wound was an exit wound, there should be an entrance wound in the back. They rolled Buchanan over, and Robey spotted the minuscule wound in his back. It looked smaller than the tip of a pencil.

"It's too small," he said. The big handgun wounds that the hospital usually sees were not that subtle. Plus, there weren't any powder burns around the wound. They rolled Buchanan back over again.

But a police officer at the hospital had become suspicious. She called her supervisor, who called the Major Crimes Division. Word also filtered to the office of the county state's attorney. There, a veteran prosecutor listened to the story and thought: That ain't no fucking lawn mower accident.

Thirty-one minutes after Buchanan went down and six miles away, a cabdriver from Pune, India, and a pediatrician from Leeds, England, pulled up to adjacent gas pumps at a Mobil gas station on Connecticut Avenue. The gas station was in the Aspen Hill neighborhood, half a block from where the bullet went through the window of the Michaels store the night before.

Premkumar A. Walekar, fifty-four, who was driving the gray taxi, lived in the county's Olney section. He was a portly, amiable man with a black beard and toupee, who attended a Seventh-day Adventist Church. He had a wife, to whom he had been wed for twenty-five years after an arranged marriage, and two children. Caroline Namrow, an urgent care doctor for Kaiser Permanente, had just delivered her five-year-old son and two other children to their school down the road. She still had her two-year-old son, strapped in a car seat in her silver van.

When Namrow pulled into the station, Walekar was already there, pumping gas into his cab. He had gone into the convenience store a moment earlier to buy gum and lottery tickets. The front of Namrow's van was across from the back of Walekar's, and she could see him clearly out the window. They exchanged smiles. She glanced down to get a credit card from her purse on the front passenger seat. As she did, she heard a bang, which she thought might have been his car. When she looked up she saw Walekar walking toward her. He had a startled look on his face. "Call an ambulance," he said, and then collapsed beside her van.

Namrow realized he'd been shot. She grabbed her cell phone and dialed 911 as she scrambled out of the van. She found Walekar bleeding heavily from his left side. There was a huge smear of his blood on the front passenger-side door of her van.

"Oh, my God, a man is dead on Aspen Hill Road!" she screamed when a dispatcher answered. "It's a Mobil station on the corner of Aspen Hill. Is this Connecticut? . . . Please call an ambulance."

"Aspen Hill and what?" the dispatcher asked.

"I don't know!" Namrow cried, her British accent making her a little hard to understand. "Aspen Hill and Connecticut Avenue." She pronounced it "Connect-ta-cut."

"What's wrong?" the dispatcher said.

"Oh, my God," Namrow yelled. "A man has been killed in front of me!"

"How is he being killed in front of you?" the dispatcher asked.

"He was shot!"

Spotting a police car, Namrow hung up and, with a gas station attendant, flagged the cruiser down. She then raced back to work on Walekar, who lay on his back. She felt his right arm for a pulse. It was very faint. She began chest compressions and mouth-to-mouth resuscitation, taking note of the heavy bleeding from Walekar's left side.

When the officer arrived, Namrow told him to take over the compressions while she continued mouth-to-mouth, something she had never done before. Walekar had a sucking chest wound, in which air was entering through the hole. Blood pooled beside her van. Walekar vomited. Now his airway was blocked. Namrow tried to clear it but couldn't. Just then an ambulance pulled up. As the medics took over, she tried to seal his wound with gauze. It was no use.

The bullet had burrowed like a poker under the skin of Walekar's upper left arm and into his left side. Fragments ripped through his left lung, one of the chambers of his heart, the trunk of his pulmonary artery, and his ascending aorta. Two of his ribs were broken. Walekar was five feet nine and weighed 225 pounds. There appeared to be no exit wound. Walekar was put in the ambulance, Medic 22, which started for nearby Montgomery General Hospital. The medics reported to the hospital that he was "asystolic," meaning he had no heartbeat. But then they couldn't get through the heavy radio traffic to update. En route, Medic 22 reached the fire and ambulance dispatcher, who relayed a message from the hospital: "If your patient is still asystolic . . . you may cease resuscitation efforts." Over the shriek of his siren and the radio static, Medic 22 copied.

At 8:37 A.M., just as the medics gave up on Walekar, an elderly man called 911 from a restaurant in a shopping center beside the Leisure World retirement community, a mile and a half north of the Mobil station. The shopping center was just off Georgia Avenue, still packed with rush-hour traffic.

"I need an ambulance and police at Leisure World Plaza at the end by the post office," the man said. "A girl just shot herself."

"She just what?" the dispatcher said.

"She just *shot* herself," the caller replied. "Settin' on the bench there. . . ."

"Are you sure that she shot herself?" the dispatcher asked.

"Well, I don't know. I was putting a letter in the mailbox, and I heard a big bang. I couldn't figure out where it was coming from. And then I looked over to the left and there, this girl, [who] was sitting there when I came in, she was all falled over and bleeding. Okay?"

The dispatcher said he would send someone right away.

Minutes later, the dispatch center reached a Leisure World security guard who had hurried to the scene.

"Do you see any weapons near her?" the dispatcher asked.

"It's hard to tell," the guard said.

"We had reports that she shot herself," the dispatcher said.

"It could be," the guard said. "I don't see a weapon."

"You don't see a weapon?" the dispatcher said, a touch of anxiety in his voice.

There was a bullet hole in the window of the restaurant behind where she was sitting, the guard said.

"Is anyone gonna do CPR?" the dispatcher asked.

"Uhhhh, probably not."

Sarah Ramos, a thirty-four-year-old former law student from El Salvador, had taken the bus from her home and was waiting to be picked up by a woman whose house she was going to clean. She was wearing jeans, sandals, and an orange blouse and was carrying a small purse.

Ramos had immigrated to the Washington area with her son and husband, a college teacher in El Salvador. Despite their education, Ramos and her husband spoke little English, and life in America had been hard for them. Her husband had not been able to teach and had grown despondent. She had been forced to take housecleaning jobs, which she had at first hated. She had been reading on the bench, her purse beside her and her head down. She wouldn't have seen the dark blue Chevrolet Caprice that a witness later reported seeing parked at the far edge of the shopping center parking lot, its front facing Georgia Avenue, its rear facing the bench where she sat.

The .223 rifle bullet entered the top of her skull, leaving its tiny entry hole and causing extensive "comminuted," or eggshell, fractures. It exited at the nape of her neck, leaving a jagged V-shaped hole in her skull and a shattered window in the restaurant behind her before coming to rest on the floor inside. She slumped to her right. Her booklet, still in her lap, quickly became soaked with blood.

Three people killed, in less than an hour. At around 8:40 A.M., fire dispatch radioed units at the Walekar shooting for help with the latest incident.

"Medic engine two-five-one," a dispatcher called.

"Medic engine two-five-one," the unit responded.

"Medic engine two-five-one, can you be released for another shooting?"

"That's negative," the unit responded.

"Can I have the ambulance?" the dispatcher asked.

"That's negative," 251 responded.

Both were tied up.

———

A few minutes after Premkumar Walekar was shot outside his cab, Patrick McNerney, the Montgomery County police detective who had handled the Martin case the night before, got a phone call from his sister, Mary Ellen Donovan. McNerney was at his home in Aspen Hill; his sister, who also lived in Aspen Hill and was a TV news editor, was at the scene.

"Hey," she said, "there's a shooting up here at Connecticut and Aspen Hill. Guy at a gas station."

"Hmmmm," said McNerney, who hadn't heard the news. "Got any more information about it?"

"No," his sister said.

"Anything odd happen about the time of the shooting, or anything like that?"

"Well, yes," his sister said. "People heard a loud bang."

"I'm on my way," McNerney said.

When Corporal Gene Curtis of the Major Crimes Division arrived at Suburban Hospital, Sonny Buchanan's body was in a body bag on a table in an operating room off the trauma bay, ready to be taken to the Maryland Medical Examiner's Office in Baltimore for an autopsy. Curtis had the bag unzipped and knew this wasn't a lawn mower accident. "This type of gunshot wound goes in small and comes out very large," he told the doctors. "Let's roll him over and make sure."

There, in the middle of Buchanan's back, was the small entry wound. Curtis telephoned his sergeant, Roger Thomson, and then hurried back to the car dealership where Buchanan had died. He had to secure the area. It was a crime scene now. This made three killings so far that morning, and four, counting Martin the night before. How many of these are we going to have? he thought. Maybe the shooter would go after a cop next.

Outside the Hines-Rinaldi Funeral Home in Silver Spring, scores of black-and-white Harley-Davidson police motorcycles were lined up, their drivers—county motorcycle officers in black boots, leather puttees, and gold-buttoned, olive-drab "green coats"—ready to escort a comrade to his grave.

Corporal William L. Foust III, a popular motorcycle patrolman who had been on the force twenty-nine years and was scheduled to retire in a few weeks, had died of a heart attack the previous Sunday at a wedding in Virginia. A cigar-smoking officer with a fat mustache and three Harleys of his own, Bill Foust worked out of the Third District station in Silver Spring. His buddies, along with motorcycle officers from around the region, were ready to take their last ride with him seven miles to Gate of Heaven Cemetery, in the county's Aspen Hill neighborhood. It was 9:30 A.M.

Third District commander Drew Tracy had been busy all morning, making sure that everything would go well at the funeral home for the family of a friend as well as a colleague. He and Foust had planned on going deer hunting in a few weeks, and Tracy had sent a motorcycle escort to bring Foust's body home from Virginia. All the department's brass, including Police Chief Charles A. Moose, would be at a funeral like this.

Tracy, who had trained as a police sniper, had been out of touch all morning, his cell phone and walkie-talkie turned off, and knew nothing of the mayhem of the last two hours. He had not heard about the Martin murder the night before either, because it wasn't in his district. He was focused on the funeral and its logistics. Just before the cortege was to leave for the cemetery, Lieutenant Alan Goldberg, head of the honor guard, got Tracy's attention.

"What are you going to do with the procession?" Goldberg asked.

"What do you mean, what am I going to do with the procession?" Tracy replied.

"What are you going to do?" Goldberg repeated. It was headed right up to Aspen Hill.

"We have this all mapped out," Tracy said. "Down New Hampshire Avenue. North on Georgia Avenue. To Gate of Heaven Cemetery."

"No," Goldberg said. "What are you going to do with the sniper out there?"

"Alan, what are you talking about?" Tracy asked.

Goldberg explained what was going on. The procession, with all its mourners and vehicles, was headed right into the hot zone.

————————

At 9:40 A.M., Fred Lofberg, an accountant and aficionado of old cars, was driving to an appointment in Kensington. He was northbound on Connecticut Avenue, which cuts right through the town, when he stopped for a red light. There was a Shell service station on the northeast corner of the intersection, which was five miles south of where Ramos had just been shot and about two miles east of where Buchanan was fatally injured. Lofberg was in a hurry and noted the time as well as the old dark Chevy Caprice with tinted windows and a New Jersey plate that was also waiting at the light.

About eighteen minutes later, at a Safeway down a slight hill from the Shell station, Maria Welsh, a pediatric intensive care nurse, had just finished loading her minivan with groceries. As she backed her car out of its parking spot, she heard a loud boom. The Caprice was probably parked about thirty yards behind her at the edge of the Safeway parking lot, and Welsh may well have been in the Bushmaster's sights herself for a moment. But Welsh had been busy moving, unloading, and returning the empty cart, so the target instead was a woman in jeans and a short-sleeved top, who now lay on the ground beside a burgundy minivan parked by the car vacuum at the Shell station.

As Welsh drove across the lot toward Connecticut Avenue, she heard someone crying, "Help, unnhh, help me," and then saw the woman on the ground. She dialed her cell phone as she drove toward her and saw that the woman was going into convulsions and bleeding from the mouth and nose.

"We need an ambulance at the corner of Knowles and Connecticut," Welsh said excitedly when the dispatcher answered. "A

woman was vacuuming her car. Something blew up. She's uncon-
scious. She's got blood coming out of her nose and her mouth."

"Do you know any more, like what happened?" the dispatcher
asked.

"I heard this huge loud noise, like a bomb," she said. "Like, it
wasn't a bomb, I mean, it was that kind of noise."

"Sound like a gunshot, maybe?" the dispatcher asked.

"Kinda," Welsh said.

The woman had fallen under the open door of her car, and
Welsh untangled her from the hose of the vacuum, which was still
running. She felt the woman's right wrist and neck for a pulse and
noticed that her lips and fingers were turning blue. She looked to see
if her chest was rising, which would show if she was breathing. It
wasn't. Welsh was still on the phone with the dispatchers: Why were
they asking her all these questions? Where was the ambulance?

Lori Lewis was nineteen when she left the tiny town of Mountain Home, Idaho, right out of Mountain Home High School. She
went to Northwest Nannies Institute, near Portland. She loved kids,
was good with them, and was determined that this would be her career and also a way to see a bit of the world. After she graduated, she
was placed with a family in Washington, D.C. When her new employer, Ellen Weiss, a senior editor at National Public Radio, went to
meet her at the airport, Lewis was carrying a single suitcase and a
thick portfolio containing games, recipes, and tips on child care,
which she insisted on showing Weiss.

Lewis was a large woman with a sweet disposition and fine blond
hair that was almost white. Portland to Washington was a big jump
for Lewis. She had found the new city a little scary. But she soon met
another nanny, a Mormon who worked in the neighborhood, and she
began getting involved in church activities. The two women joined a
Spanish-speaking Mormon group because they wanted to learn the
language, and there Lewis met an immigrant landscaper, Nelson
Rivera, who had grown up on a watermelon farm in Honduras. Although he spoke little English and she spoke little Spanish, romance

blossomed. They were married within a year and a year after that had a daughter, Jocelin.

The morning of October 3, Lori Lewis Rivera, as she would be identified in the newspapers the next day, had just pulled up to the Shell station to clean out the burgundy minivan owned by her current employer. She had just turned on the vacuum when the bullet struck her square in the back. It left a minute hole and then fragmented inside her chest, never exiting. It wrought most of its damage to her left lung, which was perforated and then collapsed.

As Welsh tried to help her, a county police officer, Terry Ridgely, who had been on patrol a few blocks away, pulled up in his car. As he did, a firefighter from a firehouse across the street raced over to help. He began CPR. Seconds later, a second county police officer, Richard Grapes, arrived and Ridgely told him to secure the scene. Grapes went to his car and grabbed a twelve-gauge shotgun and a heavy ballistic shield. He knelt with his shotgun and shield and placed himself between the open parking lot where the gunshot was heard and the desperate trio beside the minivan.

The medics examining Rivera said she was essentially dead, but when she was taken to Suburban Hospital, the trauma team tried for fifteen minutes to revive her. It was the second critical gunshot case of the morning for Robey's team, and this time they knew what they were looking for.

"This wound is the exact same place," Robey said. "Someone's just picking people off." He had already called his wife and told her to get off the streets but figured the shooter was so reckless that he would be quickly caught. "We're going to be safe tomorrow."

––––––

Back at the funeral home, Drew Tracy realized he had a potential disaster on his hands. The procession was scheduled to head straight up Georgia Avenue, right into the area where the shooting was. "Ground zero," he called it. The cortege would make an incredible target. He was the ranking officer present. Should he allow things to go forward? How could he not? He gathered together several of the police supervisors in a side parking lot and gave them the choice. "We are burying Corporal Foust right there in Aspen Hill. . . . If anyone wants to back out, by all means do."

"We're in," one said, speaking for all.

One thing about being a cop, Tracy thought. You're guaranteed a nice funeral.

Tracy decided he needed to take some precautions. Montgomery County police did not have a helicopter, so he telephoned a friend in Prince George's County, which did. Tracy explained what was going on. "I need your helicopter up here right away," he said. "I need you to follow our procession as we go to the burial grounds."

With the helicopter overhead and members of Tracy's SWAT team deployed along the route, the procession reached the cemetery, only a few thousand feet from where Walekar was killed. Tracy told the honor guard to be quick, and after a warning had been radioed of what was about to come, it fired off a salute.

Afterward, Tracy handed the folded flag from Foust's casket to his wife, Denise.

"I don't know if you really understand what's going on," he said.

"Oh no," she replied, "I know what is going on."

She might be the only person who did, Tracy thought as he headed for his car to change out of his dress uniform.

––––––

The full impact of what was happening was now clear to the police and the entire Washington region. There was a sniper stalking central Montgomery County, killing, it appeared, at random. Five people had been murdered in sixteen hours, four of them in the span of two hours and seventeen minutes. This had occurred in a densely populated part of the Washington suburbs, roughly five miles long and three miles wide. It had occurred in well-traveled areas and in daylight. Witnesses reported hearing a very loud gunshot, but none had seen anything of substance. There seemed to be no link among the victims, and they crossed racial and gender lines: There were two white men, a white woman, an Indian man, and a Hispanic woman. At the Mobil station, county detective sergeant Roger L. Thomson realized he was in trouble. He had multiple scenes and no evidence. And he was out of people.

There was, however, what seemed to be one solid clue. Juan Carlos Villeda, a twenty-year-old Guatemalan immigrant, was working with a landscaping crew on the shopping center grounds near Leisure World that morning. He told John Dassoulas, a Spanish-speaking police crime analyst, that he had seen Ramos walk past a nearby post office, pick up a booklet on top of one of the mailboxes, and sit on the bench. He saw her open the booklet. Moments later, he heard a loud explosion. He thought it was a tire blowing out. When he looked back at Ramos, he saw that she had been hit and was on the bench, shaking. Villeda then saw a white truck with a small cab and box-type rear speeding in front of Ramos. The truck turned onto a side street and headed toward Georgia Avenue.

Villeda could see exhaust smoke belching from the tailpipe as the truck raced away. The truck had an engine that sounded like a diesel. It had purple or black lettering that was in English, which Villeda couldn't read. The truck had a dent in the rear and damage to the right rear bumper. Two men were inside.

Police broadcast a lookout for the vehicle. In the coming days, as Villeda was interviewed over and over by Dassoulas, his report was to take on huge significance. White box trucks and vans were repeatedly stopped at gunpoint. They were seen by the public everywhere. White vans were, in fact, everywhere. There were over seventy thousand just in Maryland. In the midst of this frantic search, a blue Caprice became almost invisible.

Barney Forsythe and Chief Moose never made it to Bill Foust's funeral. Moose dropped his plans to fly out to Minneapolis for the convention of police chiefs later that morning, even though his wife, Sandy, had just arrived there. From the frenzy of his office at police headquarters, Forsythe ordered all available detectives to report for duty. Reporters stampeded to the county, and news helicopters clattered overhead. Local TV stations interrupted their morning programs and went live.

A county police spokeswoman assured a TV reporter that schoolchildren were safe. But most schools, public and private, stationed security guards outside and went into a "code blue" lockdown, an emergency status in which outside doors were locked and students were counted and monitored closely between classes. Forsythe ordered out the command bus, and a command post was set up at a church on Aspen Hill Road, a block from the Mobil station where Walekar was killed, to try to coordinate the investigation and the media response.

The police spokeswoman was Captain Nancy Demme, who also happened to be a lawyer. Though she had been promoted to the media job a month before, this was only her second dealing with the press. She didn't even have business cards. "Maximum disclosure; minimum delay," Moose had advised her. "Tell them or they'll make it up." She had been to the scene of the Martin murder the night before. But that was nothing compared to what she was about to face. At the Mobil station she found a horde of frenzied reporters, many worried about their own safety. They rushed toward her like spooked cattle. "Back up!" she said. "Calm down." She knew little more than they did.

Moose had gone to the gas station shortly after the shooting. When he pulled into the parking lot of a building across Aspen Hill Road, he saw Terry Ryan, a detective from the Major Crimes Division, searching the lot for evidence. Investigators were not sure where the gunshot had come from. It was probably from across Connecticut Avenue, to the east. Possibly, they thought, it might have come from the roof of a nearby supermarket. The shot into the Michaels store the night before could have been taken there, too. Ryan was looking for a spent round.

"What the hell's going on?" Moose asked. Ryan, a big, broad-shouldered detective who had posed as a hit man in a recent case, thought the chief looked worried.

"You know as much as I do," Ryan said. "We're not even sure where he was shot."

"What do you need, right now?" Moose asked.

Ryan, who had donned a flak jacket that morning for the first time in ages, said: "Be nice to have more people here, SWAT or whatever, so we can do our job without looking over our shoulders."

But there were a lot of scenes, Moose said, and they all needed cover.

"Where's Forsythe?" he asked.

Ryan said he was across the street at the Mobil station.

Moose walked over, struck that the late rush hour continued as usual, with cars whizzing along Connecticut Avenue as if nothing had happened. There were people walking everywhere. What if the killer was still lurking out there? Moose put in a call to his boss, Montgomery County executive Douglas M. Duncan.

Duncan was at a breakfast meeting in Chicago when his scheduling secretary called. "We got a message from the chief, saying call him immediately," she said. Duncan had never gotten such a call, and phoned Moose from a hallway off the conference room.

There had then been two murders that morning, Moose told him, and one the night before. They were all random but followed the same pattern. "I don't really know what's going on," Moose said.

Duncan said he would come home immediately. As he went back into the meeting to say his good-byes, his cell phone rang again. There had been another killing. In the cab en route to the airport, his phone rang again. There had been another. Duncan called his wife. During one call, she told him it might be all over. "I just saw police pull over a white box truck and had the driver on the ground," she said. For an instant, Duncan thought maybe he could turn around and go back to the conference. He decided to head home anyhow. It seemed too good to be true.

Duncan had hired Moose from the Portland, Oregon, police department in 1999, at a time when the Montgomery County police were caught up in a dispute with the local NAACP over allegations

of racial profiling. For Moose, it was an even trade. The county police department had 1,091 officers; Portland had about 1,000. Montgomery County was almost twice as big as Portland, but Portland
had more homicides. True, it was in a suburb, but the new job had
the advantage of being near the Washington spotlight.

Moose, who was forty-nine, seemed stiff and blunt-spoken beside the smooth and surefooted Duncan, a natural politician who
hoped to be governor someday. But Moose had done well in his three
years on the job. He was self-conscious about speaking in public but
was thoughtful, painstaking, and passionate about his work. He
could also be aloof, and he had an infamous temper when it was un-
leashed on members of his department, county prosecutors, and
newspaper reporters. But he knew he had a problem and sought
counseling in anger management.

As an African American married to a white woman, Moose believed he had suffered instances of what he considered especially
acute racial discrimination. He was born in Lexington, North Carolina, about thirty-five miles southwest of Greensboro. The son of a
high school teacher, he had attended segregated schools until seventh grade. Although he had planned to become a lawyer, those
plans changed when he met a recruiter from the Portland Police Department during his senior year at the University of North Carolina.
When he was offered a job, he figured he could always come home if
he didn't like it, but he quickly ascended through the ranks and decided to stay. Along the way, he earned a Ph.D. in urban studies at
Portland State University.

In 1993, he was named Portland's first black police chief, and he
made favorable headlines when he and his wife, Sandy, moved into a
house in an inner-city neighborhood. Then–Attorney General Janet
Reno called Moose "an extraordinary example of policing in America, policing at its best."

But his volatile temper dogged him. In August 1998, a small
crowd of demonstrators, upset at the closing of a local park to a rau-
cous birthday party, picketed Moose's house, yelling obscenities. The

demonstration was broken up by police firing shotguns loaded with riot control "bean bags." The city council investigated, and Moose assailed the community for not supporting him. "The decision by Sandy and myself to live in the neighborhood is a joke and a major mistake," he told the council. "Why should I work on trying to improve neighborhoods, improve job opportunities, improve schools?" The next year, Moose took the job in Montgomery County.

Shortly after 11:00 A.M., Moose stood in the bright morning sun near the command mobile center and presided at the first of what would be three weeks of press conferences that would make him famous. One of his subordinates suggested that Moose didn't have to conduct the briefings. They could be messy; a lower-ranking officer could handle them. No, Moose said. He was the chief. It was his face that should be presented to the public and to the killer. Conducting the briefings would be his most important role in the case. But his first time out, he sounded tense and a little nervous.

"I really don't want to go off into forty questions, folks," he said. "We're going to come to you every hour and roll it out to you. But we're not just going to react and compromise this investigation. Does everybody understand that?"

"Absolutely," a reporter answered.

" 'Cause I don't want to look like the asshole when I walk away and you're asking me questions. That's just what I'm going to have to do, okay?"

He ticked off the shootings, locations, and times, starting with Martin's the night before. "We strongly feel that all these are connected." He described the white truck and added that police were already inundated with calls about white vans all over the county. He said police could not yet get to every report but urged the public to continue to be observant and suspicious and to call 911. He said the suspects were "calculating" and still out there, but he added, "We don't need panic." He asked potential witnesses to search their memories. "I am convinced that someone knows who's doing this. I am convinced that someone has seen something."

The police would need the media's help, Moose said, and he invited reporters to the command bus. "We want to work cooperatively with you." Moose said the county was seeking help from the Maryland state police, and the police departments of Rockville and Gaithersburg. "We will utilize all and any available resources."

————————

Changing into his working uniform, Drew Tracy drove from his friend's funeral to the command post on Aspen Hill Road, where he was placed in charge of tactical operations. His job was to mobilize heavily armed teams of officers who could protect the police and firefighters who were on the street responding to the crimes. His teams had to be ready, if necessary, to shoot it out with the sniper. The county had about thirty police and sheriff's deputies who were trained on rifles. Tracy divided them into a series of what he called immediate action teams and stationed them around the county. The teams were armed with .308 sniper rifles, stubby MP-5 submachine guns with thirty-round clips, and AR-15s almost exactly like the Bushmaster.

Tracy ordered his people to wear uniforms of SWAT team black, so they would not be mistaken for whoever was out there shooting. The SWAT guys figured the sniper wanted a shoot-out, and one veteran officer, Jeff Nyce, predicted as he cruised the county with a partner that sooner or later he would get it. Nyce thought it would probably be like the infamous 1997 North Hollywood, California, shoot-out between police and two heavily armed bank robbers in body armor. The robbers were killed, but not before they shot ten police officers.

Promises of help came from everywhere. The FBI and the ATF offered an array of experts and facilities, as well as dogs that could track the smell of gunpowder. The Maryland state police offered troopers, the FBI offered crime scene technicians and a helicopter. The U.S. Marshals Service and the Secret Service both offered help. A police department in New Hampshire called at one point. The local summer season had just ended, and the department had two extra officers they could loan. Another offer came from Virginia. A man telephoned Lieutenant Phil Raum and said he could supply trackers.

"What kind of dogs are they?" Raum asked.

"No, not dogs," the man said. "I mean trackers, human trackers."

"We're kind of in an urban environment here," Raum told him. "I'm not sure that we're really going to be tracking anybody through the woods."

At the county prosecutor's office in Rockville, State's Attorney Douglas Gansler ordered all other work halted and summoned forty-five assistants for a mass meeting in a small conference room of the towering judicial center. Prosecutors had been getting calls from police as the cases rolled in: Martin. Walekar. Ramos. Rivera. The killer was probably some disgruntled maniac. Did the prosecutors know of anyone who had lost a case recently, or was angry over a domestic matter, or had made threats? Gansler and a deputy, John McCarthy, asked their assembled subordinates to search their minds and their cases for anything that might help.

They did, and McCarthy later hand-carried a list of initial leads to the Mobil station, where the brass was gathered.

Forsythe grew increasingly worried as the hours passed and the killer remained at large. The situation was out of hand. Innocent people dead. No suspects. And—although he didn't know it—a single quality witness whose well-meaning but inaccurate account would essentially cripple the investigation for three weeks. Forsythe hoped the county's officers searching in their white patrol cars would find something. He knew hope was a lousy technique, but there wasn't much else at this point; a huge local problem could soon become a problem for the whole Washington area. He had to figure out if he had enough investigators and enough resources.

Once he had all the scenes adequately covered, Forsythe went back to his headquarters office to begin trying to coordinate. He had information surging up from below and orders coming down from above. Here he was, two months from retirement, an aging suburban cop with a volatile boss, agitated subordinates, and a murderous sniper, whose biggest previous solved case had been the murder of a jogger in a local park. One of the first things Forsythe did was call an old FBI friend, George Layton, who worked out of the Bureau's office in Calverton, Maryland. Forsythe had heard about a slick new information management system called Rapid Start. He was being flooded with data and needed a way to control it.

"Give me an idea of what it is," Forsythe said.

"Look, it is not an analysis system," Layton said. "It helps you manage your leads."

"Fine," Forsythe said, "get it down here."

He also asked Layton for the number of the FBI's profilers in Quantico, Virginia.

———————

Out on the street, it was chaos. Detectives were dispatched, then recalled. Meetings were announced and then canceled. One detective sat in his car for forty-five minutes waiting for others who never showed up. Nobody seemed to know anything. Late in the day, the Major Crimes Division detectives were summoned to headquarters for a meeting. It was so crowded, you could barely move. Time passed. No meeting. Finally, Jim Drewry, a senior detective, gathered a group of colleagues, along with county prosecutors Katherine Winfree and John McCarthy, and went outside. They sat around a picnic table and held their own meeting. They compared crime scenes, evidence, bullet wounds, next-of-kin notifications. There was growing resentment among the detectives that Forsythe had brought in outsiders. The case belonged to them, not the feds. "What do you got?" they asked one another. After a while, someone came out and said their meeting had been scrapped.

Moose was in front of the cameras again at the church command post a little after 3:00 P.M. There hadn't been a murder in five hours, but helicopters hovered overhead, and the anxiety level was still high. Duncan was still not back from Chicago, and Moose was, for the moment, alone as the county's official spokesman on the case.

He would take questions, he said, if reporters were respectful and orderly and the briefing didn't "deteriorate." He looked tense.

Nothing like this had ever happened in Montgomery County, he said. "This is a very safe community. . . . This is unlike anything we've ever seen. This is not what happens here." The county's murder rate had just jumped 25 percent. "The pain is just starting to flow around the metropolitan area."

Moose said he didn't know much about the killer or killers, other than that this was a "very accurate marksman," "a skilled shooter" who was bold and cunning enough to kill in broad daylight under the noses of the police. He said the county was trying to set up a tip line and to come up with money for a reward. Calls to 911 were already in the process of tripling over the previous day. White vans and box trucks were being stopped all over the area. He again appealed to the public for help.

"This is not some lightning bolt from the sky. Somebody knows. Somebody saw it."

Detective Ryan had been trying to find Rivera's husband, Nelson, who worked for a landscaping company, to tell him his wife was dead. He was out on a job, and Ryan had been unable to track him down. Ryan wanted to make the notification in person. As a homicide detective, he had this duty a lot, and he never did it over the phone. But he was afraid Rivera might hear about it on the radio or TV. He discussed it with other detectives and decided to try to reach him on his cell phone.

When Rivera answered, Ryan asked to speak to someone who spoke English, and his brother came on the line. Ryan identified himself and said he had bad news.

The brother understood immediately and began screaming and crying. He told Rivera, and Ryan could hear him wailing in the background. The brother told Ryan they were in Arlington, Virginia, and would start immediately for the Shell station. An hour later, Nelson Rivera arrived with his brother and some other men. They were all distraught. Already a small shrine had been erected at the car vacuum machine. Rivera knelt in front of it and prayed. What am I going to tell my daughter? he kept repeating in Spanish. Ryan handed him a plastic hospital bag. In it was his wife's jewelry—a necklace and her wedding ring.

———————

As evening approached, Chief Moose asked Forsythe to talk to a group of about thirty friends and relatives of the shooting victims who had gathered in the county's public service training facility in Rockville for counseling. It was unusual for the chief of detectives to do this. Such talks were normally handled by the individual detective on a case. He was trying to figure out his next move and didn't really have time for it. But he realized that this was an extraordinary case. He got into his unmarked green Dodge and made the short drive to the training facility.

The relatives and friends of the victims were assembled at desks in a large classroom. There were about thirty of them, their eyes red and puffy from crying. They were a diverse group, Forsythe thought, typical of the county. He could feel their grief in the room. He stood beside a lectern in front of the blackboard, wearing a blue blazer with an American flag lapel pin, gray slacks, and a silver 9 mm Smith & Wesson pistol holstered on his right hip.

Forsythe was introduced as the person heading the investigation. He didn't know what to say. He felt guilty. He wanted to say: We got the guy. We've got answers for you. But he didn't want to sugarcoat the story, either. He thought about his younger brother, Kevin. They were fourteen months apart and had grown up together. They had delivered newspapers together. Both had been in the army. Both had become police officers, Kevin in Phoenix, Arizona. They were extremely close. In 1984, his brother had been run over and killed instantly at the scene of a traffic accident.

Forsythe remembered hearing the news from his father, who was so upset that he couldn't finish the phone call. Facing the room full of grieving relatives, he said he knew what they were going through. He told them the story of his brother, how he was gone in a flash, and how he felt a part of his life had been ripped away. He told them he had no answers for them, but the department was working hard. "I will keep you in my prayers," he said. He asked for their prayers in return. He took questions for a few minutes, but there were only a few: Was there any connection among the victims? Any explanation why they were chosen to be killed? No, Forsythe said. When the questions were over, Forsythe hurried back to headquarters. He tried not to think about the pain he had seen in the room.

A little after Forsythe left the relatives, John Muhammad walked into a Jamaican restaurant in Washington and asked to use the portable phone. The restaurant, the Tropicana, was on the corner of Georgia Avenue and Kalmia Road, just over the Montgomery County line, about four miles south of the morning's killing zone. The Tropicana served curry goat and chicken, jerk chicken, and fried plantains. It was a small, tidy place with a counter and three booths. It was frequented by police officers from the D.C. police's Fourth District headquarters nearby.

Muhammad made a calling card call, then left. In the midst of a police dragnet, Muhammad and Malvo had been cruising the area all day. At about 2:00 P.M., Muhammad had walked into a Boston Market restaurant in the same shopping center as the Michaels store where the window was shot the night before. He had ordered a quarter chicken, soda, and two side dishes and sat by the windows with a newspaper for about half an hour. He was two blocks from the Walekar crime scene. The area was crazy with police and reporters. But things around the Tropicana were much quieter. This was a mostly African American neighborhood in the city, where their invisibility was complete. Here they might pause for a moment and plan the next move.

At 7:01 P.M., a D.C. police officer stopped the Caprice while it was headed north on Georgia Avenue about two miles south of the restaurant. The intersection was near a cluster of schools and playgrounds in the Petworth neighborhood. Officer Henry A. Gallagher Jr. had "lit up" the Caprice for running two stop signs. Gallagher, a former officer with the U.S. Capitol Police, loved car stops. You nabbed car thieves, drug dealers, all kinds of interesting people. Gallagher had watched the Caprice go through one stop sign, then another. He followed and then sounded his siren once to get the driver to pull over. Gallagher got out of his car. The driver was an adult black man wearing a short-sleeved yellow T-shirt. John Muhammad looked as though he had just awakened from sleep or was very tired. He was unshaven but respectful. The car was filled with soda bottles, newspapers, and other junk. Gallagher didn't smell alcohol, and Muhammad didn't look drunk.

"I'm Officer Gallagher with the Metropolitan Police Department Fourth District," he said. "The reason I stopped you, sir, is you just ran two stop signs. You didn't even stop for this one right here."

Was there any reason he had not stopped? the officer asked.

"No," Muhammad replied.

Gallagher told him he was going to run his tag, and if everything was okay, he would give him a break and let him go. Gallagher told him to stay in the car. "Yes, sir," Muhammad replied.

Gallagher didn't see anyone else inside. Malvo was likely in the trunk. Gallagher went back to his cruiser and ran the tags and driver's license. Again, the computer reported that all was proper with the car. It reported, as did the other checks, on Muhammad's domestic troubles in Washington State. But there appeared to be no family or anyone else in the car, and Gallagher wasn't worried about the report. Be more careful, he told Muhammad. "What you need to do for me is stop at these stop signs," Gallagher said. "If I see you do it again, I'm going to give you a ticket."

"Yes, sir," Muhammad replied.

Shortly after 9:00 P.M., thirty-three blocks north, Gail Howard, owner with her husband of the Tropicana, walked out to a parking lot behind the restaurant to put several thousand dollars in receipts into her black Lexus. She was wary as she walked to the car. It was dark, and there were few other people around. An employee, Karl Largie, who knew old cars, was catching a smoke in the lot, talking on his cell phone, and keeping watch.

Both noticed an old, dark-colored Caprice with tinted windows parked on Kalmia Road, an east-west side street that intersects with Georgia Avenue in front of the restaurant. They noticed that the car was facing west, with its rear facing Georgia Avenue. The area was quite dark, because the nearest streetlight was broken and flickering on and off. As Howard loaded the car, there was suddenly a loud boom. It sounded like a blown tire or a car backfire. Then came the sound of a bus screeching to a halt on Georgia Avenue. Largie told Howard that the boom was either a bus backfire or a gunshot. It was loud, but sounded slightly muffled. Seconds later, they noticed the Caprice sliding west on Kalmia with its lights out. "Look at the idiot with his lights off," Largie said. Howard got in her car and headed home. Five minutes later, Largie called Howard on her cell phone. Guess what? It was a gunshot.

Pascal Charlot had left Haiti so many years before that friends couldn't recall how long he had been in the neighborhood. He was a skilled carpenter who walked with a bowlegged gait and could build anything. He had a gray mustache and was seventy-two. He lived with his invalid wife in a redbrick row house that had lawn chairs and potted plants on the front porch. He grew tomatoes and bell peppers in a back garden.

At 9:20, after taking the bus from his house, Charlot was standing under a streetlight in a green-and-white polo shirt on the southeast corner of Georgia Avenue and Kalmia Road, about to cross the street. The Tropicana was across the road. He was gazing up and had just raised his right hand to his chin when a bullet crashed through his palm near the base of his thumb. It fractured the bones and left a two-inch hole before punching into his chest near his left collarbone. The bullet ripped a three-inch-long wound, shattered the collarbone and several ribs, and tore open a major vein and artery nearby. It then fragmented, and the tip of its copper jacket dug into his right collarbone. Other fragments scattered through his upper chest, neck, and shoulders.

A witness sitting in her car happened to be looking at Charlot and thought he was smoking. She saw a puff of what detectives think was probably a spray of blood as the bullet struck him. He collapsed. Malvo would recall shooting an old man on a street corner.

In Montgomery County, police hoped that the killing in the District was unrelated, that it was just another piece of the crazy violence that plagued some of the tougher Washington neighborhoods. But Charlot had no enemies. He'd been by himself. He was not accosted. There had just been this boom, and down he went. It had to be the sniper.

But this time there were witnesses. One woman saw a red Toyota drive away quickly from the scene. She said she had actually seen smoke coming from the car. Police tracked down the Toyota a short time later in Montgomery County and found it was driven by a man who had nothing to do with the shooting. He, too, said he had heard the shot.

It was not until two days later that Tony Patterson, the lead D.C. homicide detective on the Charlot case, was canvassing the neighborhood and interviewed the reluctant witnesses at the Tropicana. He had been wondering who this old man could have pissed off, and when he heard the description of the Caprice, he was intrigued.

This was no white van. It was probably not even a white man's car. This sounded like a "hoopty," a fellow detective said when he heard of the Caprice. "Man, that's a brother's car." On October 7, two days after he interviewed the witnesses, Patterson sent out a police teletype alerting fellow officers across the region to be on the lookout for the car that Howard and Largie had seen the night of the murder.

Largie described the car as dark colored, possibly burgundy, but he wasn't sure. The alert said it was burgundy, "an older model Chevrolet Caprice or vehicle of similar style . . . 4-door with dark tinted windows." The alert was addressed to all area law enforcement agencies and was to be read at all roll calls. "Any officer coming into contact with similar vehicles, please stop and identify all occupants."

About 10:00 P.M., on October 23, as stunned police realized that the sniper was not finished and had probably now hit Washington, an off-duty officer was driving in for his shift with the Prince George's County police. The officer was southbound in a marked cruiser on the Capital Beltway, which goes through the county east and south of Washington. As he drove near the community of Oxon Hill, southeast of the capital, a dark Chevy Caprice sped past, also southbound, and then braked suddenly, as if the driver had seen the police car. The officer was suspicious and entered into his computer the car's New Jersey license number, which he had glimpsed: NDA-21Z. The computer reported nothing unusual. The Caprice had slowed to the speed limit. The officer headed on to work. A few miles ahead, the Beltway crossed the Potomac River over the Woodrow Wilson Bridge and continued into Virginia.

That night, in Brentwood, Tennessee, a suburb of Nashville, Jim Cavanaugh heard about the sniper shootings on the TV news. This was ATF stuff, he thought. Somebody in the agency would get called on this. As a former street cop, he figured the shooter was one very angry guy, on some kind of personal mission.

5

Tunnel Vision

Shortly after 6:30 A.M. on Friday, October 4, Chief Moose appeared in the darkness outside county police headquarters for his first press conference of the day. He had not had much sleep. He had worked late, and his wife, Sandy, had arrived home from Minneapolis well after midnight. An aide sent to pick her up had missed her at Baltimore-Washington International Airport. At 1:30 A.M., Moose had to drive forty miles from his town house in Gaithersburg to get her himself.

With County Executive Doug Duncan by his side, Moose tried to sound reassuring. Overnight, there had been no more shootings in Montgomery County. "All was quiet," he said. He did not mention, and was not asked about, the Charlot killing, barely mentioned in the day's newspapers. There was lingering confusion about that case from the night before.

Police had received 150 leads, Moose said, a number that would seem laughably small later. The county had set up a tip line and was offering a $50,000 reward. He said he was 90 percent sure the fatal bullets were high-velocity .223-caliber rounds fired from a high-powered rifle. He told the public that schools would be open on time, under the protection of police. "We feel very comfortable that we're going to be able to get the day off to a positive start," he said. He asked the public to remain alert and closed by saying, "Have a safe day."

At 8:30 A.M., Maryland's chief medical examiner, Dr. David R. Fowler, assembled his pathologists and trainees for morning rounds in the basement autopsy suite of the state medical examiner's office in downtown Baltimore. Those doing autopsies that day were in purple scrubs. Fowler was in shirtsleeves. Before them on stainless-steel gurneys lay the previous day's sniper victims. They were in "as is" condition, just as they had come from where they were shot or taken the day before. They had been photographed and were ready for examination.

Fowler was already being criticized for moving too slowly on the autopsies. Though Martin's had been performed the day before, frantic Montgomery County police wanted the rest done immediately. They had a madman, or madmen, on the loose. They were desperate for any clues, especially bullet fragments, the medical examiner could supply. Were the shots from one gun? Or more? What kind? But the bodies had not started arriving in Baltimore until around 4:00 P.M., too late in the day, by the office's strict protocols, to begin postmortem examinations. Many of Fowler's staff finished at 4:00, and he was adamant that the best plan was to start fresh the next morning.

Moose asked the county's deputy state's attorney, John McCarthy, to try to intercede. But Fowler, a native of Zimbabwe who got his first training as a medic when he was drafted into what was then the Rhodesian army, insisted that office protocols be maintained, especially in such a case. Departures could cause problems later in court. "It would be much better to take a deep breath," he said. "We'll do all these cases in the cold light of day, step by step, following our usual protocols." He did have X-rays taken and provided the information from them to police. But the autopsies had waited.

Copies of those X-rays now hung on a light box in the autopsy room. A clipboard containing an investigative report was with each victim. A dozen pathologists and investigators gathered around the first gurney and then moved down the line, victim by victim. Several of the X-rays showed bullet fragments in the bodies, and those of

Walekar and Rivera showed the classic "snowstorm" pattern of a fragmented ultrahigh-velocity rifle bullet that had come apart upon impact.

X-rays of Charlot's body taken later that day by the Washington, D.C., Medical Examiner's Office would show the same thing. Maryland didn't see a lot of high-velocity rifle homicides; most were committed with handguns. Fowler, to help illustrate, went to the files and pulled the case of a previous .223 rifle homicide with the same snowstorm-type X-rays. As he and his staff studied the victims, he indicated the entrance wound in Walekar's left arm. "Have a look at this wound," he said. "What do you see?" The burrowing of the bullet under the skin, and its associated damage, was another classic indicator of a high-velocity round. There were others everywhere.

The postmortems began, supervised by Deputy Chief Medical Examiner Mary G. Ripple. They were all fairly simple, single-shot cases. All had small entrance wounds, along with massive internal injuries. Three had large exit wounds. Two showed the snowstorm X-ray pattern. There was no soot near any of the wounds, which would indicate a close-range shot. All evidence pointed to a high-velocity rifle.

Numerous bullet fragments were recovered. The jagged, almost complete copper jacket of a .223 bullet was picked from Walekar's left lung. Other pieces were found elsewhere in his chest cavity, including one that looked like the base of the bullet's lead core. Fragments of a jacket and core were also recovered from Rivera's chest. The fragments were labeled, placed in an evidence envelope, and handed over to the police. They would quickly become the most crucial pieces of evidence in the case and would definitively link the shootings to the Bushmaster rifle and those who were pulling its trigger.

———————

To the good fortune of Montgomery County, one of the nation's premier laboratories for examining spent bullets and bullet fragments was located about a mile from police headquarters in a large gray building in the Rockville research sprawl. The National Laboratory Center belonged to the federal Bureau of Alcohol, Tobacco and Firearms.

Officially, the ATF dated only to 1968, but its roots stretched back through Prohibition and the Whisky Rebellion. Over the years, its ever-changing mandates were centered chiefly at the messy crossroads of alcohol, tobacco, and taxation, but responsibility for firearms regulation was added in the 1930s and explosives in the 1960s. The ATF was a perennial little brother to the larger FBI, with which it occasionally feuded. In the sniper case, the ATF lab would play a critical role, especially in the ballistics, which was largely done by a former D.C. narcotics detective named Walter A. Dandridge Jr.

When a bullet is fired down the barrel of a rifle, it is rotated like a spiraled football. The passage marks the sides of the bullet, leaving a pattern of alternating raised lines called "lands" and gouged lines called "grooves." These patterns and even more minute impressions, which can be examined and measured under a microscope, are unique in every firearm, even the same type.

But an individual weapon leaves the same marks on almost every bullet fired. Some experts have likened the marks to a bar code. It is therefore possible to say that a series of recovered bullets did, or did not, all come from the same gun. If the gun is in hand, it can be test-fired into a tank of water and the spent bullet recovered. The marks can then be compared to the marks on other spent bullets to see if they came from the tested gun. Similar comparisons can be made with a bullet's shell casing, the small brass canister that holds the gunpowder and that is left behind when the bullet is fired. The weapon's loading, firing, and ejecting mechanisms leave unique marks on the casing that can be scrutinized and compared.

The process is sometimes called "ballistics fingerprinting." It is one of the arcane forensic sciences, upon which TV shows now are based, and Dandridge was a leading practitioner.

The bullet work usually went well when an examiner had the entire slug to study, magnified forty times under one of the lab's Leica stereo microscopes. Dandridge could study two bullet samples side by side, rotate them 360 degrees under the microscope, and line up the patterns to see if they matched. The patterns could also be photographed, projected onto a videoscreen, and entered into a database of other such bullet patterns to see if they matched an earlier crime. But the operation became more difficult and sometimes impossible if the bullet fragment plucked from a victim or a wall or a car was too small. A patch of bullet two square millimeters in size was generally large enough to make a comparison; anything less was most often no good.

By midafternoon on October 4, Dandridge had what bullet evidence had been recovered from the scenes and the autopsies and was examining them under his microscopes. The ATF had been involved in the case from the first day, when it dispatched several agents from the Baltimore office to assist county police. Earlier that day, Michael Bouchard, the special agent in charge of the office, sent twenty more agents, gunshot trajectory experts, and gunpowder-sniffing dogs called EDCs (for "explosive detection canines").

That morning, at Moose's request, one of Bouchard's top assistants, Joseph M. Riehl, of the Baltimore ATF office, presided at a press conference at county police headquarters where agents displayed .223 cartridges and several kinds of rifles that fired them. One was a bolt-action hunting rifle. Another was a sleek, black AR-15, just like the military's M-16. No one knew it then, but it looked almost exactly like Muhammad's Bushmaster. Later that day, Bouchard ordered in more ATF agents and then went to Rockville himself.

Bouchard, a fifteen-year veteran of the ATF, would soon join Moose as a familiar face on national television. Arriving at police headquarters, he found a chaotic scene. There were so many investigators, and so little room, that some meetings were held in the ground-floor cell block.

Across the county, people tried to heed the advice of the police: Go on with life. But be vigilant.

It was difficult. Callers dialed 911 to report car backfires and eccentric neighbors. At gas stations, customers began what came to be called the Montgomery County quick-step: bobbing, weaving, ducking, and hiding while trying to fill the tank. Some squatted behind their cars for cover. Some left their doors open to use as shields. Some sat inside the car while the pump ran. Later, gas stations would hang tarps to block the view of the pumps from the road. Parents sent children to school but often drove them to the door or had them wait in the car at the bus stop. Recess and outdoor lunch were still canceled, but after-school activities like track meets and football games were given a tentative okay. The local soccer league lifted the ban on practices and games it had imposed the day before.

This was a community that only a year before had been targeted in two separate terrorist attacks—the plane flown into the Pentagon and the deadly anthrax poisoning, which had killed two people in the Washington area and closed one of the U.S. Senate's office buildings for months. The Pentagon repairs had just been dedicated, amid solemn fanfare. But those had been, for the most part, carefully targeted—the nation's military command in one case and Congress and the media in the other. The sniper attacks were entirely different. The targets had been selected at random and slaughtered for maximum shock effect, Malvo would explain later. The public got the message: It could be anybody. It could be me. Much more so than with 9/11 or anthrax, the terror was real, and it was spreading.

Moose came back before the cameras at noon. He announced that the FBI would shortly provide a profile of the killer or killers. He cautioned that a profile was just a tool. Investigators were worried that it would create "tunnel vision" and would cause the suspects to be missed by the public or police. "We want to stress that when we release that information that we not release it in a way that somehow now eliminates people and causes us to get too focused on a path and potentially miss the suspect," Moose said.

Moose could not know that the very trap he had hoped to avoid had already been tripped. A reporter asked him at the press conference: What were the chances that the suspects were still in the white truck? Moose said he had to proceed as if they were. "We don't eliminate anything until the evidence eliminates it," he said. His investigators were trying to "fine-tune" the description of the white truck and get the update out later.

Moose said the Charlot killing had been the cause of some confusion. Police had hunted down a burgundy Toyota seen leaving the scene of Charlot's slaying and the driver had been arrested on an unrelated charge. But that did not mean the shooting was unrelated. In fact, he said, he was "very much interested" in the case and was consulting closely with D.C. police chief Charles Ramsey. Investigators were awaiting results of the autopsy and ballistics tests by the city police firearms examiners.

"Patience," he told reporters. "If we rush now and lose it later, how sad would that be." The morning rush hour had now passed without incident. Things seemed to have calmed down, but Moose said he was still worried. "The quietness of this morning, and how good that felt, will be almost nothing to how good I'm going to feel when we make an arrest."

The Reverend Curtis Latimore, pastor of Antioch Baptist Church in Clinton, Maryland, was getting tired of people leaving their cars in the church parking lot. He would occasionally jot down a license number and ask members of the congregation if they knew who owned this or that car that had been left in the lot. In October, a particularly sorry-looking car started appearing. It was a dark blue Chevy Caprice with tinted windows and New Jersey tags. Latimore, a former D.C. police officer, noticed that it had a hole in the trunk that appeared to be stuffed up with some kind of cloth. He never saw anybody in the car.

Antioch Baptist was three blocks from Margellina's, the Italian restaurant where Paul La Ruffa was almost killed back in September. It was also less than a mile from where Muhammad's ex-wife Mildred lived with their children. Mildred often took the bus from a stop across the street from Margellina's. The liquor store where Muhammad Rashid was shot was also just down the highway.

Mildred had moved in with her sister on Quiet Brook Lane early in 2001 to help take care of their ailing mother, Olevia, who died later that year. She brought her children there in September 2001 and began working at an administrative job at the nearby Southern Maryland Hospital Center. Mildred believed that only a handful of people back in Tacoma knew where she lived. But she still was edgy.

One day, while driving to work with a friend after the shootings began, she saw a dark Chevrolet Caprice parked near her sister's home. It had New Jersey license plates and she noticed that the two men in the car held newspapers up to shield their faces when they drove up. The car looked so suspicious that she called the police. She also called her son, John, and told him to be careful because there was an odd car in the neighborhood. The police never called her back, she would say later. The next day, a neighbor's car was stolen. She wondered if there might be a connection between the car theft and the men in the dark blue car. She never saw the car again.

Muhammad and Malvo seem to have haunted the area where Mildred lived. Latimore thinks he may have seen Muhammad on the street near the church. A neighbor thinks he saw the Caprice one evening in early October, parked a few doors from Mildred's home. One friend called her during the sniping spree and asked if she thought Muhammad was behind the shooting. No, Mildred said. Her husband wanted to kill only her.

———————

At 2:00 P.M. on October 4, Moose gave another briefing. He said the FBI profile he had expected by day's end would not be released. "Maybe I misspoke," he said, explaining that psychological profiling was tricky and that the FBI needed more time and information. In fact, Moose never did release the profile developed by the bureau.

Though it would remain secret, the FBI would develop a theory that the killings were probably the work of a single shooter. "Multiple offenders" would be extremely unusual, though if there were two, one would be dominant.

The sniper was likely angry, self-centered, and fascinated with weapons and violence. Probably the sniper had recently suffered a domestic or job-related setback. He would stay in the Washington area, keep the same method of operation, and scout his shooting locations. The sniper was almost certainly male, was probably not a juvenile, and was not likely to display any sign of mental illness.

The profilers were unsure about the sniper's race but guessed he would frequent gun shows, be interested in books and movies about the military, and take pride in his prowess with firearms. He would be a taker of calculated risks, would not be confrontational, and would not be involved in a long-term relationship. He could come and go as he pleased. He would be hypersensitive and suspicious and pay close attention to media coverage.

While suddenly downplaying the psychological profilers, Moose announced that a geographic profiler was being brought in who specialized in determining where the shooter might live. Geographic profiling is an emerging science that uses a computer to analyze the locations, times, and dates of a series of crimes to try to indicate the area where the perpetrator might live or work. The theory is that most criminals stay in an area that is close, but not too close, to a zone of familiarity. It seemed logical. It had worked in some earlier cases. And it was pretty quick. In this case, it would turn out to be useless.

If the investigators were cautious about profiling the killers, the media was not. In the days ahead, a procession of retired law enforcement profilers and criminologists speculated on the airwaves and in print on the sniper's identity and motivation. They compared the sniper to almost every serial killer of recent memory: Charles Whitman, who killed fourteen people from an observation tower at the University of Texas in 1966; David Berkowitz, the psychotic "Son of Sam" killer, who murdered six people with a .44-caliber revolver in 1976 and 1977; Theodore J. Kaczynski, the Unabomber, who killed three people and wounded twenty-three others in almost eighteen years of mail bombings that ended in 1996; and James E. Swann Jr., the "shotgun stalker," who killed four people in northwest Washington in 1993.

The consensus of TV profilers was that the person responsible for these shootings was most likely a white man with a military background, familiarity with firearms, and a grievance. Detectives chuckled that it was the same profile the experts always seemed to produce, no matter what the case. One retired FBI profiler, Gregg McCrary, could see no real motive. "You're down to thrill of the kill," he said. "Playing God. Having the power over these individuals. Life and death. That's real heady, a real rush. He's on a high now."

As the hours passed without another shooting, Muhammad and Malvo were executing a new phase of what Malvo would later say was their "strategy." This was all planned out, he would brag to investigators later. It was a military operation, just like those at the Pentagon. Phase one was Montgomery County. The overwhelming shock attack. Too many bodies in too short a time for the cops to cope. "We did five in one day, knowing you couldn't handle it," he would explain to his interrogators later. Now it was time for phase two.

At about 2:30 P.M., seventy-five miles south of Montgomery County police headquarters, Caroline Seawell, a forty-three-year-old mother of two, drove her minivan into a sprawling shopping complex called the Spotsylvania Mall. The mall was in the northern Virginia suburbs about halfway between Washington and Richmond, but psychologically closer to Richmond. Spotsylvania County, where the mall was located, was chiefly known as the location of four major Civil War battlefields.

The mall was just west of Interstate 95, right near two of the exit ramps. Seawell pulled into the shopping center and parked in front of a Michaels arts and crafts store, where she was a regular customer. She did some shopping and was loading packages into the van. She was moving around a lot, which Malvo later said made her a tough target because he didn't want to wait too long.

At almost the same moment, a couple from nearby Bowling Green, Alex and Doris Jones, pulled up in their car behind Seawell. They saw her loading her stuff and decided to wait for her spot. Just as Seawell was closing her van's rear hatch, Jones heard a loud pop and saw Seawell fall down. He got out of his car and rushed over to her. "I've been shot!" she shouted.

"This woman's been shot!" Alex Jones yelled, and then suddenly realized his own vulnerability. If the gunman could see her, he could see him—and his wife.

Jones dashed back to his car, told his wife to get down, and then, ducking low himself, steered to the safety of a nearby furniture store out of the line of fire. As he drove, he noticed a dark-colored car with New Jersey license plates heading out of the lot right in front of him. A furniture store worker had seen a black teenager in the same car parked earlier but dismissed it. Jones thought the car seemed funny, out of place. And its back window seemed to be covered with something so Jones couldn't see inside. He mentioned the car to his wife, who was crouched in the back. But she hadn't seen it.

Seawell had been luckier than the others, perhaps from Malvo's impatience. She had been struck in the lower right back. The bullet had come out under her right breast and slammed into the outside of the hatch door, where it cut an oblong, three-inch gouge in the metal. Miraculously, it had not injured her fatally. Seawell remembers that one of the people who came to her aid didn't even believe she'd been shot. She was rushed to Mary Washington Hospital in

Fredericksburg and then flown by helicopter to a hospital in Fairfax in stable condition.

Police quickly deduced the attack was almost certainly the sniper's. The similarities to the other shootings were unmistakable. The target. The backdrop. The sound. The wound. Only the outcome and the location were different. The shooting zone had now been broadly expanded, from the ten-square-mile area in Maryland to a seventy-five-mile corridor more than halfway to Richmond.

In Montgomery County, the police were stunned. Now they had a whole new game. And it really looked like a game, a contest. C'mon, the killer seemed to be saying, let's play. See if you can figure this out. Seventy-five miles was a long way away. Had the killer been scared out of the area by all the police activity? Could it still be someone from Montgomery County, as the first day's spree seemed to suggest? What was the connection to Michaels stores? And what on earth was the motive? As Barney Forsythe had feared, Montgomery County's problem had become regional.

At police headquarters in Rockville, Nick DeCarlo summoned Patrick McNerney, the detective who had been put in charge of the Martin murder as well as the shooting at the Michaels store in Aspen Hill. McNerney had become convinced that the latter shooting was no practice run. He had gone to the scene with some sniper experts, who showed him that the shot had probably been taken from low to the ground, had missed the head of the person for whom it was intended, and had hit the store window on an upward trajectory. That should have been the first murder in Montgomery County. Somebody out there was walking around lucky.

Now there was another Michaels case. It may have just been a coincidence. Police would shortly be checking Michaels employee records, along with records of local Shell and Mobil employees and records of gun owners, gun dealers, certain military personnel, rifle club members, people who leased or owned box trucks, and anything else they could think of.

DeCarlo wanted McNerney in Spotsylvania right away. Okay,

McNerney said, but it would take him a while to drive down there, even with running lights and his siren. He wouldn't be driving, De-Carlo told him. There was an FBI helicopter waiting at the county's public service training academy a few miles away. McNerney drove to the academy and boarded a dark purple UH-1 Vietnam-era heli-copter. Two law enforcement snipers were on board. As the heli-copter reached altitude, McNerney heard the pilot radio his call sign and route to air traffic control. The controller replied that the route was through restricted airspace and that the helicopter would have to be vectored around. The pilot replied that the controller must have missed his high-priority call sign and repeated it. The con-troller apologized and cleared the flight through. As the chopper raced south into Virginia, McNerney saw, and heard over the radio, the medevac helicopter carrying Seawell to Fairfax passing in the opposite direction.

————

McNerney's helicopter landed in the mall parking lot. There was lit-tle information to be shared, just as with the other cases. The sniper had fired a single shot and then vanished. People had heard the shot and the victim's cries. No one had seen much of anything. The po-lice were, however, able to dig the mangled bullet out of Seawell's van. It was a critical piece of evidence. They planned to drive it up to the ATF lab in Rockville and see if it could be matched to the other sniper bullets. McNerney made them an offer. If they wanted, he had his purple helicopter waiting and would be glad to carry the bullet to the ATF lab, which was right down the street from his of-fice. The Spotsylvania police turned the bullet over to McNerney in a paper evidence bag. By now it was dark, and as the chopper sped north, McNerney was so worried about this precious piece of evi-dence that he was afraid to put it in his pocket. He clutched the bag in his hands the whole way back.

By the time Moose talked to reporters that night, his once quiet Friday had long ago gone bad. Not only was there a new shooting in Virginia, but word had come from the D.C. ballistics lab that the multiple fragments taken from Charlot's body by the District's medical examiner had been positively matched to fragments recovered in the shootings of Walekar, Ramos, and Rivera. Though no fragments had been recovered from Martin and Buchanan, Moose said their shootings were almost certainly related to the others.

"Whoever is involved in this madness, rethink what you're doing," Moose said. "Turn yourself in. Surrender to law enforcement." It sounded so futile, but it was the opening of a bizarre and inept dialogue that would continue until the saga's end.

––––––

The next day brought confirmation that ballistics tests had linked Seawell's shooting with those of Walekar, Ramos, Rivera, and Charlot. And Moose had to downplay the importance of a Rockville man, a native of North Carolina, who for a time on Friday had seemed like a prime suspect. His family in Rockville had reported him missing, and the North Carolina state police had broadcast a lookout, saying he was armed with a .40-caliber handgun and a .223 rifle. Michael Bouchard, of the ATF, tried to wave the media off the report. This didn't look like the guy. Besides, Moose said, he had a blue pickup, not a white box truck.

Duncan, the county's highest elected official, had been urging people to go about their business despite the threat, and he tried to set an example by taking two of his sons to an outdoor food festival in Bethesda. SWAT police were stationed on the rooftops, a plainclothes security detail met him when he arrived, and a helicopter hovered overhead. Duncan walked the streets, shaking hands and thanking people for coming. They thanked him back. He tried to keep moving.

That evening at St. Mary's Catholic Church in Rockville, Cardinal Theodore McCarrick, the archbishop of Washington, D.C., celebrated a mass for the victims. The 189-year-old parish, known locally as the burial place of F. Scott Fitzgerald, was located at a busy crossroads, within sight of the county courthouses and the executive office building. Bells tolled and candles were lit for the victims.

McCarrick reminded those in the packed church that they must not let evil take over their lives, that they must not give in to their fears, that they must continue to be courageous and generous and take care of one another. "Do not let fear turn us back to where we cannot live our lives," McCarrick said. "Anxiety can keep us from doing the things God wants us to do."

The day was almost over. It was the first in four days that there had not been a shooting. Tuesday, the last day of peace, seemed an eternity ago. It was amazing how much had changed. Maybe the sniper would take the weekend off. Maybe he was finished.

At 10:17 P.M., John Muhammad placed a telephone call from an Exxon station on Bladensburg Road, in Washington. It was on the east side of the District, just off the east-west New York Avenue corridor that feeds into the Capital Beltway, twenty-five miles from the church. He called his old lover, back in Tacoma. She had moved since he had last seen her. He sounded sweet as usual, telling her he had something he wanted to send her. He had often done that in the past. He'd send her sentimental greeting cards, which he would never sign, saying she knew who sent them. But now, he said, he didn't know her new address. She thought for a second.

Muhammad had been out of her life for many months. Painful as it had been, she did not want to let him back in. The old revolving door would start all over again, and she didn't want that. So she lied, poorly. She told him she was still in the process of relocating and wasn't sure where she'd be. He knew her daughter's address, she told him. He could send things to her there. She sensed immediately that he saw through her lie. He said something about not having a pencil to write anything down. It was okay, he said, he'd talk to her later. The call lasted less than five minutes. She would later wonder why he had called.

———

On Sunday, the funerals began. Premkumar Walekar was mourned at a service in Sligo Seventh-day Adventist Church, a monumental white structure in the county's Takoma Park section, just over the

Lee Boyd Malvo and John Allen Muhammad in an undated photo.
(Polaris Images)

Malvo's childhood
home in Jamaica.
(Mary Beth Sheridan,
The Washington Post)

John Muhammad's California
driver's license photo.
(courtesy of the U.S. Marshals Service)

Mildred Muhammad,
ex-wife of John Muhammad.
(Dudley M. Brooks, *The Washington Post*)

The Bushmaster XM15 E2S, the weapon used in the national sniper spree,
in the trunk of Muhammad's Chevrolet Caprice after his arrest.
(law enforcement sources)

Scene of the James D. Martin shooting, Shoppers Food Warehouse, Wheaton, Maryland, October 2, 2002, 6:02 P.M. (courtesy of Bill Cornett, Gamma)

A Montgomery County police officer takes measurements after Sarah Ramos was killed in Silver Spring, Maryland, October 3, 2002, 8:37 A.M. (Bill O'Leary, *The Washington Post*)

Police search a white box truck hours after four shootings in Montgomery County, October 3, 2002. (Marie Poirer Marzi)

From left: Montgomery County state's attorney Douglas Gansler, Montgomery County police captain Bernard (Barney) Forsythe, and Montgomery County police chief Charles A. Moose at a press conference in June 2001.
(James A. Parcell, *The Washington Post*)

A customer at a Texaco gas station in Fairfax County, Virginia, is shielded by a tarp the station put up after sniper attacks began.
(Michael Williamson, *The Washington Post*)

Students leave the Benjamin Tasker
Middle School in Bowie, Maryland,
on October 7, 2002, the day after
Iran Brown was shot.
(Bill O'Leary, *The Washington Post*)

Chief Charles Moose cries during a
press briefing after the Brown shooting.
(Marvin Joseph, *The Washington Post*)

ATF special agent
Jim Cavanaugh and
Police Chief John Wilson
of Montgomery, Alabama.
(Kevin Glackmeyer, *Montgomery Advertiser*)

The gas station in Massaponax,
Virginia, where Kenneth Bridges was
shot on October 11, 2002.
(Gerald Martineau, *The Washington Post*)

Fairfax County police
cadets prepare to search
the scene of Linda
Franklin's shooting at
Home Depot in Fairfax
County, Virginia.
(Larry Morris,
The Washington Post)

Michael Bouchard, an ATF special agent, addresses the media after police announce that a witness to the Franklin shooting lied about what he had seen.
(Lois Raimondo, *The Washington Post*)

Area police officers search the wooded area behind the Ponderosa restaurant in Ashland, Virginia, site of the Jeffrey Hopper shooting on October 19, 2002.
(John McDonnell, *The Washington Post*)

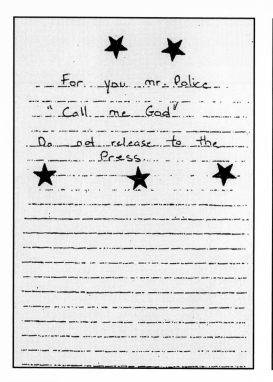

★ ★

For you mr. Police

"Call me God"

Do not release to the Press

★ ★ ★

Pg 1.

"For you Mr. Police
Call me God."

Do not release to the press.
We have tried to contact you
to start negotiation, But the
incompitence of your forces in
(i) Mongomery Police "Officer Derick"
at ▆▆▆▆▆ Friday,
(ii) Rockville Police Dept "female officer"
at ▆▆▆▆▆
(iii) Task force "FBI" "female"
at 1888-324-9800 (four times)
(iv) Priest at ashland.
(v) An Washington DC at ▆▆▆▆▆
These people took of call
for a Hoax or Joke, so your
failure to respond has cost
you five lives.
If stopping the killing is

Pg 2.

more important than catching us
now, then you will accept our
demand which are non-negotiable.
(i) You will place ten million
dollar in Bank of america.
account no. ▆▆▆▆▆
▆▆▆▆▆
Pin no. ▆▆
Activation date 08/01/01
Exp. date 09/04
Name: ▆▆▆▆▆
member since 1974
Platinum Visa Account.
We will have unlimited withdraw
withdrawl at any atm world-
wide.
You will activate the bank
account, credit card, and Pin
number.
We will contact you at

Pg. 3

(AshLAND, VA)
Ponderosa Buffet tel # ▆▆▆▆▆
6:00 am Sunday Morning.
You have until 9:00 a.m.
Monday morning to complete
transaction.
"Try to catch us" withdrawing
at least you will have less
body bags."
(BuT)
(ii) If trying to catch us now
more important then prepare
you body bags.
If we give you our word
that is what takes place
"Word is Bond"

P.S. your children are not
safe anywhere at any time.

Letter written by the snipers to the police. It was found tacked to a tree
in the woods behind the Ponderosa shooting scene.
(*The Washington Post*)

Scene of the shooting of Conrad Johnson on a Ride On bus in Aspen Hill, Maryland, October 22, 2002.
(Ricky Carioti, *The Washington Post*)

Traffic backed up on I-95 while police stop cars after the Johnson shooting.
(Bill O'Leary, *The Washington Post*)

Investigators comb the yard in Tacoma, Washington, where John Muhammad allegedly shot his Bushmaster at a tree stump, testing a homemade silencer.
(Mike Urban, *Seattle Post-Intelligencer*)

John Muhammad's Chevrolet Caprice is pushed into a police garage for inspection. (courtesy of Gary Hite)

A government vehicle believed to be transporting John Muhammad leaves the U.S. Federal Courthouse in Baltimore after his arraignment, October 25, 2002.
(Susan Biddle, *The Washington Post*)

A press conference in front of the Joint Operations Command center of the Montgomery County Task Force to announce the apprehension of the sniper suspects in Myersville, Maryland.
(Bill O'Leary, *The Washington Post*)

Paul B. Ebert, the Prince William County commonwealth attorney, speaks at a press conference at which Attorney General John Ashcroft announced that the sniper suspects would be tried in Virginia, where they could both face the death penalty. (Susan Biddle, *The Washington Post*)

Robert F. Horan, the Fairfax County commonwealth attorney, addresses the press on January 15, 2003, following a hearing at which it was ruled that Lee Boyd Malvo would stand trial as an adult. (Robert A. Reeder, *The Washington Post*)

Sniper shooting survivor Iran Brown is greeted by First Lady Laura Bush on December 13, 2002. (James A. Parcell, *The Washington Post*)

John Allen Muhammad is led into Prince William County
Circuit Court for a hearing on November 13, 2002.
(Jahi Chikwendiu, *The Washington Post*)

Lee Boyd Malvo is escorted out of a hearing at a Fairfax
County court, December 30, 2002.
(courtesy of Sarah L. Voisin, *The Washington Post*)

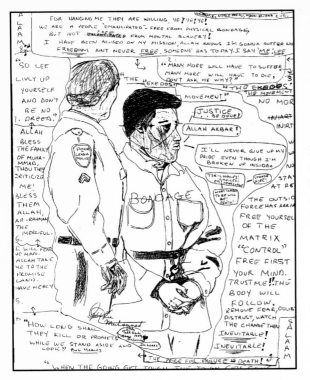

Drawings by Lee Boyd Malvo, confiscated from his cell at the Fairfax County Jail.
(*The Washington Post*)

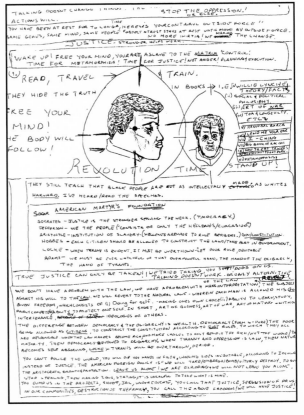

border from northwest Washington. Duncan was one of the speakers, and he was so taken with Cardinal McCarrick's words the evening before that he paraphrased them: "If we let the fear, the anxiety, overcome us, then we lose our generosity, we lose our caring, we lose our compassion, we lose our kindness, we lose our goodness. Then what will become of us? Evil will have ruled the day."

Caroline Namrow, the pediatrician who had ministered to Walekar, was another speaker. She described the shooting and how she did CPR to try to save Walekar. She described how he looked peacefully up at the sky and didn't seem as though he was in pain. She didn't mention the blood, or the vomit, or how she had screamed in terror to the 911 operator.

By that afternoon, there hadn't been a shooting in forty-eight hours. It was a beautiful day, sunny, breezy, and cool. A hint of fall. The county police had had two days of relative quiet to regain a measure of equilibrium. In Rockville, Forsythe and Raum, weary from trying to mesh their moderate-size suburban police department with the cogs of what had become a local, state, and federal task force, were ready for a break.

As the hours passed, the two men decided to slip outside, something they had not been able to do in days. Forsythe, for one, had been a prisoner in his office. People from above were looking for the captain; people from below were looking for the captain. The FBI, the ATF, the Maryland state police, the Secret Service, the U.S. marshals, the profilers, the negotiators, the prosecutors, the detectives, the chief—all were looking for the captain. It was an enormous chore just keeping the new names straight. He was swamped. Forsythe believed he needed to be where he could be found, even if he didn't have a lot of answers. But now, maybe for an hour, he could step out. "Phil," Forsythe said, "let's go somewhere else. I need some fresh air." Pale and tired, he walked out with Raum into the sunshine and headed to an Italian restaurant, That's Amore, that was just down the road from headquarters. At the bar, the Washington Redskins–Tennessee Titans game was on television. They tried to clear their heads. Forsythe mentioned his ailing parents and his pending retirement. It felt good to talk about something other than the sniper, although the talk eventually came back to that. They watched a little of the game. They ordered salads and some soup.

––––––––––––

As Forsythe and Raum tried to relax that afternoon, James Griffin, a retired Washington, D.C., police officer, pulled into the parking lot of Fox Hill Park, a neighborhood recreation area in the community of Bowie, Maryland, thirty miles away. Bowie was in Prince George's County, east of Washington. The park, on Collington Road, was a pleasant expanse that included tennis courts and football and baseball fields. Just to the south, separated by a belt of trees, was the Benjamin Tasker Middle School, a modern, low-rise building with a big flagpole out front. Generations of schoolchildren had carved their names in the bark of the trees beside the school, which was named after a Colonial mayor of Annapolis. South of the school was Route 50, a broad highway that ran east and west and linked Washington and the Maryland capital.

Griffin, driving with his wife in their minivan, was drawn to the lot by a Jeep Cherokee parked there with a sign saying it was for sale. People with cars to sell often brought them to the parking lot. As the Griffins pulled in, they spotted a thin, disheveled black man beside an old blue Chevrolet Caprice. The man was wearing a filthy T-shirt. Griffin's wife thought he was going to beg for money and rolled up her window. Later, Griffin would identify the man to the FBI as John Muhammad.

A few hours later, three other people spotted the Caprice on London Lane, a residential side street that ran off Collington Road a block and a half from the school. The car stayed there overnight but was gone early the next morning.

6

"Call Me God"

Iran Brown had been banned from his school bus for three days for eating Twizzlers. Eating on the bus was against the rules at the Benjamin Tasker Middle School, but Iran was thirteen and careless of such strictures. On Monday morning, October 7, unsure if the three-day ban was up or not, he got a ride to school with his aunt, Tanya Brown. Iran had been living with his aunt and uncle in Bowie for a year. His mother had sent him there to try to get him away from some unsavory characters in the apartment complex where she lived twenty minutes away. Iran was an eighth grader, and she wanted him to be safe. He was a good kid, with a shock of curly hair. He had taken to the strong Christian values in the household of his mother's brother, Jerome, who worked at the Pentagon, and his aunt, a nurse at Children's Hospital in Washington.

That morning they would have to get to school early, but Iran could hang around outside near the big flagpole for the few minutes before the doors opened. At 8:09, they pulled into the driveway and Iran got out, wearing his backpack over his white football jersey. As Tanya Brown began to drive away, she heard a boom, a child's scream, and then Iran yelling, "Aunt Tanya!" She stopped, looked back, and saw Iran on the ground.

A teacher standing in the doorway heard the shot and ran to the boy's side.

"What's wrong?" the teacher asked.

"I've been shot," Brown replied.

"Are you kidding?" the teacher said.

No, Brown said, he wasn't kidding.

His aunt, meanwhile, had backed the car up. Iran got to his feet and again said he'd been shot. She could see blood on his shirt. He managed to walk back to the car and got in. His aunt buckled him into his seat belt, dialed 911 on her cell phone, and raced for a nearby emergency clinic, the Bowie Health Center. Iran, sitting beside her, looked terrified. He told her it hurt. She could hear congestion in his chest as he tried to breathe. Color drained from his face.

"Aunt Tanya, I love you," he said.

"It's all right, baby, you're going to be okay," his aunt replied. "Nothing is going to happen to you."

She drove frantically the mile and a half to the health center, honking her horn and running a red light. She pulled up next to a police car and began waving her arms. But the officer just looked at her and drove off. She raced up to the health center, jumped out of the car, and yelled, "I need help!" When no one came out, she yelled again, "I need help *right now*!" A security guard came out and then a nurse. They hurried Iran inside in a wheelchair. Tanya called her husband, who reached Lisa Brown, Iran's mother, at work. She collapsed when she heard the news.

Lee Malvo, older than Iran Brown by only four years, later told his interrogators in Virginia that he hadn't wanted to shoot the boy in the head. There were other children around, and a head shot would be too messy. But he had wanted to shock. Malvo, who was in the trees just north of the school, aimed for the body instead. The Bushmaster's .223 round penetrated Iran's upper left abdomen and then fragmented, lacerating a lung and his spleen, his diaphragm, liver, and pancreas. He and Muhammad had another mission that day—they wanted to deliver their first communiqué to police. The police wouldn't find the communication until a little later.

————

Iran was stabilized at the Bowie clinic, where X-rays showed the familiar "snowstorm" pattern of scattered bullet fragments, and then rushed by state police helicopter to Children's Hospital, where his aunt was a nurse. There, a trauma team was waiting. They would have to remove his damaged spleen and part of his pancreas and work hard to save his life.

At one point early on, in the confusion, an announcement was made that the boy's shooting was not connected to the others. But as the attack became known, a wave of fear unlike anything so far began to spread through the whole metropolitan area. The week before, Moose had tried to calm fears by insisting that children were safe in school. Now, deep inside, people knew better.

Frantic parents rushed to Tasker to retrieve their children, leaving their cars parked helter-skelter outside on the roadside. Kids arriving on school buses were told to run, not walk, into the building. Younger children cried with relief when their parents picked them up. "Why would you shoot a thirteen-year-old boy that did nothing?" Brandon Tyler, a friend of Iran's, told a local television station. "He doesn't even see you shoot him. You're hiding and shoot him. It's a coward."

Schools throughout the region went into code blue. Outdoor activities were canceled, including after-school sports. Some restaurants sat empty, and others removed their outdoor seating. Private security officers guarded supermarkets. Even members of Congress were advised to limit outdoor activities. "We have a level of fear we're not used to," Moose said. Outside the White Flint shopping mall, not far from where Muhammad had been seen by the security guard, an eleven-year-old boy, Moses Hart, later summed up the fear with a ditty:

> *Watch out for the killer*
> *Cuz he'll shoot you in the head.*
> *And then you're dead.*

At Children's Hospital, Iran Brown was rushed into surgery. Doctors opened the boy's chest and hurried to drain away blood and find and repair what damage they could. They first treated Iran's injured left lung, decided to remove his smashed spleen, and did a minor repair to his nicked pancreas. The liver, like the lung, was damaged but largely able to heal itself. The surgeons then moved to his lacerated stomach, which they repaired successfully. Finally, Dr. Martin Eichelberger, chief of the hospital's pediatric surgery, dug from the boy's chest wall a thumbnail-size fragment of the bullet. It was placed in a cup and turned over to an ATF agent who was waiting outside the operating room.

The doctors had done all they could for the boy, and it looked as though it might be enough. All the damage had been fixed or controlled, and Iran was alive. But plenty could still go wrong. "There is a lot of luck involved here," Eichelberger would say later. "I hope I'm a lucky surgeon."

The fragment from Iran's chest was hurried to the ballistics lab, where Dandridge and his staff quickly matched it to the others and notified police headquarters. When Moose began his news conference that afternoon, his eyes blinked with tears and his voice quivered.

"Today it went down to the children," he said. "Someone is so mean-spirited that they shot a child. . . . Now we're stepping over the line because our children don't deserve this."

Moose faltered and shed a single tear. "So, parents, please, do your job tonight. Engage your children. Be there for them. We're going to need it . . . shooting a kid, I guess it's getting to be really, really personal now."

Deputy Chief Bill O'Toole put his arm around Moose as they went back into headquarters. It was a dramatic moment, replayed on national television, that showed the anxiety of the community and the passion that Moose brought to the case. The chief "showed what everyone is feeling," said Duncan, the county executive. "How could someone stoop so low as to shoot a child? We're all feeling anger and outrage, and on top of that we're working sixteen- to twenty-hour days."

Moose later said he regretted his show of emotion. "I shouldn't have done any of that," he said. "We're supposed to be dealing with the evidence and the facts."

One person who watched Moose thought he was funny. The chief's breakdown, Malvo said later, made him laugh. Shooting a child had been designed "to hurt Moose, let him know [we] mean business," he later told prison guards. And it had "worked," because Moose couldn't handle it. "If he's upset, he can't think straight."

The shooting of a child and the shooter's striking of yet another jurisdiction elevated the case to a new level. More reward money began to flow in. Maryland's governor, Parris N. Glendening, added $100,000 to the pot. A California businessman, Tim Blixseth, after seeing Moose weep on TV, sent the county $50,000. President Bush weighed in, calling the shootings "cowardly and senseless."

Moose wrote to the Justice Department, officially requesting federal help under a law that dealt with serial killings. The government pledged all available help. Gary M. Bald, the FBI's new special agent in charge of the Baltimore office, hurried back to Maryland from the police chiefs' convention in Minneapolis. He was a tall, angular man who had been with the Bureau for twenty-five years and had investigated organized crime and corruption as well as internal misconduct. Bald, who had never met Moose, was worried that the Montgomery police might take his arrival the wrong way. Some did, at first. Drew Tracy initially found him to be a starchy bureaucrat, "a pain in the ass in a tie," but changed his mind when he saw how committed Bald was to the investigation.

Kevin Lewis, an FBI assistant special agent in charge in Baltimore, was already in Rockville after getting a call from Moose that

morning. He and Moose knew each other from a black law enforcement professional organization. But Lewis got bad personal news
that day. His mother, Armenal Mitchell, had been hospitalized, later
to be diagnosed with terminal cancer. Lewis agonized over whether
he should go home to Michigan until she passed the word: Don't
worry about me. He was doing an important job. He should stay. He
would make the ten-hour drive to the Lansing hospital as soon as he
got a break.

Adding the federal government to the investigation greatly expanded its resources but caused friction in the task force and planted
the seeds of a bitter backroom legal battle weeks down the road. The
friction was evident almost immediately. When Moose began seeking formal help from the Justice Department, Lewis told him that
it would also involve the presence of federal prosecutors from the
U.S. Attorney's Office in Baltimore. Lewis asked Moose if he was
okay with that. Moose, who had an often tense relationship with
Montgomery County's chief prosecutor, State's Attorney Douglas
Gansler, said he didn't mind the feds at all.

———————

Later that day, the U.S. attorney for Maryland, Thomas M. DiBiagio,
arrived in Rockville from Baltimore for an evening press conference
designed to be a show of unity. Beforehand, DiBiagio and Assistant
U.S. Attorney A. David Copperthite were sitting at a small conference table in Moose's headquarters office when Gansler walked in.
Earlier Copperthite had been drafting Moose's request to the Justice
Department for help. DiBiagio would remember that Gansler didn't
say hello.

There were raw personal feelings between Gansler, a Democrat,
and DiBiagio, a Republican. Among other things, Gansler was still
angry over a partial gag order DiBiagio's office had gotten a federal
judge to issue against him in a recent murder case. Gansler, who was
the chief target of the motion, felt he had been "slammed" and
hadn't forgotten it. He had no problem with Copperthite, but, in

front of DiBiagio, he told Moose he believed the federal prosecutor was untrustworthy.

DiBiagio and Copperthite would recall that Moose brushed Gansler off, saying, "This case is bigger than any of us. We need help, and that's what we're doing." DiBiagio promised whatever federal assistance Moose wanted and said he wasn't there to take over the case. The group then adjourned to the press briefing, publicly pledging its solidarity. DiBiagio emphasized that Moose was running the investigation. Gansler said the cooperation was unprecedented. "We're all together on this," he said.

————

Across the county, funeral services for the victims continued. Sarah Ramos was remembered, mostly in Spanish, during services at St. Camillus Church in Silver Spring. Her mother and other members of her family had traveled from El Salvador to participate.

After the service, they were driven to the shopping center bench where she had been murdered the week before. Her mother, Maria Benitez, placed a single white rose on the bench, along with the bouquets of flowers left by others. She then knelt, covered her face with her hands, and cried. "I will miss everything about her," she said. "Everything that she had become." A little later, relatives of Lori Lewis Rivera gathered for a wake in her memory at the same funeral home where Corporal Foust's mourners had been gathered when Rivera was shot the week before. Rivera's father, Marion, blinked back tears as he read a statement to reporters outside. "We miss her deeply," he said. "I'll never forgive the people who took her away from us."

At the gas station where she had been murdered, local children had erected a makeshift memorial near the car vacuum where she had died: One sign there simply read, WHY? At the same time, in Virginia, Caroline Seawell was released from the hospital. She had been seriously but not critically injured. Friends said her survival was miraculous. Police kept her name secret, because her attackers were still at large.

Meanwhile, at the Tasker school, investigators were swarming over the area. Busloads of Montgomery County police cadets were brought in to help the Prince George's police scour the grass, woods, and bushes for bullet fragments, casings, and other clues. The ATF sent a mobile crime lab. From the TV helicopters overhead, it was impossible to see that progress was being made on the ground. But it was.

Late in the day, Forsythe got a phone call from Dr. William Vosburgh, a former dentist who was now director of the Prince George's County police forensics lab. Vosburgh told Forsythe that something unusual had turned up. The searchers had found a tarot card. He didn't say that there was a message on it, but he asked if Forsythe had found anything like it at his crime scenes. Forsythe hadn't. Vosburgh didn't want to say more just yet.

The Tasker school searchers had started out that morning with little idea where to begin. They weren't even sure where the shot had come from. Somewhere across the street seemed the most likely spot. The U.S. Marshals Service brought in a search dog, a half black Lab, half golden retriever named Beacon, who had flunked out of guide dog school but was later trained to sniff out explosives. Beacon and his handler, Deputy Marshal Michael Pyo, entered the dense woods north of the school, guarded by three SWAT officers. As Pyo was ducking in the underbrush, one of the SWAT officers yelled, "Hey, look at your dog." Beacon was up on his hind legs, sniffing a tree branch. The dog then "alerted," by sitting. Pyo realized it was the perfect spot from which to fire on Iran Brown.

The ground looked disturbed, as if someone had been lying there in wait. Prince George's police then brought in a bloodhound, Miss Demeanor, that they used in tracking. The dog retraced a trail through the woods and along the tennis court to a parking lot and one specific space, where the scent was lost. Police then went back over the trail Miss Demeanor had followed, looking for clues, when an ATF agent suddenly spotted something in the underbrush.

It was a tarot card. Used in Italian parlor games as long ago as the fifteenth century, the cards have more recently been associated with the occult—and sometimes with crime. In a famous case in California, a killer left a tarot card in the home of a family he had just slain.

The card, perhaps predictably, was the so-called death card, one of seventy-eight in the classic Rider-Waite tarot deck designed in 1909. On the front was depicted a skeleton in armor riding a white horse and carrying a black flag. The horse's reins were decorated with skulls and crossbones. Across the bottom of the card was printed the word *DEATH*.

But across the top, neatly lettered in blue ink and bracketed by quote marks, was a message: "Call me God," it said. And on the back, two scrawled lines divided the card into three sections. The top segment contained the salutation "For you mr. Police." In the middle was written: "Code: 'Call me God.' " And on the bottom was a warning: "Do not release to the press."

Police put the card in a bag and had the bloodhound sniff inside. The dog then followed the scent from the card along the same path she had first traced, indicating that the card was likely connected to the shooting site.

When Joseph Bergstrom, the lead homicide detective, was shown the card, his instinct was to hide it. It was an absolute ace in the hole, he thought, and he didn't want anyone to see it. And the search turned up more. Scouring the area with rakes, Montgomery County police cadets found a shell casing from a .223 rifle bullet that police thought might have been ejected from the shooter's gun.

While there was a chance the card was a fluke, it had the possibility of providing a treasure of evidence. And it was apparently an overture, one that had to be handled with utmost care. Police revealed publicly only that they had found the shell casing.

The next day, Prince George's County police chief Gerald M. Wilson sent some of his police officials to Rockville to brief Forsythe and two dozen other high-level task force members. They showed the shell casing and a copy of the card. They detailed the history of

tarot cards and their meanings. Bergstrom, uncomfortable with the
size of the meeting, introduced himself and told the group he was
worried that someone might leak information about the card. The
group discussed what, if anything, should be said publicly about it.
Should Moose hint it had been found? Someone mentioned that in
the Vietnam War movie *Apocalypse Now*, an American officer left
playing cards—"death cards," he called them—on the bodies of
dead enemy fighters. Vosburgh remembered that "God" was the
nickname of the chief sniper in a recent movie about navy SEALs.

But the secret could not be kept. That night on the eleven
o'clock news, Mike Buchanan, a veteran reporter with a local TV station, WUSA, reported that a tarot card had been found. Buchanan
later said he got a tip from the wife of a police officer. *The Washington
Post* confirmed the story and reported it in its late editions. Both
got the wording on the card slightly wrong, reporting that the salutation read, "I am God." Neither news organization initially reported
the press warning.

The police were incensed. The sniper had specifically warned
them to keep quiet. Any chance of continuing the dialogue now
seemed lost. At a news conference the next morning, Moose made
his feelings clear. "In Montgomery County, our citizens have asked
the Montgomery County Police Department and all available federal
resources to work this case," he said angrily, his voice raised, his
hands clasped behind his back. "I have not received any message that
the citizens of Montgomery County want Channel 9 or *The Washington Post* or any other media outlet to solve this case. If they do,
then let me know. We will go and do other police work and we will
turn this case over to the media and you can solve it."

He went on angrily in this vein for several minutes. It looked like
a classic Moose temper outburst. Much of it, he would say later, was
an act. He believed the sniper was probably watching, and he was
trying to communicate that the leak had not been his fault, that he
was upset by the violation of the request. He was trying to keep the
lines open. "You want to make sure that the people who left the card

know that you're upset," he would say later. He had a conversation under way, but not the kind that either party wanted.

———————

Muhammad and Malvo kept moving. Judging from the Griffins' sighting and others, they were living out of the Caprice. Their next stop was Baltimore. The night of the Tasker shooting, Muhammad appeared at a Subway sandwich shop in Baltimore's Remington neighborhood. It was just before 9:00 P.M., and two employees, Marty Ruby and Holly Thompson, were closing up for the night. Muhammad, wearing shorts and a T-shirt, came in the shop, said he was from out of town, and asked politely if they were still serving. Ruby and Thompson said they were not. Muhammad asked if he could rest in his car outside, and the two employees said fine.

Muhammad then went next door to a Mobil minimart, where he bought potato chips, a brownie, and a soda. He said he hadn't slept in two days. An hour later, when Ruby and Thompson were locking up and taking out the trash, Muhammad came out of the Caprice in his bare feet. They could see a laptop computer on the front seat, its blue screen illuminating the interior. Again Muhammad asked if it was okay to rest there.

"You're fine, you're okay, hon," Ruby said, impressed at Muhammad's politeness. "But don't stay too long. The police will come. They don't let people sleep in cars here because it's unsafe for us workers."

Ruby was right about the police. At 1:00 A.M., James Snyder, a Baltimore police officer, spotted the car in the parking lot of the Donut Connection next door. When he returned two hours later, the car was still there and the windows were steamed up. Suspicious, he pulled up and radioed the car's tag number to police dispatcher Derrick K. Evans for a computer check. Snyder had no way of knowing, but it was the seventh time in eleven days that the Caprice had been investigated by police.

Evans said there was no problem with the car, but Snyder

knocked on the car window and woke up Muhammad, who told Snyder he was traveling from the Washington area to visit his father near Camden, New Jersey. He asked for directions. A block off Interstate 83, which runs north to central Pennsylvania, Muhammad was a long way from Interstate 95, the route to New Jersey. Snyder saw no one else in the car but noticed that the backseat was filled with clothes, as if someone were living in the vehicle.

Another Baltimore officer arrived as backup. Officer Snyder requested a check of Muhammad's driver's license, which produced nothing of concern. The officer told Muhammad to move on, and he drove off.

Malvo would later say he had a pregnant woman in his sights in a Baltimore cemetery, but Muhammad called off the attack because a police helicopter was overhead. And police would find under the front passenger headrest in the Caprice the handwritten names of three schools in the city. One was a preschool. One was an elementary school. And one was the Maiden Choice School, a center for severly disabled children.

On Tuesday, a week after the shootings began and with no virtually no progress in solving them, Jim Cavanaugh, the ATF's special agent in charge in Nashville, joined the investigation. Robert Switzer, the deputy assistant director of field operations in Washington, had tracked Cavanaugh down the day before en route to an assignment in Memphis. Technically he would be the ATF's deputy incident commander, behind Michael Bouchard. But he was the seniormost special agent in charge in the country. He had been a supervisor longer than Bouchard had been with the ATF, and he brought priceless experience and wisdom.

Cavanaugh, forty-nine, had been involved in some of the biggest national crime cases of the previous twenty years—the Unabomber, the Atlanta Olympic Park bombing. But he was best known as the ATF negotiator who spent days on the telephone with Branch Davidian leader David Koresh at the 1993 siege at Waco. It had been the biggest gun battle in the history of U.S. law enforcement. The Davidians fired 12,000 rounds; the federal agents fired 1,200 back. Cavanaugh, who had witnessed at agonizingly close range and under fire the deaths of four ATF agents killed in the shoot-out with Koresh's followers, begged and cajoled Koresh into releasing eighteen of the children inside the compound. But he was later replaced by FBI negotiators in the standoff, which ended with the compound burning to the ground, killing all those inside. He was haunted by Waco, the agents' deaths, and the more than eighty people he had not been able to get out. The psychic scars were just beneath the surface.

Cavanaugh arrived outside the Rockville police headquarters in an airport cab in the middle of Moose's morning news conference. Wearing an $800 business suit with a white linen handkerchief in the breast pocket, a $1,200 watch, and a $300 pair of shoes, he had a .40-caliber pistol strapped to his left ankle as he stood behind the throng of reporters and took in the scene: Media tents and satellite trucks seemed to have dropped from the sky. SWAT police were on the rooftops. Traffic was inching past. The chief was castigating reporters. Chaos, he thought. A goat rope of epic proportions.

Cavanaugh was low-key, witty, and charming. He always had a story to tell. He quoted Winston Churchill, Humphrey Bogart, Yogi Berra, and Fred Smith, the head of FedEx. He dressed like a CEO, wore black driving gloves in his Grand Marquis, and spoke like a motivational guru. But Cavanaugh had the Cheshire grin of a salesman and often finished his sentences with "You know what I mean," which could be a question or observation. He was a wiseguy catcher as a kid and now was a gentle hustler, selling people on themselves and on the patented Jim Cavanaugh method of leadership.

He was obsessed with leadership, fascinated by its smooth exercise. He believed that one wielded power by giving it away. Subordinates loved to bring commanders what Cavanaugh called "the leaky bag," the messy problem. Cavanaugh always gave it back. Fix it and brief me. He never raised his voice and was a quick judge of character. One Virginia state trooper reminded him of Clint Eastwood. He thought a ranking FBI official looked like the father of cartoon figure Dennis the Menace.

Cavanaugh referred to ATF and FBI executive offices in Washington as "mahogany row" and to himself as a "broken-down, empty holster," which he wasn't. He had the power to pick up the phone and order one hundred more agents, which, to the amazement of the county police, he shortly did. He also got along well with the FBI, and had often worked with its agents on big cases. The FBI, with thirty-three thousand employees, was like a battleship, Cavanaugh would say. The ATF, with four thousand, was more nimble, like a cruiser. FBI guys always seemed to be on the phone, he joked, probably talking to "the brain in a jar" downtown.

As the new guy from Nashville, he wanted to be careful not to offend anyone in Rockville. He needed Forsythe. If he was to be effective in the job, he knew he would have to have the respect and goodwill of the local captain, the guy in direct command who gave the orders and answered to the chief. Their relationship, in fact, became a kind of model of the alliance between the federal government and local law enforcement that was envisioned in the aftermath of the terrorist attacks of September 11, 2001. If the war on terrorism was going to succeed, it could not be won solely by federal agents. But local police had to feel they weren't there just to take orders from the FBI or the Justice Department. For that reason, Attorney General John Ashcroft and his top aides would strongly resist calls for "federalization" of the sniper investigation, even though the resources in the case were mostly theirs.

Cavanaugh and Forsythe hit it off from the outset. Forsythe was born in the same neighborhood in Newark where Cavanaugh grew up. They were about the same age and at about the same level of experience; they might have swapped career paths. Both were from Irish-Catholic families. Both had been altar boys. Both had ancestors who were Newark firefighters.

But Cavanaugh, in his nice suits and snazzy shoes, was at ease at the center of a big national investigation. Forsythe, with his sweater vests and grubby trench coat, was not. Cavanaugh was flashy and outgoing. Forsythe was a background guy, "a grinder," a cop you'd never give a second look. At home, the phone stayed on his wife's side of the bed. He valued routine.

Cavanaugh drove a big Mercury. Forsythe, who had a wood-burning stove in his house and a plaque on the wall that said, BECAUSE NICE MATTERS, drove a Honda. Cavanaugh loved battle-scarred cops like Forsythe, imperfect guys who hadn't solved every single case, guys who had had their own little Wacos. Forsythe was impressed with the tall, dapper federal agent.

"I've never done one like this," Forsythe told him later. "You've got to show me."

"Barney, it ain't hard," Cavanaugh said. "It's an orchestra. You're the conductor trying to make music. If you're running around playing the flute, you're a loser. You've got to step up there and grab the baton." But Forsythe was a jazz fan and not used to conducting. He ran a bunch of suburban detectives with twenty murders a year who had just had hell dropped on their heads. That was okay, Cavanaugh said. Just remember: You're world-class police. Cavanaugh would later say their friendship was natural. "He knew I wasn't going to screw him."

Cavanaugh took care to make sure Forsythe was always kept in the loop. "Go get Barney," he'd say. "Barney, do you know about this?" He made sure to introduce Forsythe to visiting VIPs: "This is Captain Forsythe, the chief of detectives." He'd tell Forsythe their main job was making decisions. "We're not supposed to do any ac-tual work," he'd joke. Forsythe would joke back: "I like your style." But Cavanaugh was serious. It was important, he believed, that as they sat in their wheeled desk chairs they appear unstressed, re-laxed, and available to make decisions.

After he had introduced himself, Cavanaugh joined a small meet-ing of commanders around a table in Forsythe's office. It was not long before they were discussing a favorite subject of Cavanaugh's—lead-ership in big cases. Cavanaugh mentioned that in *Chief!* by Albert A. Seedman, a former chief of detectives in the New York Police Department, Seedman described how he solved a difficult shooting case that had no motive and no witnesses. When his detectives told him they had no leads, he pointed to a random spot on the map and told them to start there. The point was: It didn't matter where they started. They just needed to start. They did, and the case was eventually solved—a man shooting seagulls had hit the victim by accident.

As Cavanaugh told the story, Forsythe left the table. Cavanaugh was afraid he had bombed. When Forsythe returned moments later he was carrying his own copy of Seedman's book. This guy gets it, Cavanaugh thought.

Cavanaugh had worked out of big joint command centers in the past and knew that the one in Rockville, jammed almost shoulder to shoulder with investigators, was too small. And too tense. He was determined to lighten things up a little if he could. He was not overly concerned about the tarot card leak. Leaks always happened. The important thing was to know your priorities. "Keep the main thing the main thing," he liked to say.

It seemed possible that the day would wind down without further incident. But at 8:10 P.M. an urgent call came in that there had been another shooting. This one was in Virginia, in Prince William County, thirty-five miles away, just south of the old Civil War battlefield at Manassas. It wasn't yet clear if it was the work of the sniper. The sniper had struck only once before in darkness, in the Charlot case a week earlier. But this was at another gas station, as in the Walekar and Rivera cases, and near a major highway, as in the Brown and Seawell cases. And it was a weekday. The sniper had so far always struck on a weekday.

A call came in from Prince William police chief Charlie T. Deane asking for help from the ATF on ballistics. Joe Riehl, the assistant special agent in charge in the ATF's Baltimore office, said he was going down there to take a look. Forsythe said he would go, too. So did Cavanaugh, and they rode together. As Riehl, a former schoolteacher who had eventually followed his father into the ATF, speeded south along the interstates, Cavanaugh joked that it would be okay if they got there in one piece.

7

Striking at Will

On March 8, 1970, a twenty-year-old army rifleman named Dean Harold Meyers volunteered to go on a patrol near Phuoc Vinh, South Vietnam, about fifty miles north of Saigon. One of four brothers from a family in rural Pennsylvania, Meyers didn't smoke or drink and played the piano beautifully. While many young men his age were trying to avoid military service, he let himself be drafted out of a sense of duty. He'd been in Vietnam since May of 1969 and would be able to leave in about three months.

Meyers and his unit were surprised by a group of enemy soldiers, and he was directly in their path when they opened fire. He was badly hit in the upper left arm and bolted for cover. Luckily, some of Meyers's unit saw where he ran and went out looking for him. They found him in some underbrush, bleeding profusely and in shock. They patched him up as best they could and called in a medevac. He was ghostly white when they put him on the helicopter and sent him away from the war. Several of the men on that patrol didn't survive Vietnam. Others wouldn't hear about their injured comrade again for thirty years.

On the night of October 9, 2002, Meyers, now fifty-three, had worked late as usual at his office in Manassas. Meyers was a civil engineer. He designed storm drainage systems for residential developments. He was good and thorough at what he did. He worked late almost every night. He was a lifelong bachelor and had a town house in Gaithersburg, up in Montgomery County, forty miles from his job. He had lived there for twenty-five years. Meyers had come back from Vietnam with a Purple Heart and the army's Commendation Medal for Heroism, but he was grievously injured and disillusioned. He spent months in a military hospital in Valley Forge, Pennsylvania, and underwent numerous operations on his arm, which was substantially disabled. "I've lost the direction my heart would lead," he wrote on the back of a hospital menu in 1971. "I've grown out of the dreams of my youth. . . . I've cast them down, and now I'm lost, searching for a purpose in my life."

But he recovered, studied engineering at Penn State, and landed a good job in the Washington area. He owned five acres near the Rappahannock River, a vintage Corvette, and a motorcycle. He still was generous and decent and still didn't smoke or use bad language. Though he never spoke about the war, he was in many ways the same person who left the jungle in 1970.

A little after 8:00 P.M., he decided it was time to go. A colleague in the next cubicle who was also leaving bade him good night. Okay, Meyers said, see you tomorrow. But Meyers had a long ride home and needed gas. He pulled his black Mazda Protegé into the Battlefield Sunoco station on Sudley Road a block or so from his office, flipped open the door to the gas tank, and put in the hose nozzle. The station was less than a thousand feet from Exit 47 on the big east-west highway, Interstate 66, that ran fifty miles from Washington all the way to the Shenandoah Valley. A half mile north on Sudley Road, just beyond the interchange, was the dark and quiet of the Civil War military park, where two bloody battles were fought in 1861 and 1862.

Meyers stood bathed in the modern white lights of the pump island, a perfect target. It was cold and wet, and his car windows were up. As he stood there, a gunshot cracked and a .223 bullet from a rifle much like the one he had carried in Vietnam struck him behind the left ear, killing him instantly. Meyers fell on his back, his left foot bent against a rear tire, his injured left arm at his side as if he were asleep. His head was propped on the curb of the pump island. A thick stream of his blood quickly spread underneath his car, like a bad oil leak. Malvo would later say it was an excellent hit, a devastating head shot, in a place far from where the other shootings had occurred, designed to thin out police defenses.

Inside the gas station, the attendant thought he heard a tire explode. Somebody dialed 911 and reported a suspected shooting. The shot sounded as though it had come from the direction of Sudley Road. The Lake Jackson Rescue Squad was one of the first on the scene, along with Prince William County police officer Anthony Notarintonio. There was little they could do. Notarintonio saw Meyers's awful head wound and noted that he wasn't breathing. He radioed that the shooting was confirmed and asked if anybody had any information on a vehicle or suspect.

Prince William County police chief Charlie T. Deane, an elegant, gray-haired man with a soft Virginia accent, had gone home for the night when he got the call about the shooting. Deane, fifty-seven, was among the most senior police chiefs in the area. He had been the chief of the Prince William County Police Department for fourteen years. The son of a rural county sheriff, he had started out in law enforcement as an FBI file clerk and had been a Virginia state trooper until he joined the county police department when it was founded in 1970. He was the last of the original force still working.

Deane had already been in on the daily police conference call on the sniper case. Now it looked as though the sniper had come to Prince William County, a big wedge of northern Virginia that stretched from Possum Nose on the Potomac River to Lookout Road on the Fauquier County line. Like many of the outer Washington suburbs, the county was booming with housing tracts, golf courses, and shopping centers, and with a population of nearly three hundred thousand, it had become the third most populous jurisdiction in the state.

Deane was told the attack had been a long-distance shot at a gas

station right off the interstate. The victim was dead. Deane knew
Prince William didn't have a lot of murders by distant gunshot.
Aside from the sniper, there wasn't much else this could be. "Whatever size crime scene you have, I want you to double it," he told his
officers at the gas station. "I don't care how big it is, I want you to
expand it." An area half a mile deep was roped off and barred to
anyone except investigators. Deane alerted the Montgomery County
task force, and a dragnet operation went into effect. He had already
planned with Chief J. Thomas Manger, head of the adjacent Fairfax
County Police Department, that if the sniper struck either place,
they would "lock down" the road system as best they could. If the
police were quick, and the killer was not, they might be able to bag
him downstream.

But what were they looking for? For miles up and down Interstate
95, Virginia police raced to take up position, closing down the exits
and entrances to the interstate at Sudley Road. There was a fresh report about a white van seen speeding away, but the police quickly
tracked it down. The van was owned by a family that was having dinner at a restaurant near the gas station. When the parents heard the
shot, they had taken their kids and left immediately. They had called
in when they heard the police were looking for their van.

The Sunoco, like many of the Montgomery County crime scenes,
was in a busy commercial area ringed by restaurants and other businesses. There was even a county police officer right nearby. Malvo said
later that he saw him. They could have shot him, he said, if they had
wanted.

The shot could have been taken from almost anywhere: the Bob
Evans restaurant parking lot across the street, some nearby hedges.
When Deane arrived, he used notebook paper to cover the Mazda's
license plates. He didn't want Meyers's identity to get out prema-
turely. He told his investigators to be cautious and sent them comb-
ing through the lots and shrubs for evidence.

Two detectives reported that they had found something interesting near the Bob Evans lot: a map of Baltimore and Baltimore
County. The map, which had been stolen from a library in Mary-

land, was one of several items found at the crime scene and wasn't considered to be of much value. It wasn't immediately examined or processed for fingerprints, but instead was stored by Prince William County police in a locker. Forsythe and Cavanaugh were never even told about it. After Malvo and Muhammad were arrested, their fingerprints were found among the many on the map. Cavanaugh later believed that if the prints had been found at the time the map was discovered, Malvo and Muhammad might have been caught much earlier.

Dozens of FBI and ATF agents descended on the gas station, along with Cavanaugh, Forsythe, Riehl, and forty Virginia state troopers. Deane was grateful for the help but felt his people were probably more experienced at handling crime scenes than the feds. Forsythe understood. He wouldn't want people walking through one of his crime scenes, either. "When you're ready for us, let us know," he said. He and the others waited for almost an hour outside the police tape.

Once admitted to the county's police command bus, Forsythe was helpful, describing for Deane the Maryland murder scenes. The two joked about the bus, which used to belong to Montgomery County. Later, Deane set up a bigger command post in a local hotel. There Forsythe stood up and introduced himself as the chief of the Maryland investigators working the case and offered to share what information he had. He noted that while no one was yet certain, the Meyers killing sure looked like the work of the sniper. On the way back to Maryland, Forsythe and Cavanaugh talked about how just when they were getting a handle on the case, it spread somewhere else. Deane, meanwhile, called the county's chief prosecutor, Paul B. Ebert.

Ebert, sixty-five, was a legend in northern Virginia. He had been the Prince William County commonwealth attorney for over thirty-four years and was nearing retirement. Ebert had played football at Virginia Tech and was nicknamed Butch. He had a dog and a pickup truck and loved to fish and hunt. In court he was folksy and plainspoken. Every Christmas, he hosted a bash at the rescue squad building behind the courthouse, across from the jail, in Manassas. He

served bear and elk meat and invited lawyers, judges, law enforcement officers, and reporters from as far away as Washington, D.C.

Ebert was famous for other things. He was so effective with Virginia juries that since the reinstatement of the death penalty in 1976,
he had sent a dozen killers to death row, more than any other prosecutor in the state. Since then, Virginia had ranked second in the nation in executions, with eighty-seven. Ebert was also known as the
man who in 1993 prosecuted Lorena Bobbitt, the woman who had
cut off the penis of her sleeping husband. The focus of international
publicity, Ebert said later that the only thing that changed for him
was that he now slept on his stomach. More recently, he had received
a taunting letter from a murder convict whose death sentence had
just been overturned on a technicality. The convict boasted of further heinous offenses he had not revealed in the case and mocked
Ebert for "fuckin' up and saving me." Ebert promptly filed updated
murder charges, based on the contents of the letter.

When one of Ebert's assistant prosecutors, Richard A. Conway,
heard about the Meyers killing that night at his home in the Virginia
countryside, he thought, If this is the sniper, he just made a fatal
mistake.

––––––––––

The next day, Dr. Frances P. Field, the assistant chief medical examiner for northern Virginia, conducted an autopsy on Meyers's
body at the Northern Laboratory of the state's Division of Forensic
Science, in Fairfax. Field began removing pieces of bullet fragments
from his brain. Ralph Daigneau, a Prince William County police officer who attended the autopsy, counted fourteen pieces. One of
them was a jagged piece of copper about a quarter inch in size that
Daigneau thought looked like the back end of the bullet. Most of
them were turned over to the ATF laboratory in Rockville.

After a night of fruitless searching, Virginia police realized that
their traffic lockdown had not been tight enough or broad enough.
At a meeting at the Fairfax Police Academy, they planned a dragnet

that next time would be much more extensive and prevent the killer from returning to Montgomery County if that was where he was based. They were virtually certain he would attack again.

In Rockville, Moose deflected questions about whether the Meyers case was linked to the sniper but announced that there was a new consolidated tip line. He gave out the number and repeated it twice. Twenty miles away, at the Washington Field Office of the FBI, the new phone number was a cause for consternation. The task force had been working on the extremely complicated task of coordinating tips from what was becoming a huge geographic area. It was overwhelming. Van A. Harp, the assistant director in charge of the field office, volunteered to set up the hot line in downtown Washington.

The day before, assistant special agent in charge Toni M. Fogle and special agent Vincent Montagnino pulled together tables and computers and telephones and set up a call center in a first-floor classroom of the FBI office, not far from the U.S. Capitol. The computers were loaded with software so the tip takers could enter and catalog data for "Major Case 194." Fogle was told to have everything ready by 9:00 A.M. the next day, when the number would be broadcast on television. Fogle got twenty-three phone lines ready and worked out the staffing. She planned three shifts, with the first crew coming in at 6:00 A.M. to get briefed for the 9:00 A.M. announcement. She thought she had everything ready.

At 6:00 A.M., Fogle got a shock. The number was going public not in three hours, as she had been told, but in an hour. She gave her staff a quick briefing, and everyone took their places. A big TV screen in the front of the room was tuned to CNN. Shortly after 7:00 A.M., the new tip number flashed on the screen. Instantly, every one of Fogle's phone lines lit up. In seconds, the call center was swamped.

Fogle realized that it was taking too long to open the software reporting form and enter the data. Callers were put on hold and then hung up. It was like trying to fit a ten-gallon hose through a one-gallon pipe, Montagnino thought. The crush shut down all calls coming into the entire field office. Fogle made a quick decision. She ordered the computers removed and replaced with pens and legal pads. It was old-fashioned, but faster. Fogle arranged for fifty-nine more lines and more room on the third floor. It still wasn't enough.

At times, calls were coming in at the rate of 20,000 to 30,000 a day. Montagnino figured a tip taker could spend maybe a minute or so with each caller and could realistically handle about 35 calls an hour, which was 3,500 calls per person per one hundred hours. At first, Fogle had FBI agents manning the phones. She then drafted researchers and analysts to help.

There was a tremendous sense of urgency. The killer was out there. The next caller might have the key to the case. The classroom got hot and noisy. The work seemed endless and numbing. The calls came from all over the country and around the world. Sometimes callers were angry or frustrated. Gradually, a system was worked out. If a tip taker got an especially promising tip, the taker would raise a hand, then be taken to investigators for a quick exchange of data. The most pertinent tips were then immediately faxed or couriered to the task force in Rockville. The vast majority of the tips in this flood turned out to be of no use, but one call would later be critical.

The tips, and the investigation, turned up dozens of likely suspects and scores of weird, armed characters. Parents reported on disgruntled children. Girlfriends called about oddball boyfriends. At one point, someone put up a sign in Rockville: NO MORE EX-WIVES AND EX-GIRLFRIENDS. Unbalanced people called to identify themselves as the sniper.

Some people saw mystical signs in the pattern—Rockville to Bowie to Spotsylvania. One day, a navy captain and his wife came to the Prince William County command center with a Bible and a map of the shootings that had been published in the newspaper. They thought that the sniper might be a member of a religious cult. Look, the captain said, the shootings form a cross. He showed investigators how the shootings in Montgomery County formed the head of Jesus and the other attacks represented wounds in the hands and feet. He predicted that the next sniper attack would be in an area of Virginia that represented the traditional lance wound of Jesus in the side. The man said he was a religious person and just felt he had to tell someone. That night, U.S. marshals were sent to conduct surveillance in an area near Fredericksburg that corresponded to the point in the cross where the man predicted there could be another shooting.

Teams of investigators knocked on doors, staked out houses and workplaces, "sitting on" possible suspects and tailing them in their cars. At times, investigators surreptitiously attached tracking beacons to the cars of suspects so they could be followed electronically. The case seemed to bring out the strangeness in people. "There are a lot of people who don't think on the same wavelength as us," the ATF's Bouchard noted, "but can legally possess guns." Police "borrowed" dozens of rifles from owners so they could be test-fired at the ATF lab. None produced bullets that matched the sniper's.

Police observed one man who, aware they were watching, crawled out to his mailbox every day and then crawled back with his mail. Another person, a medical professional, owned a rifle and had a suspicious map on the wall designating the shooting locations. Early in the probe, a gunpowder-sniffing dog led investigators to a home in which police learned a male resident had not been to work lately. Further investigation showed the man was innocent and had stayed home to care for his sick wife.

Other times, though, police had what looked like prime suspects. At one point, Moose recalled later, investigators were watching four at the same time. All had guns. All had strange histories and shady comings and goings. All had access to white vans. They couldn't all be a coincidence, could they? Three times, Duncan, the county executive, was alerted to expect the phone call: "We've got them." Then another shooting would happen, and all those being watched fell off the suspect board. All coincidences.

Later on the day after Meyers was shot, officials in Virginia announced that the shredded bullet fragments taken from his brain were found to match the others identified as the sniper's. Paul Ebert, at a press conference, said: "This case, if I have anything to do with it, will be prosecuted in this jurisdiction to the full extent of the law." The match wasn't much of a surprise. Almost everyone on the task force already believed the Meyers killer was either the sniper or a copycat. Now he had struck for the second time in Virginia, but much closer to Washington than with Seawell in Spotsylvania. This time, there was no cryptic message, as in the Brown case. At least no written message. Malvo would indicate later that the Manassas shooting was all part of one big threatening message: We are in control. You can't stop us.

He and Muhammad had it down to a system. Using the laptop they stole from Paul La Ruffa and a global positioning navigation device they had in the Caprice, Malvo navigated them easily around the area. Maps printed out from their software appeared to indicate some of their travels. "You have the computer," Malvo would tell the authorities later. "It's all on there."

One map highlighted a Virginia route that went from Manassas to Haymarket to Centreville, with a detour within sight of where Meyers was killed. Another map showed a route right past the Tasker school, where Brown was shot. Several spots were designated with small skull-and-crossbones icons. One marked a spot across the street from where Walekar was killed. Another marked the White Flint Mall, near where Buchanan was killed. Another marked a place a few blocks from the shopping center where Martin was killed.

Other skull icons marked spots where there had been no reported shootings: the Howard University Campus in Washington, D.C.; a spot near Quincy Street off Brookville Road, in Chevy Chase, Maryland; the busy intersection of Connecticut Avenue and Viers Mill Road, not far from the area of the October 3 shootings; Indian Spring Drive near a YMCA in Silver Spring, Maryland; and the Martinsburg Mall in Martinsburg, West Virginia, about ninety miles northwest of Washington.

Some maps featured places marked with smiling or frowning face icons. The National Naval Medical Center in Bethesda got a frowning face in the middle of the hospital grounds. But a spot near rural Fairplay, Maryland, south of Hagerstown, earned a smiling face and a box that read "potential area." Some of the maps also contained spots denoted with exact addresses. Two were for YMCAs in Maryland and North Carolina. Three others were for schools just outside Washington, D.C.: the Rosaryville Elementary School in Upper Marlboro, Maryland; the Mary Harris "Mother" Jones Elementary School in Adelphi, Maryland; and the Berwyn Heights Elementary School near College Park. All were brand-new, in recently built or refurbished buildings, and had just opened a few weeks before.

Other maps traced routes between Washington and Fredericksburg, Virginia, and south into North Carolina. Several map locations in southern Virginia and North Carolina had small computer screen boxes that read "good spot," "good spot off I-95," "good spot, drag effect," and "eastern move, many ways out."

Malvo would later laugh to investigators about a shot he said had missed a boy, who then swatted the air as if at a bee. He wasn't specific about where that was. Some investigators concluded it could have been the first Michaels shooting. But the maps hint that it could have been any of the other locations the pair seem to have cased.

Malvo said they watched the media and the police response carefully. "You said this so we did this or that. . . . The media would say this so we would do another thing. We had something for everything."

Malvo indicated that he and Muhammad took turns with the Bushmaster, deciding who it would be before they went out for the day. One would set up to shoot, while the other spotted, not to aid the shooter but to look for trouble. Police would later find, in a sock left in the car, a second rifle scope besides the one Malvo called the "battlescope" on the gun.

Sometimes the shooter would be in the car, sometimes out of it. Often, shooter and spotter would not be together. Malvo said they used walkie-talkies to communicate. They selected a location and a time window. It was the call of the "sniper" whether or not to take the shot. Escape was made cautiously, so as not to arouse suspicion.

But knowing they were still invisible, they sometimes came back, as in Manassas, and hung around to watch the expressions on the faces of the bystanders. Malvo even asked policemen what had happened and would be asked, in turn, if he had seen anything suspicious. He and Muhammad also would test the roadblocks to see if the car caught police attention. It never did.

The two seemed to have scouted out rest stops along the interstates, according to the computer maps, noting the location and the facilities available. One particular map highlighted a rest stop off Interstate 70 in Maryland. It was near mile marker 39, just west of the little town of Myersville, near Frederick. It was a very secluded stop, well off the highway, and couldn't be seen from the interstate. It had rest rooms, vending machines, telephones, and a picnic area. It would be a perfect place to lie low for a few hours, if the time came.

———————

In Rockville, police were preparing for a long siege. County police headquarters had become a circus. The office was trashed, the carpet ruined. The Major Crimes Division smelled of stale coffee. Cavanaugh at one point wound up sitting on a laundry basket. Food was now available in the cell blocks. Michael Mancuso, a county police lieutenant, found an office building next door with empty space. Mancuso grabbed thirteen thousand square feet on the fourth floor. When he was told to get more, he took space on the third floor and later the first as well. It all totaled $40,000 a month. Plus there was furniture, electricity, air-conditioning, and heat for the twenty-four-hour-a-day, seven-day-a-week operation. Mancuso worried about the cost. George Layton, of the FBI, said it was not a problem. "Whatever we need," he told Mancuso. To get the funding, though, the operation had to have a name. He asked around. "SNIPMUR" didn't sound quite right, but SNIPEMUR people liked. So that's what the operation was named. It wound up on the title page of most of the investigation's top secret documents.

Now the operation began migrating next door, and it too had a new name—the Joint Operations Center, or JOC. There would be more room, and more equipment. The FBI was setting it up, rounding up computers, TVs, and telephones. It would be like a small city. The ATF's Cavanaugh knew the value of a well-equipped and manned JOC. "Boiler rooms," he called them. They had to be big enough and organized enough or they would be counterproductive. He and Forsythe would be sitting a foot from each other in this one for the next few weeks, along with their FBI counterpart, a quiet, knowledgeable special agent in charge named Stephen Wiley. Chief Moose would remain across the parking lot in headquarters. When Cavanaugh was first shown the proposed space, he said, "It's too small." Remember, he said, this is the biggest active criminal investigation in the world. When more space was acquired, Cavanaugh said he also wanted satellite TV. But the weekend was coming on, and he was told it could be a problem. He put a hard-driving subordinate, Michael Mund, on the job and overheard him on the phone.

"I ain't asking for an NFL Sunday ticket," he said.

"I want the news, man. . . ."

"The sniper doesn't take weekends off."

Mund hung up and turned to Cavanaugh: No problem, boss.

Cavanaugh also wanted a podium, with a sound system. It seemed an odd request. This wasn't an auction house. But Cavanaugh knew it would help the command center gel and was a fast way to get information to people spread out in a big room. Cavanaugh also had a chart with pictures of all the sniper victims moved from headquarters into the JOC as a reminder. "We need to keep the main thing the main thing."

Friday morning around nine o'clock, Kenneth H. Bridges, a fifty-three-year-old Philadelphia businessman, pulled his silver Buick into an Exxon station near Massaponax, Virginia, and telephoned his wife, Jocelyn, on his cell phone. It was drizzling and he had gotten off I-95 at Exit 126 to buy some gas near a spot called Four Mile Fork in

Spotsylvania County. He had been warned by friends about stopping in the area. This was sniper country. One of the earlier victims, Caroline Seawell, had been wounded seven days earlier in a shopping center five miles away. Bridges's wife, whom he called his "queen," had warned him, too. As he sat in the gas station right off the interstate, he let her know where he was. Jocelyn Bridges thought about warning him again but didn't. He'd be out of there shortly and safely out of the sniper's range. Besides, there was a Virginia state trooper fifty yards away working a fender bender. No one would fire a rifle with a trooper so close.

Bridges was a smart, dynamic African American entrepreneur with six children. He had a degree from the Wharton School at the University of Pennsylvania and a notion that black Americans needed to support black American business. His late father had been a pioneering black army paratrooper during World War II. Five years earlier, Bridges had cofounded an organization called MATAH, a distribution network for products of black businesses. MATAH was based in Oaklyn, New Jersey, across the Delaware River from Philadelphia.

On Wednesday, Bridges had driven down to King William, Virginia, northeast of Richmond, to work out a new distribution deal with an importer and a North Carolina cosmetics firm. The meeting had been held at Aspen Grove, the Virginia estate of Dr. Walter P. Lomax Jr., a Philadelphia physician and friend of Bridges. Bridges had started home Thursday and was halfway there when he got a phone call asking if he could come back to help with final details. He backtracked over a hundred miles, sealed the deal, and was starting for home a second time on Friday morning.

"Why don't you buy your gasoline around the corner?" Lomax urged him. There was a good, safe spot nearby, miles before you hit I-95.

"Okay, okay," Bridges said.

But he didn't need gas right away, so he drove fifty miles north on the interstate before stopping. At 9:28, he stepped out of his car and put the fuel nozzle into his gas tank. Suddenly there was a boom, and he slumped beside the gas pumps, shot in the back. The state trooper, David Gray, heard the shot, ran to Bridges, and began working on him. When the rescue squad arrived a few minutes later, Bridges had no pulse. He was rushed to Mary Washington Hospital three miles away, where he died.

Seventy miles north, where the task force was moving to its new quarters, phones began ringing. Forsythe was shaken. Everybody was already going flat out. What in God's name is going on? he thought. Nobody needed to think hard about this one. The sound, the gas station, the interstate—the invisibility of the killer. Virginia police activated their new dragnet plan. Scores of police, clad in flak vests and cradling rifles and shotguns, stood along the highway and watched from overpasses as the traffic streamed along I-95, the East Coast's main north-south artery. At the Springfield, Virginia, interchange, where almost half a million motorists pass each day, officers choked off the highway to a single lane and peered into vehicles.

Hundreds of white vans were pulled over—176 in Alexandria alone—not just on the interstate, but also Route 1, the other north-south route. Witnesses had seen the pale ghost at the Exxon—this time a white Chevy Astro with ladder racks. Police concentrated their search on northbound traffic because a white van had been seen headed for a northbound on-ramp. The tie-up was monumental. As the morning wore on and the net remained empty, the frustration was painful. The Virginia state police superintendent, Colonel W. Gerald Massengill, said the dragnet had been quick but "obviously not quick enough."

Among the first to reach the Exxon station was Jeffrey R. Roehm, the ATF's special agent in charge for Washington, D.C., and Virginia. Roehm had been involved in the investigation since the October 3 Charlot slaying in Washington but had become more involved since the killing came to Virginia. Roehm was stunned at the size of the police response. There were cops with dogs, cops with metal detectors. The FBI crime bus was there; a helicopter landed to rush a bullet fragment recovered at the scene to the ATF lab in

Rockville. Officers canvassed local hotels. Bloodhounds led officers to room 109 of the Ramada Inn across the street from the Exxon, where they briefly detained a Georgia man with brown hair and a mustache who later said police told him he looked like a suspect.

A businessman killed on his way home from a trip, Roehm thought. His anxious family and friends would be devastated. Who would do this? What could possibly possess someone to do this?

In Philadelphia, Bridges was long overdue. His wife was worried. Colleagues couldn't reach him on his cell phone. They had heard about the shooting but didn't fathom that it could be Ken. Then, at Bridges's office in New Jersey, someone watching on TV recognized the victim's car. Finally, about 2:00 P.M., Bridges's partner, Al Wellington, called Lomax. Wellington was distraught. The police were saying the shooting victim might have been Bridges.

"No," Lomax said. "That's impossible."

Wellington called back an hour later.

"Yes," he told Lomax, "it was Kenny."

––––––––––

At 7:40 that night, John Muhammad began making a series of phone card calls from a Shoney's restaurant in Hagerstown, Maryland, more than 100 miles from the gas station at Exit 126. The Shoney's was in a mall right near the intersection of two other major interstates. From there, the pair could head east or west on I-70, or north or south on I-81, through the eastern Appalachian Mountains. The I-95 corridor, 60 miles to the east, was still crawling with police. They headed south. Two days later, they were 350 miles away, in a YMCA in Burlington, North Carolina.

8

False Hope

As police in Virginia scrambled over the interstate that Friday morning, hundreds of federal, state, and local law enforcement officials were assembling in a makeshift conference room at a branch of the University of Maryland in Rockville. The sniper spree was ten days old. Eight people had been murdered and two grievously injured. The region was terrorized and the nation transfixed by the case. Montgomery County police issued press credentials to 1,300 members of the media from around the world. Many of them were at Camp Rockville—as the encampment was soon called—day and night. And in ten days, the police had gotten nowhere.

There was coffee and doughnuts, pizza and soda, in the room that morning, and lots of men in uniform with stars and eagles on their shirt collars. Moose, Bald, Bouchard, and a few others were in the front on folding chairs, facing the group, and gave brief overviews of the investigation. The mood was tense. The chiefs in the audience knew that any of them might get the sniper's next shooting. Preoccupied by the Bridges attack, Forsythe showed up late, to Moose's irritation. But Forsythe, who was always respectful of Moose, stood up and thanked him for being the public point man for the investigation. He said he could never have done it along with everything else in the case.

The Washington police chief, Charles Ramsey, overheard Bald mention that with all the work to be done in the investigation he had better things to do than sit in another meeting. The remark irked Ramsey, who thought that Bald had nothing more important to do than explain where things stood. But he thought the PowerPoint demonstration they had to sit through was nothing but a dog-and-pony show. Save it for someone else, he thought. He didn't want the whole history of the case. "Pissed me off," he would recall later.

When the presentations were over, Ramsey made clear his complaints. He wondered, he said, if the task force was really on top of everything. What, for example, was going on with the lookout, the burgundy Caprice with the tinted windows that had been seen at the Charlot killing? The white truck thing, he said, was out of control.

Ramsey's friend and former top assistant, Terrance Gainer, chief of the U.S. Capitol Police, was also upset at not being kept informed of task force deliberations. But, sitting a few rows behind him, he became concerned that Ramsey was losing it. He sent Ramsey a text message on his pager. "Take a deep breath and sit down," the note said. "Let's not do this in public."

At fifty-two, Ramsey was a burly man with a strong voice and an imposing presence who when in uniform usually wore a lanyard emblazoned with the word *Gonzaga,* for the Jesuit high school where his son played football. After the shootings began, Ramsey stopped wearing the lanyard for fear the sniper would see it on TV and target his son's school. Ramsey had been chief of the Metropolitan Police Department (its official name) for four years. After nearly three decades rising through the ranks of the Chicago Police Department, he was the first outsider to head the D.C. police in thirty years. He was chosen by a selection committee that had also considered Moose but preferred Ramsey, a chief with experience in a bigger city. Unlike his suburban counterparts, he was used to the spotlight, organizing security for high-profile protests like those against the World Bank and leading the investigation of several sensational cases, including the disappearance of former intern Chandra Levy.

A few on the task force were stung by the criticism. There just wasn't that much information to be had. The case was frustrating. The killings didn't seem to fit any pattern. They didn't yet jibe with the five standard motives for homicide—greed, power, revenge, hate, and escape—or any combination of them. Even veterans like Cavanaugh were baffled. The investigators still had almost nothing to go on. There were the bullet fragments and the tarot card, which linked the killings. But those clues told detectives only what the killer wanted them to know, that this was the work of a single, ruthless enterprise.

Cavanaugh felt the police were responding to each shooting quickly enough and were investigating each one as aggressively as possible. But the killer was nimbly staying ahead and giving police little to work with. In most crimes, victim and victimizer are physically close, with good potential for transfer of evidence—blood, fibers, DNA, fingerprints. Not with the sniper and his rifle shots. At least not so far. Cavanaugh knew that for more evidence there would have to be more killings. He urged detectives to "think three murders ahead." Anticipate. Where would the sniper go next? What could be his next goal? "You gotta think like he thinks." Cavanaugh remembered Waco and Koresh. If they could just get him on the phone.

Some investigators worried that the sniper might get rid of his rifle, which would end any link to the bullet fragments found in the victims. Cavanaugh tried to reassure them. "Nah," he would say, "he'll never get rid of the rifle. It's his signature."

But a grim logic had developed. As much as Cavanaugh and the others wanted the shooting to stop, they knew that if the sniper kept on killing, they would have a better chance of catching him. If the sniper suddenly stopped or left the country, he would probably never be caught.

Police released a composite graphic of the beat-up white box truck they said several witnesses reported seeing October 3, the day of the mass attacks. The graphic was also posted on the Web sites of the Montgomery County police, the FBI, and the ATF. Moose stressed that the graphic was not a photograph. It depicted the truck that Villeda saw. Rear damage. Mysterious purple or black lettering. Because Villeda couldn't read the writing on the panels, the graphic showed the truck with UNKNOWN WORDS UNKNOWN WORDS printed on the side.

Moose said at a press conference on October 12 that more than one person had seen the truck, but he wouldn't say who or where. He also said investigators were still interested in the Chevy Astro with the ladder racks seen near the Bridges shooting, prompting reporters to ask whether he was suggesting the killer was using "multiple vehicles."

And why the continued emphasis on white vehicles? Wasn't it a mistake to concentrate on one color? "Is this perhaps limiting the effectiveness of the investigation?" a reporter asked.

"Well, sir, we're all welcome to our own opinion," Moose replied. "Any other questions?"

There were, though not for Moose. Later that day, Allan Lengel, a *Washington Post* reporter, called Ramsey. On October 7, D.C. detective Tony Patterson had put out a BOLO teletype—Be on the Lookout—to all law enforcement agencies in the area for the Chevrolet Caprice that witnesses had described leaving the neighborhood where Pascal Charlot was shot. For some reason, Patterson's bulletin had not captured the attention of investigators in Rockville. But one of Lengel's police sources had read him the teletype message, and for two days Lengel had filed memos on the bulletin. With an avalanche of information coming in every day from reporters in the field, nothing had appeared in the paper. Lengel figured that if he could persuade Ramsey to mention the Caprice on the record, he might have some success.

Ramsey confirmed that D.C. police were looking for an older-model burgundy-colored Chevrolet Caprice with dark-tinted windows, and a two-sentence mention of the car appeared in Sunday's *Post*. The morning the story appeared, CNN's Wolf Blitzer asked Moose about the report as the chief sat in a director's chair at Camp Rockville for a round of TV interviews. "That is also a lookout that has been put out there," Moose said, "and I think there's been more law enforcement focus on that, not a big push for public feedback about that."

The focus of investigators was still the white truck. "We remain interested in that," Moose said. "Has someone brought one into your shop to have a bumper repaired? Has someone brought a truck of this type in to have it painted since these events have started to unfold?"

There were many pieces, many nuances, to an investigation like this, he said. "But the puzzle has yet to come together."

————

Anxiety and fear had now spread through the entire region, from Baltimore to Richmond. In Fredericksburg, near where both Bridges and Seawell were shot, the Reverend Larry E. Lenow, pastor of the Fredericksburg United Methodist Church, tore up his planned Sunday sermon. Instead, he referred his congregation to the book of Isaiah. "We really aren't in control," he said. "Life is fragile, and we just never really know, do we?" Death might come from a car crash, a heart attack, a stroke, and now a sniper. "The hard, cold reality is that we are not in control."

At the 8:00 A.M. service at Montgomery United Methodist Church in Damascus, Maryland, Barney Forsythe took his usual seat on the right near the front. Forsythe was well known in the congregation. He'd been attending the church for seventeen years. He'd taught Sunday school and was normally an usher at the 11:00 A.M. service, where his job was to tidy up the pews, making sure the Bibles and hymnals were in place, and to greet people at the door.

At one point that morning there was an opportunity to request special prayers. Forsythe rose, as he often did, to get the ball rolling. The church got very quiet. He said he and the task force badly needed prayers. Everyone knew that. He paused, telling the congregation that this was hard for him to say, but he believed they also ought to pray for the killer. He knew firsthand the personal devastation the sniper had wrought, and it was difficult to request prayers for such a person. But it was the Christian thing to do.

When the Washington Redskins played the New Orleans Saints that afternoon at FedEx Field—their stadium off the Beltway in suburban Maryland—tailgaters hung tarps to shield themselves in the parking lot. There was a brief scare when someone set off firecrackers in nearby woods. In Stafford County, Virginia, in the heart of the Virginia sniper zone, the manager of a Burger King who wanted the day off was arrested after he called 911 and described a hooded rifleman on a roof. The day ended quietly, but with great apprehension. "People are very anxious about what the coming week may bring," said Sean T. Connaughton, a member of the Prince William County Board of Supervisors. "They don't really know what to expect."

Monday was Columbus Day, a holiday for many people in the area. Three full days had now passed since Bridges's murder. It was the longest period without a shooting since the sniping began. But the fear persisted, even as people went about their business. Halloween pumpkin patches were empty, and schools were still operating under a code blue emergency. The parents of a student at Sidwell Friends School in Washington, D.C., were so upset by this policy that they took out a full-page ad in *The Washington Post* that read: "Homecoming is cancelled due to paranoia and bad judgment." But a new poll by *Newsweek* suggested the sense of threat was no longer confined to the Washington area. Nationwide, it found, people were more afraid of being killed by a sniper than by terrorists.

At the White House, President Bush, who was being briefed daily on the investigation by the FBI, said he was "sickened" by the situation. "The idea of moms taking their kids to school and sheltering them from a potential sniper attack is not the America I know."

But as the day went on with no violence, there was a faint, irrational easing of the tension. Why couldn't the killer simply move on? It was possible. The afternoon passed, and evening came. Still nothing. The task force spent its first official working day in the new JOC, which would shortly become a warren of desks, metal folding chairs, telephones, computers, copiers, wires strung from the ceiling, shredders, TVs, tiny American flags, and photos of the victims. Task force leaders lingered late to make sure nothing happened. The overnight shift arrived and was briefed; the day shift headed home.

———

Malvo and Muhammad spent part of Sunday afternoon at the YMCA in Burlington, North Carolina. They arrived around 3:30, Malvo in a white T-shirt and black shorts, Muhammad in a green tank top and green shorts. Rodney Burnette, a mailman who worked Sundays at the Y, was on the front desk. The two showed him out-of-town membership cards. Muhammad was pleasant; Malvo said nothing. Malvo shot baskets alone, but Burnette was not sure where Muhammad went.

Before they left, around 5:30 P.M., Muhammad used the courtesy phone in the lobby by the water fountain. He made several calls using his phone card. He called his son Travis in Baton Rouge and made several calls to Washington State. Muhammad sounded agitated to Burnette, as if he were hearing things he didn't want to hear. But he thanked Burnette when he left. Muhammad and Malvo probably departed Burlington that night or the next day, October 14. It was a three-hundred-mile, five-hour drive to Fairfax County, Virginia.

———

Just before 7:30 P.M. on Monday, Ted and Linda Franklin drove their 1991 red Mercury Capri into the lower-level parking lot of the Home Depot store in the Seven Corners Shopping Center, near Falls Church, Virginia. They had been married for eight years and had recently weathered some bad times together. Linda Franklin, a forty-seven-year-old analyst at the FBI, had recently undergone a double mastectomy for breast cancer. She had taken four months off from work to recover and was still in physical therapy. She had two children from a previous marriage, and one, her daughter, Katrina, was about to make her a grandmother.

Franklin had been a teacher at U.S. military schools in Japan and Belgium and also in Guatemala, where she once fended off a man with a machete who tried to steal her car. Her specialty was middle school math and science. She had met Ted in Okinawa and in 1998 had landed a job with the FBI as an intelligence operations specialist in the National Infrastructure Protection Center, a new agency that guarded against threats to utilities, banks, and public safety.

Linda and Ted wandered around Home Depot for about an hour and a half with a big shopping cart, picking up some shelves and other odds and ends for a house they were about to move into. A little after 9:00, they wheeled their packages out to their car and started putting things in the trunk. It was dark, but the lower lot was well illuminated. One of their shelves was giving them trouble. It was too long to fit in the trunk, so they put down the backseat and tried to slide it into the car through the trunk. It didn't work. Standing by the open trunk, Ted held the cart to keep it from rolling away, while Linda then tried to wrestle the shelf in the passenger-side front door. She was having trouble.

"Why don't you come and hold the cart?" Ted asked her. "I'll see if I can put it in." They switched places, and as Ted wrestled with the shelf, ducking in and out of the car, he heard a loud noise and felt something spray his face. The noise, he thought, was probably from the store, where they were always dropping pallets and boards. The spray, which was blood from his mortally wounded wife, got his attention.

When he turned toward Linda, she was down on the pavement. He ran over, knelt beside her, and put his hand on her hip. A .223 rifle bullet had entered the left side of her head near her temple and come out the right side above her eye. It had split her skull and then fragmented, a small piece burying itself in the rubber seal around the rear window of a Ford Bronco parked beside her car. There was nothing he could do for her. He got out his cell phone to dial 911 and noticed shoppers running for cover. Inside the Home Depot, there were screams, and customers began backing away from the front entrance.

"Shut the door! Shut the door!" the store employees were shouting. "Someone's been shot!"

———————

Fairfax County Police Chief J. Thomas Manger had just arrived home from work. Still in his gray-and-blue uniform, he played with his one-year-old son for thirty minutes or so and had just gone upstairs to change when his pager went off. Manger had been police chief in the big, populous county outside Washington, D.C., for five years. He had a 1,300-person department and over a million citizens to police. Usually the pager didn't bother him. As he stood in his bedroom and glanced down at his pager, his heart missed a beat. "Shooting at Home Depot, Seven Corners," said the readout. "Possible sniper related."

Manger called downstairs to his wife, Jacqueline. "We got one in Fairfax!" He didn't need to explain. He kissed her and his son and hurried out the door. He reached the Home Depot in ten minutes. In the parking lot, shoppers were still milling around as police tried to identify witnesses. Franklin's head had been covered with a yellow safety blanket. Her distraught husband was being taken care of inside an ambulance. Their shopping cart stood by the open trunk. The white shelf was still protruding from the passenger door of their Capri. There was little question it was a sniper case. The circumstances were too familiar: the random victim, the long-range shot.

Hundreds of federal and local law enforcement officers descended on the store in a sea of "raid" jackets with FBI or ATF on the back. From a distance, Manger thought, they looked like ants. A police helicopter swept the area with a searchlight. Manger, who had sent a detective to watch how Chief Deane in Prince William County handled the Meyers killing, had a job keeping the reinforcements out. Major Frank J. Kitzerow of the Fairfax County police, who oversaw the crime scene, was worried that with all the federal agents and state and local cops arriving, someone might trample on key evidence, which could hurt a prosecution down the road. Some of the newcomers were unhappy with the strict perimeter and sulked in a nearby Starbucks.

June Boyle, a Fairfax County detective, approached Kevin Lewis, the senior FBI agent on the scene, and told him she had spoken to Franklin's husband. The victim worked for the FBI, the detective told Lewis. It took his breath away.

Brad Garrett, another FBI agent on the scene, had responded to an urgent page from a Fairfax homicide lieutenant with whom he had often worked. After a Pakistani named Mir Aimal Kasi killed two CIA employees on their way to work at the agency's headquarters in Langley, Virginia, in 1993, Garrett, a former marine with a Ph.D. in criminology, tracked him for four years before helping with his arrest in Pakistan. At Kasi's request, Garrett attended his execution, staying with him in his last few moments. Garrett, who was assigned to the Bureau's Washington Field Office, was also renowned for his role in solving a brutal triple murder at a Starbucks in Georgetown in 1997.

Garrett, who liked to dress entirely in black, was a film buff and was handsome enough to have once been a model. Quiet and intense, he was known for his skill in interrogating suspects. He sensed that, at their core, they needed to explain their deeds, and he had an innate ability to reach that need. He was more confessor than interrogator; his questioning was oblique rather than direct. Later, with Malvo, he would get another chance to demonstrate his skill—and his knowledge of movies.

As the hours passed, Manger could see the glow of TV cameras in the distance. Once again, a gigantic dragnet was thrown out, and the highways swarmed with police. TV news helicopters showed the taillights of cars backed up for miles on I-95 and flashes of blue from the dome lights of massed police cars. Checkpoints with SWAT teams were established on the major bridges over the Potomac River. As far away as Chevy Chase Circle, on the border between Maryland and Washington, police were slowing vehicles to peer inside at their occupants. But the net stayed empty. As Virginia state police lieutenant Tom Martin put it: "It's hard to find something when you don't know what you're looking for."

At the scene, police had discovered two other bullet fragments—one a piece of copper jacket from the end of the bullet—and shipped them to the ATF lab in Rockville. But this time they also had something else—a witness who said he had seen the whole thing. The next day, Manger would say he was confident the tip would lead to an arrest.

As the ranking FBI official on the scene, Lewis, who lived fifteen minutes from the Home Depot and often shopped there, began questioning the witness, Matthew Dowdy.

"I was inside the store," Dowdy told him. "I just came out. I had a cart. I was going to put some stuff away. I was looking. There were some guys over here on pay phones. I looked up and saw this guy come out of a van." Dowdy said it was a cream-colored Chevy Astro van with a silver ladder rack and a dead right taillight. The gunman, he said, had olive skin and a mustache and wore a denim jacket. He said he saw the man raise a rifle he described as a version of the AK-47, fire, and then dash away in the van.

Hard evidence, a solid description of the getaway vehicle, and an actual sighting of the shooter. Police broadcast a description of the gunman to patrol cars. It seemed odd that the sniper had been so careless, and strange that only one person had seen him. But with the white van and the rifle, it all seemed to fit. At last, one of the murders had yielded a useful clue. Finally, Cavanaugh thought when he heard Dowdy's account, we're getting somewhere. We're getting something to work with.

One of the other people who got the news about Dowdy that night was the Fairfax County commonwealth's attorney, Robert F. Horan Jr., who was notified whenever there was a homicide in the county. At seventy, he had been the county's top prosecutor for thirty-five years. During that time, Fairfax County had experienced tremendous growth, and Horan had handled much of the crime that seemed to go along with it. As a prosecutor, Horan was known for his legal scholarship and spartan style. While defendants often marshaled teams of lawyers, Horan sat alone at the prosecution table with nothing but a legal pad and a folder of legal briefs. He and Ebert of Prince William County were close friends. They would both play key roles in the case in the coming months.

————

Hidden in the car in the Home Depot parking lot that night, Malvo explained later, he had set up and watched several people walk in and out of his gun sight. Most were moving around too much to hit. He got a bead on Ted Franklin, but Ted moved. When Linda came into his "range," he wasted no time: "Within two seconds . . . I fired." In telling the story, Malvo laughed and pointed to his head to show where he had hit her.

He and Muhammad had no trouble with their escape. At about 9:30, an off-duty Fairfax officer driving on nearby I-66 spotted a beat-up Caprice caught in the same traffic jam that ensnared her. It had tinted windows and New Jersey license plates. As she pulled closer to the car, she saw that the license number began NDA. As she passed the car, she noticed that it was being driven by an African American male. She didn't think much about it at the time. The fish had been caught in the net. The police just didn't know what it looked like.

Later that night, still in their car, Muhammad and Malvo took a little break. They slid a favorite DVD into their stolen laptop—*We Were Soldiers,* the Vietnam War film with Mel Gibson. A heroic account of a 1965 battle between four hundred members of the Seventh Air Cavalry and two thousand North Vietnamese troops, the movie begins with a French soldier being sprayed in the face with the blood of one of his buddies who had just been shot.

Malvo was fascinated by the Vietnam War. He also liked *Platoon,* another movie about the war. He had written three school papers on the movie. Malvo felt he was a soldier, too. He had to be disciplined. He had to use tactics and strategy and the element of surprise. And the stakes were the same. "You fail, you die," he said later. In the Caprice, Muhammad and Malvo had a copy of Sun Tzu's 2,500-year-old treatise, *The Art of War*, which stresses stealth, cunning, and intelligence. He had read about Hannibal, the African general of ancient times who was tutored and sworn by his father to be the eternal enemy of Rome. Malvo knew a bit about Thomas Jefferson and the philosophers Socrates, John Locke, and Thomas Hobbes. He was familiar with the teachings of Islam. He liked Jamaican reggae music.

But if there was a key to his thinking, he would tell his questioners, it was *The Matrix*. Evil machines in the movie ruled mankind using a computer program that simulated life. Modern life was really only a virtual world; real life was a decayed wasteland that the machines hid from view to keep humanity enslaved. The machines' brutal enforcers—who wore dark suits and sunglasses, the traditional look of movie FBI agents—did battle with the hero, a young messianic seeker, who was schooled by a father figure. Watch *The Matrix*, Malvo said.

Vietnam, *The Matrix*, Jefferson, Islam, Hannibal, reggae, John Muhammad, life, death, reality, unreality, honor. All were brewing in the fetid interior of the Caprice as *We Were Soldiers* played on the laptop. The movie closed with a military glee club singing the hymn "Mansions of the Lord": "No more bleeding, no more fight / No prayers pleading through the night. . . . / Where no mothers cry and no children weep . . ."

Meanwhile, the police were searching frantically for the olive-skinned man in the cream-colored cargo van.

———————

At the Rockville command center, the Franklin killing was a particular shock. In an instant it wiped out days of hard work on the task force's leading suspects. There were four of them—their names written in black on the white marker board to the right of the command table. They were under surveillance. The shooting eliminated all of them. They couldn't have been in two places at once.

Someone walked over and, one by one, erased the names from the board until it was clean. The suspects may have looked good, but now they were gone. It was frustrating. The task force was back to the beginning. Forsythe, who was already home when he heard about Franklin and had rushed back in, tried to be positive. At least they didn't have to waste time and energy on these guys. They'd already had tens of thousands of leads. There would be more. And now they had Dowdy's eyewitness account. As the hours passed, Forsythe waited, hoping Dowdy's shooter would turn up in the dragnet. Meanwhile, he talked to the task force analysts about a list of Chevy Astro van owners in Montgomery County who also owned .223 rifles.

———————

The day after Linda Franklin was shot, Muhammad's old army friend Robert Holmes decided he shouldn't wait much longer. He had been sitting in his little house on Proctor Street in Tacoma watching the sniper spree unfold on TV. He grew more uneasy with each shooting. He knew Muhammad. He knew Muhammad had a rifle and had been obsessed with getting a silencer. He knew Muhammad hated his ex-wife and that she lived in the Washington, D.C., area. He knew Muhammad had a teenage sidekick. And he hadn't seen either of them in several months.

One night, as coverage of the shooting played on TV, Holmes said to a visiting friend, Nathan Perry: "Hey, man, you know that's John doing that on the East Coast."

Holmes would recall Perry replying, "Are you fucking crazy, man? That's not even funny to say some shit like that."

Holmes told Perry he thought Muhammad had suffered a nervous breakdown over the kids. But he hadn't been hospitalized, Perry said. Holmes replied that you didn't necessarily go to the hospital with a breakdown.

"It's him," Holmes said. "When it's all over and done with, you watch."

The day Bridges was shot, Holmes was again watching the TV

coverage when someone mentioned that there might be a team of killers, a shooter and a spotter. Goddamn it, Holmes thought, remembering Malvo. That's John. I know that's John.

Holmes hadn't seen all the TV coverage. It wasn't until the night of Franklin's killing that he saw pictures of the rifles police thought the sniper might be using. As Holmes watched, a gun flashed on the screen that looked almost exactly like the Bushmaster Muhammad had fired into Holmes's tree stump.

Aw, shit, Holmes thought, that's John.

He decided to call the FBI tip line.

9

"Incompitence"

The next day, Amy M. Lefkoff was working the 7:00 A.M. to 3:00 P.M. shift as a dispatcher for the Rockville City Police Department, where she had worked for fourteen years. She was the only one on duty in the first-floor dispatch room of Rockville City Hall, twenty-five miles from downtown Washington, D.C., where the FBI's big call-taking center was located, and three miles from county police headquarters at the other end of town.

Calls poured in to her anyway, at the rate of about one a minute, five hundred by the time she finished her shift. People saw the name Rockville on TV, got the number for the Rockville police, and called Lefkoff—one person even phoned from Australia. It was madness. Shortly after 11:00 A.M., four hours into her shift, the phone rang again.

"Rockville City police, Lefkoff," she said. "This line is recorded."

"Good morning," a male voice said. "Don't say anything. Just listen. We're the people that are causing the killing in your area. Look on the tarot card. It says, 'Call me God. Do not release to the press.' We have called you three times before, trying to set up negotiations. We have got no response. People have died—"

"Sir . . . ," Lefkoff interrupted.

The male voice tried to continue. "Get your people—"

"I need to refer you to the Montgomery County police hot line," Lefkoff said, following the instructions she had been given about sniper calls. "We are not investigating the crime. Would you like the number?"

It was a young man's voice, with a slightly clipped cadence. There were pauses with each sentence, as if the caller were reading from something written. He had a smooth, distinct voice. It was Lee Malvo. He was calling from a pay phone at a Texaco gas station right off I-95, outside Dale City, Virginia, about thirty miles south of Washington, D.C. He hung up.

What was that? Lefkoff wondered. A prank or the real thing? Calls continued to roll in, and she kept answering. When she got a break, she called her supervisor, Captain Mike England, who was in an office down the hall. Lefkoff told him she'd had a strange call that he ought to hear. She rewound the tape for him when he came to her office. "Listen to this and see what you think," she said. England thought it was interesting enough to send to the task force.

Muhammad and Malvo were trying to initiate the next phase of the strategy. First, they had left the tarot card with the message "Call me God," so the police would know it was really them when they called. With the code established, the two could simply call the cops, give the code, and start things going. They had a financial arrangement they wished to discuss.

But then things got screwed up. "Do not release to the press," they had said, but the media had reported their code anyway. They got the wording wrong—it wasn't "I am God." While Moose had launched a tirade against the leak, investigators were secretly re-lieved that the press hadn't gotten it quite right. The code was still potentially viable, though few now knew its correct wording. With the task force worried about leaks, the wording was so closely held that people on the tip lines didn't know it.

Muhammad and Malvo kept on trying. All they had to do was get through the telephone chaos they had created. Thousands of people were trying to call in—tipsters, complainers, crazies—and the FBI's main call line was swamped. Calls were also coming in to police in Maryland and Virginia, in some cases getting only recorded messages. Altogether, more than eighty thousand tips came in to authorities.

For the snipers, the issue was money—for now and for later. It had been six weeks since Paul La Ruffa had been shot and robbed of his $3,500—money, he would lament afterward, that had financed the whole sniping operation. Since September, Muhammad and Malvo had covered a lot of ground and used a lot of gas, and they needed cash. On October 16, they walked into an Eagle Financial Institution in Suitland, Maryland, just off the Capital Beltway and a mile from Andrews Air Force Base. Muhammad wanted to get a Western Union wire transfer of funds from somewhere in New Jersey. But his driver's license identified him as John Muhammad and the Western Union system identified him, from prior transactions, as John Allen Williams, so he was turned down. Muhammad succeeded in frightening the clerk but still got no money. It sounded too fishy. The staff watched the two drive away in a blue Caprice with New Jersey license plates.

At about 2:30 that afternoon, they showed up at the YMCA in Ashland, Virginia, right off I-95 about ten miles north of Richmond. Muhammad presented desk clerk Tracey Brown with a membership card from the Tacoma Y. Brown said he was welcome to use the Ashland facilities. Just a moment, Muhammad said. He wanted to get his son from the car. They were traveling together from Washington State and were both pretty tired. Brown thought Muhammad looked road weary, but he was soft-spoken and polite.

Muhammad went out to what Brown would remember as an old, dark, "nondescript" car and came back with Malvo. The two signed in as Thomas Lee and Thomas Lee Jr. It was an alias Muhammad had used two years earlier in Antigua. Malvo went to the locker room with a gym bag, but Muhammad lingered at the front desk. He asked Brown if she knew of any Catholic churches in the area. She didn't, but she pulled a phone book from the desk drawer to see if she could find one.

When she couldn't find anything, she telephoned the Richmond diocese, which gave her the number for St. Ann's, a redbrick church with a white spire ten blocks away on Snead Street. She copied the number on a piece of paper and gave it to Muhammad. He then picked up the telephone on the desk, asked Brown, "Is it all right if I use this?" and made a brief telephone call. He then joined Malvo in the locker room. Other patrons that day would describe an almost overpowering odor from the two in the locker room. Both took long showers. Muhammad shaved.

In Fairfax, investigators were still questioning Dowdy about the Franklin killing, but he was frustratingly vague. "Because of darkness and distance and perhaps, you know, excitement and adrenaline at the time, they are unable to come up with a composite," Nancy Demme, the task force spokeswoman, said to reporters. "We don't have a refined description to go by."

Police were urging motorists to seek cover when outdoors and to always carry a blanket, phone, and extra clothes in the car in case they got stuck in a dragnet. They were issuing instructions on how to be a good witness: Separate permanent identifiers, like body build, from temporary ones, like facial hair. Always carry a pen or pencil, and jot down descriptions on your hand if necessary.

Twentieth Century–Fox announced that it was postponing the November 15 opening of its new thriller, *Phone Booth*, about a maniac sniper. A SWAT officer sent friends an e-mail advising them to travel in pairs, zigzag when walking, and, when shopping, place packages in the backseat rather than the trunk because it was quicker. Newspapers printed instructions on how to stay sniper safe. Maryland banned the outdoor discharge of firearms everywhere except shooting ranges. The Guardian Angels and Black Panthers came to help pump gas and lend moral support. Gas stations offered full service for the price of self-service.

People wondered how long the shootings would last. Halloween was two weeks away. Children could never trick-or-treat with the sniper loose. The November election was the week after that. Election day would produce target-rich environments at polling places everywhere. Would the killing last that long?

On October 16, a detective in Fairfax County was poring over surveillance tapes taken inside the Home Depot in the minutes after Linda Franklin was shot two nights before. Suddenly, there was Dowdy on the videotape. A time stamp said it was 9:21 P.M., and frightened bystanders were running into the store from the shooting in the parking lot three minutes earlier. Dowdy had apparently not yet gone outside. So how could he have witnessed the murder?

Police had always been a little wary of Dowdy's account. He had spent time in prison. It wasn't long before they concluded he was lying. His whole story—the cream-colored van, the broken taillight, the olive-skinned man with the mustache and denim jacket, the rifle—was made up. Dowdy would later say he had not seen the shooting but was relaying the account of a homeless friend named Linda who was afraid to go to the police.

The next day, Tom Manger, the Fairfax police chief, stood before reporters and announced that Dowdy's story was "not credible." Searchers were sent back to the Home Depot to do a fresh sweep of the area. Dowdy was arrested the next day. Horan, the Fairfax prosecutor, said his lie was "outrageous." A New York tabloid featured the story on its front page. Under a picture of Moose and Manger the headline read, CLUELESS. Nothing, however, dispelled the notion of the white truck, which was about to cost the authorities their best chance yet of grabbing the killers.

And the background noise on the case was now so loud that critical pieces of information were getting lost in the racket. In Tacoma, Robert Holmes, Muhammad's old friend, called the FBI tip line on

October 17 to say he thought he knew who the sniper might be. His information was typed onto a form in the agency's Rapid Start database for sniper leads. But it was five days before Holmes was interviewed.

Muhammad and Malvo were having troubles of their own, wandering from pay phone to pay phone trying to get through to someone who would listen to them. On October 16, they had been seen near a Home Depot in Baltimore and a video store near Bladensburg, Maryland. Shortly before 1:30 P.M. on October 17, they made a series of phone card calls from a Uni-Mart in Frederick, Maryland, fifty miles west of Baltimore and Washington, D.C. Muhammad again appeared to be trying to reach his son Travis in Baton Rouge and friends in Washington State. There were five calls in six minutes. The calls were all short, lasting a few seconds to just over a minute. Perhaps he was leaving phone messages.

Investigators would later find a piece of paper under the driver's seat in the Caprice bearing the handwritten phone numbers for the Rockville police, the police in Raleigh, North Carolina, the Montgomery County, North Carolina, Sheriff's Department, and the FBI tip line. The Raleigh number was crossed out. The killers were trying to lay out what seemed like simple instructions, but they couldn't get through to the authorities.

———

Late on the afternoon of Friday, October 18, they tried again. Montgomery County police officer Derek Baliles was at his desk in the media services office on the second floor of police headquarters in Rockville. Just after 4:30, a phone call was transferred to media services from Chief Moose's office. Someone had called Moose's number, which was in the phone book, and said he had information about the sniper. According to department protocol, all such calls pertaining to the sniper investigation were to be transferred to media services for screening. Baliles took the call.

"Shut up and listen," the caller, in all likelihood Malvo, said in a menacing tone. "And don't ask any questions." He told Baliles that he knew who was responsible for the sniper killings. But before he would say anything, he wanted Baliles to "verify" something for him. He told Baliles to call a Sergeant Martino at the Montgomery, Alabama, Police Department and gave him Martino's number. He told Baliles to ask about a liquor store holdup on Ann Street back in September in which two women had been shot, one fatally. Check it out, the caller said. He would telephone back a little later.

Okay, Baliles said, ask for "Officer Derek" when you call back. A recording came on the line announcing that more money had to be deposited for the call to continue, and then the line went dead.

Baliles didn't know what to make of the call. He had scribbled down the number from his caller ID. He didn't know it then, but the call had come from a pay phone at a gas station right near the Ponderosa Steakhouse in Ashland, Virginia, where Muhammad and Malvo had dined in September. Baliles had fielded hundreds of sniper calls in the last two weeks and, before that, regularly took tips on a county crime solvers line. But he was struck by the caller's ominous tone of voice. It sounded like the same tone crime victims described hearing from stickup men.

Baliles called Kristen Poole, a county police officer at the command center, and relayed what the caller had said. Then he called Sergeant Scott Martino, a detective and part-time public affairs officer with the Montgomery, Alabama, police. Martino gave him the details of the September 21 murder of Claudine Parker and the wounding of Kellie Adams outside the liquor store. The store was actually on Zelda Road, he said, but it was a block from Ann Street. Police and witnesses had chased two suspects, but they got away.

Forsythe then called from the command center. If the caller rings back, he warned Baliles, be careful not to give him any details from the investigation.

At 5:40 P.M., the person called back, asking for "Officer Derek." He was put on hold for a moment. Baliles picked up the phone and recognized the voice. Again, he wrote down the caller ID number, which this time was different. This call came from a pay phone at a Fastmart store, about a mile away from the Ashland gas station. The caller told Baliles to speak quickly because he didn't have much time. Baliles gave him the general details of the Alabama crime. The caller told him he was correct.

But he told Baliles he would have to call him back when he found some more change, as well as a pay phone that was not under surveillance. The call was then disconnected. Baliles reported back to the command center that the person had called again. But he never called back. "I got a really weird phone call today," he told his wife that night.

Weeks later, investigators would find a notation in the electronic organizer found in the Caprice. OFFICER DERRICK IS DEAD, it read.

Baliles and Lefkoff were apparently not the only ones Muhammad and Malvo tried to contact. They would write later that they tried the FBI tip line four times. Someone named George at the tip line was listed three times in their electronic organizer, the last time under the heading PEOPLE TO DIE LATER. The CNN Washington bureau had also been contacted in vain. FUCKERS AT CNN, MUST DIE, appeared in the organizer. Weary of phone operators, media leaks, and bungled calls, Muhammad and Malvo had now taken a desperate step. They had become so frustrated at their inability to be taken seriously that they had decided they had to prove themselves. With fractured logic, perhaps they thought that if the police realized they had also committed terrible crimes elsewhere, they might get some respect. "People weren't listening to us," Malvo would say later. The killers needed to establish their criminal credentials. They needed to say, as Jim Cavanaugh later put it, "We're big, we're bad, we're national." They also needed to get through on the phone. But it was risky. They wanted the shock effect the Parker case would give them, but they didn't want to compromise their present mission. They apparently didn't seem to think mentioning Alabama could do that. As far as they knew, the police there had nothing that would help the task force. The call to Baliles was their first successful phone call. He was the FIRST RECIPIENT OF THE MUHAMM . . . AD NEGOTIATIONS, they wrote in the electronic organizer.

But they needed to press home their message. Who else could be used to safely get the word out? At 8:30 P.M., four hours after Malvo had first called Baliles, he and Muhammad telephoned St. Ann's Church, whose phone number they had gotten at the Y. The after-hours message on the church answering machine provided the pastor's home phone number. If they were still hanging around the Ponderosa area, where they had called Baliles, St. Ann's was only a mile away. They didn't need much change. They reached Monsignor William V. Sullivan, the pastor.

Muhammad got on the line first and said he'd been trying to reach the priest. Then he said, "I've got somebody here who wants to talk to you." Sullivan figured it was a desk clerk at one of the local hotels with a guest who wanted the mass schedule. He got a lot of calls like that. He could hear noise in the background, as though the phone were in some public place.

Then Malvo came on. He had an accent Sullivan couldn't place. It was nothing like Sullivan's light southern drawl or like anything you might hear around Ashland. Malvo said he knew who was doing the sniper shootings. Then he began talking about some crime in Alabama, and something about doing ballistics tests, and the same gun being involved, and a woman at Seven Corners who didn't have to die. He was rambling, and Sullivan wasn't getting it.

Malvo told him to start writing some things down. Sullivan grabbed his grocery list and began scribbling. He may have dropped the phone at this point. Malvo thought he had scared him. "For you Mr. Police," Malvo said. "Call me God. Do not release to the press." Malvo made reference to this writing being on some kind of card. Sullivan didn't know what he was talking about. Then it clicked—the tarot card. "Oh, yeah," he said. "I remember reading about that."

Malvo went on about a liquor store and somebody named Ann, and people being for real. Sullivan thought it didn't make much sense. It sounded as if the guy were just repeating stuff he had seen on TV. He suggested maybe the caller should be talking to the police.

"Why did you call me?" he asked.

"Because they will record what I have to say," Malvo replied. "I know you're the church and you're not taping this."

The conversation turned over and over, and finally Sullivan got a little impatient. "I'm not going to stand here forever. . . . What do you want me to do?" Why didn't the caller just contact the police? There was no response, and the call ended.

Later, Malvo would try to explain to investigators. "We wanted to let them know it was us," he said, "to take us seriously." But he was wasting his time. During the conversation, Sullivan had thought of his caller: Oh my, he's got a great imagination. He never called the police.

Muhammad and Malvo had their own thoughts about Sullivan. PREIST [*sic*], they noted in the electronic organizer, FUCKING SCARED.

———————

Just before 8:00 P.M. the next day, October 19, Jeff Hopper and his wife, Stephanie, were walking to their white Cadillac in the parking lot of the Ponderosa Steakhouse in Ashland. They had just had dinner, a solid Ponderosa meal of steak and salad. They had been on the road for nine days. They'd left their home in Melbourne, Florida, where Hopper worked as a computer consultant, and driven to Lansdale, Pennsylvania, outside Philadelphia, to visit Stephanie's sister, who was about to undergo major surgery. They had left Lansdale that morning, planning to drive straight through. Hopper and his wife were anxious about the sniper. On the way north, they had been careful not to stop for gas in the Washington area. That morning, they had gassed up in Lansdale before leaving. They'd been on the road for over four hours and covered 250 miles. They thought that Ashland was out of the danger area and a safe place to stop for food and fuel. The Ponderosa was a block and a half off the interstate.

It had been almost five days since the Franklin murder. It was a Saturday, and the sniper had never attacked on a weekend. There had been two more funerals that day. In Washington, D.C., services were held for Pascal Charlot, the elderly victim of the October 3 shooting. In rural Pennsylvania, not far from where the Hoppers were visiting, Dean Meyers was buried behind a brick church down the road from where he had grown up. While Meyers's family was gathered under a green tent in the churchyard, his town house in Gaithersburg, still filled with his belongings, was burglarized.

The Hoppers were holding hands as they walked across a side parking lot when they both heard a loud noise. Stephanie, who was on Jeff's left, thought it was a car backfire. Jeff thought it sounded like an explosion. For a split second he looked for fire and smoke in the darkness. Then he felt a concussion in the air and an ache in his stomach. He was pushed against his wife. He brought his hand to his abdomen, slowly fell to the ground, and said, "I think I've been shot." Stephanie knelt over him. "I love you," he said. She replied, "I love you." They said the Lord's Prayer together. Then she started dialing 911. But she couldn't get her cell phone keyboard unlocked. She hollered to bystanders to call 911. Her husband had been shot.

The bullet, a .223, struck Hopper in the abdomen below the sternum and fragmented. It had ripped through his stomach, damaged his liver, spleen, pancreas, diaphragm, and a kidney. It then struck, and broke, a rib on his left side. But the bullet did not exit. Its core and a jacket fragment were recovered later when Hopper was rushed to Virginia Commonwealth University's Medical College of Virginia Hospital, in Richmond. When the medics arrived, they kept asking Hopper how old he was. "I'm thirty-seven," he replied, "and I hope to reach thirty-eight."

One of the first investigators to reach the parking lot was Ashland police officer Patrick Meacham. He arrived within two minutes of the first 911 call. Moments later, a man coming out of the Ponderosa told Meacham he was a retired New York police officer. While Meacham stayed with the victim, he asked the retired cop to go to the patrol car and pan the adjacent woods with the vehicle's spotlight. Witnesses thought the shot had come from the woods. But the spotlight penetrated only about five yards into the trees, and there wasn't much to see.

As the medics were hurrying Hopper to the hospital in Richmond, police poured into the area. Dogs were brought in, along with a human tracker from the ATF. The scene was reminiscent of the Tasker school shooting, with woods bordering the open area where the victim was hit. These were the only two shots thus far that seemed to be taken from outside cover. It was promising that police at least had an area in which to look. But it was just starting to rain.

Again the dragnet went out. This one was the most extensive, but like the others, it was futile. Again, Virginia authorities were touchy about their crime scene. Hanover County sheriff V. Stuart Cook felt strongly that he didn't really need these excited federal agents from the North thundering upon them. Cook had avoided the big sniper conference calls. They seemed to include every police chief on the East Coast, and he felt he got much better information from CNN than he did from Rockville.

When the feds arrived, he redirected many of them to a secondary command post nearby. When one ATF investigator got too pushy, Cook's people threatened to arrest him. Cook had 150 officers and believed they could handle it. But it was an ATF dog and his handler that made the first breakthrough on the case.

Twenty or thirty feet inside the wood line, ATF special agent Ray Neeley, using a flashlight, was working his way down a path with his gunpowder-sniffing Labrador, Garrett. Neeley and Garrett had worked together for seven years. Neeley thought the area he was searching would have been a good place from which to take a shot. As they searched, Garrett suddenly sat down, signaling he had found something. Neeley shined his flashlight, and there in the beam sat an empty cartridge casing from a .223 rifle round.

An ATF agent specially trained in tracking traced the escape path used by whoever had left the casing, while Sergeant James S. Sizemore of the Hanover County Sheriff's Office covered him. As the two worked their way through the woods, Sizemore suddenly spotted something on a tree. It was a Ziploc Halloween bag attached to the tree with two white thumbtacks, and inside it was a folded piece of pink paper with stars on it. Sizemore passed the word, and a county sheriff's forensics expert pried the bag off the tree and dropped it into an evidence envelope. The tacks were still attached.

For the second time, Muhammad and Malvo had sent a written message to their pursuers. It was a replay of the scenario twelve days earlier with Iran Brown—a message punctuated with an attack. Like Brown, Hopper had survived—Malvo would say later it had been a "bad" shot because Hopper had been moving around too much, bobbing his head, as he walked through the parking lot.

Muhammad and Malvo had a lot they needed to say, and the message was printed carefully on several pieces of lined paper, the first of which had five stars on it. They had complaints. They had threats. They had demands. They began with the same lines from the tarot card:

> For you mr. Police
> "Call me God."
> Do not release to the
> Press.

"We have tried to contact you to start negotiation," they continued on the second page. They listed the calls to Baliles, "Officer Derick" [sic], and a "female officer" at the Rockville Police Department, presumably Lefkoff. They also listed calls to the priest in Ashland and to CNN in Washington. They indicated that they had tried to call the task force hot line "four times." Like angry store customers, they listed the phone numbers they called and blamed "the incompitence [sic] of your forces.

"These people took [the] calls for a Hoax or Joke," the message continued, "so your failure to respond has cost you five lives." Actually, nine people had been killed thus far, but there had been five shootings, including Brown's, since the tarot card had been left.

Now they came to the heart of their demands, part of the rationale, Malvo would later say, for the shootings: The snipers wanted $10 million placed in a Bank of America account, whose number,

PIN, activation date, and expiration date they provided. It was a "Platinum Visa Account," they wrote, in the name of "Jill Lynn Farell," the Arizona Greyhound bus driver whose credit card had been stolen back in March. "We will have unlimited withdrawl [*sic*] at any atm world-wide," the message continued. "You will activate the bank account, credit card, and Pin number."

The message then explained that the snipers would contact authorities at 6:00 A.M. Sunday, the next day, at the Ponderosa "Buffet" and left a telephone number they planned to call. "You have until 9:00 a.m. Monday morning to complete transaction."

Option two, so to speak, was ignoring option one and "trying to catch us." If the police chose option two, "then prepare you [*sic*] body bags." To underscore that threat, they wrote a postscript: "your children are not safe anywhere at any time." The writers tried to apply a kind of authoritative seal to the message: "If we give you our word [then] that is what takes place. 'Word is Bond.' "

It was a dizzying amount of information for investigators. Here, apparently, was revealed a motive behind the murderous spree. The killing was for money. It was a giant, bloody extortion scheme. And here was a trove of potential evidence, too, from the calls and the stolen credit card to the handwriting and the Ziploc Halloween bag. The handwriting would later be linked to the tarot card by the U.S. Secret Service Questioned Document Section. The sharp-eyed Sizemore had also found a suspicious empty bag of CinnaRaisin snack food behind a nearby tree. Police would later find Malvo's thumbprint on the bag.

But the message also contained instructions, demands, and deadlines. Time would quickly become a factor. The Ziploc bag was not found until late and not handed over to ATF investigators at the scene until just before 2:00 A.M. By the time the bag was transported to the lab, opened, and analyzed, and the letter finally examined, it was past 6:00 A.M., the time when Malvo and Muhammad said police should expect their call. And there was another problem. The phone number the snipers had left for the Ponderosa was incorrect. They had transposed two digits. It was the number for someone's home, not the Ponderosa. Once again, communications between pursuer and pursued were not going smoothly.

But the note still gave investigators plenty to go on. Detectives scrambled to identify the priest, "Officer Derick," and the others who supposedly had received calls. It didn't take long. St. Ann's was the only Catholic church in Ashland. Investigators showed up there Sunday morning and told Sullivan they thought the sniper might be a member of the parish. A little later, Forsythe summoned Baliles to the Rockville command center. He didn't say why, and Baliles wondered if he'd done something wrong. On the way over, he bumped into Moose.

"Derek," Moose said, "I just wanted to say I'm very proud of what you've done, and thank you very much."

"You're welcome," Baliles replied, still not sure of what he had done.

At the command center, Baliles was questioned by the FBI and the ATF. Had he gotten any strange calls? He knew immediately what they were referring to and explained what had happened. Later, he was taken to an ATF audio–video truck outside, where agents placed a CD into a laptop and gave Baliles some headphones. The CD contained a recording of the Lefkoff call. Was it the same person? Yes, Baliles told the ATF. It was the same guy. Baliles said he thought it sounded like a black male.

By now it was well past the deadline. At 9:40 A.M. Sunday, someone, either Malvo or Muhammad, called the FBI hot line from a Fastmart, on West Broad Street in Richmond. "Don't talk," the caller said. "Just listen. Call me God. I left a note at the back of the Ponderosa. I'm trying to reach you at the Ponderosa. Be there for a call in ten minutes." But nobody was. The hot line call takers had no idea what the Ashland letter said.

The task force had to reestablish contact. Cavanaugh had an idea. Why not go public with an appeal for the sniper to call again? To simplify things, they would ask him to call back the number he had left in his letter. Police commandeered the correct Ponderosa number and the incorrect number in the letter. The sniper would be able to get through on both numbers, without operators or transfers or protocols.

———

Muhammad and Malvo stayed in the Richmond area but once again attracted the attention of police. At 3:00 that afternoon, just northwest of Richmond, Henrico County deputy sheriff D. W. Stone spotted the Caprice, became suspicious, and ran the tag but saw no problem. At 4:53 P.M., about five miles away, the tag was run again by a Virginia state trooper who saw the Caprice traveling on Broad Street in Richmond. The trooper followed the car until it got onto Interstate 64, noting that he couldn't see in the tinted windows. He didn't stop it. The car's tag had now been run nine times since September. Muhammad and Malvo were still invisible. But with the Ponderosa note, they had given the task force critical clues. The note was a kind of Rosetta stone that connected things that had seemed unrelated. Its mention of the Visa card connected the sniper to Tacoma, where records showed it had been used to buy gas in April. Its mention of Baliles and a priest connected the shooter somehow to the Alabama shooting. And, although the authorities didn't yet know it, Alabama held the key to the case.

———

Montgomery, Alabama, police chief John H. Wilson III had driven over to Atlanta for some football. He spent Sunday afternoon with his brother, a Georgia police sergeant, watching the Atlanta Falcons whip the Carolina Panthers. When the game was over, they went out to a restaurant for dinner and then back to his brother's place to watch another game on TV. Wilson planned on making the two-and-a-half-hour drive home the next morning.

At about 7:00 that evening, Pat Downing, chief of detectives for the Montgomery, Alabama, police, called Wilson on a walkie-talkie. Could the chief telephone him at home? Downing asked. He had a sensitive matter he didn't want to discuss over the air.

"This is going to sound real farfetched," Downing said when Wilson called him back. One of his sergeants, Scott Martino, had just been contacted by the sniper task force outside Washington. The task force thought the sniper might be connected to the Parker/Adams liquor store shooting in September. The suggestion was not a complete shock—the possibility had even come up at one of the chief's daily morning staff meetings. But it seemed remote. Ours was a robbery, Wilson had thought. Theirs were totally random sniper shootings, with no apparent motive at all. Besides, eyewitness accounts and bullet fragments recovered from Parker initially indicated that the weapon used was a .22 pistol, not a rifle.

Montgomery, Alabama, had only a few more murders every year than Montgomery County, Maryland. For the most part, they were drug shootings and domestic disputes. The shooting of Claudine Parker and Kellie Adams was unusual because it occurred in a busy, upscale area in early evening. The scene had been chaotic. One suspect, now believed to be Malvo, fled and was pursued by bystanders. The second suspect, believed to be Muhammad, fled and was pursued for a quarter mile by Dwight Johnson, a rookie police officer who was heartsick afterward because he hadn't been able to run fast enough. Malvo later told a prison supervisor that it was Muhammad who had fired the shots at Parker and Adams.

Police were at first skeptical that the first suspect was even involved in the case. When the police sirens are wailing, Wilson knew, anybody with a parking ticket is going to "haul buggy." The suspect had been in such a hurry that witnesses saw him drop something, which turned out to be a catalog for ArmaLite rifle accessories. There was a gun show in town that day. It could have been someone from the show. Two Montgomery detectives, Don Favor and John Bowman, decided to pick up the catalog as evidence, even though they weren't sure the guy who ran away had anything to do with the case.

The magazine had a number of fingerprints on it, and police also found a suspicious print on a receipt stapled to a small paper bag Adams was carrying. But the prints didn't match anything in local or statewide databases or anything in neighboring Georgia. Alabama was not one of the nineteen states electronically linked to the FBI's new national fingerprint database, so investigators in Montgomery decided to ship the prints to the FBI to see if there were any matches. The prints were prepared for shipping, but they had not yet been sent.

Now, Downing explained to his boss on the phone, the sniper task force was looking into some calls believed to be from the sniper. He boasted about a liquor store shooting in Montgomery, Alabama. The task force wondered if a local FBI agent, Margaret Faulkner, a former Montgomery police detective, could bring the evidence— bullet fragments as well as the fingerprints—back to Maryland for analysis.

No problem, said Wilson. Faulkner could fly up to Washington with the evidence on Monday. He was happy to help the task force and eager for new leads on his case. But the sniper could easily have heard about the Alabama killings on the news. It could turn out to be nothing.

About the same time the two Alabama policemen were talking, Moose was holding a press conference in Rockville. He looked tired and squinted as he spoke. "Tonight, we will not take any questions," he said. ". . . And we just ask you to understand." He praised Sheriff Cook, in Hanover County, where the shooting the night before had occurred. Then he added: "I would like for people in the media to carry this point. Carry it clearly and carry it often. To the person who left us a message at the Ponderosa last night, you gave us a telephone number. We do want to talk to you. Call us at the number you provided." He did not mention that the deadline had passed thirteen hours earlier.

10

"Your Children Are Not Safe"

It was raining on the morning of Monday, October 21, as José Morales walked across the parking lot of a convenience store outside Richmond to call his wife in Guatemala. Morales had entered the United States illegally five months earlier. He earned $8 an hour working as a roofer from dawn to dusk and slept on the floor in a crowded apartment with six other immigrants. He had five children back home.

Across the street at an Exxon station, Edgar Rivera García, a carpenter from Mexico, was sitting in a white Plymouth minivan with a roof rack, talking on a pay phone. He had been on the phone for thirty-five minutes, parked close enough to the phone kiosk so that he didn't have to get out of the van and get wet. It was 8:32 A.M., and the lives of two immigrants were about to change—and not for the better.

Responding to Moose's appeal the night before, Malvo and Muhammad had indeed called back. Thirty-five minutes before, they had called the Ponderosa number from a pay phone at the same Exxon station where García was talking. Baltimore FBI agent Jackie K. Dalrymple took the call, which had been automatically forwarded to the command center in Rockville. Dalrymple had been on duty since 7:00 A.M. and had already taken several calls on the Ponderosa line. Someone had asked about the chicken wings, someone else about the work schedule that day.

When the phone rang at 7:57 A.M., it was Lee Malvo.

"Is this the Ponderosa?" Malvo asked.

"Um, who is this?" Dalrymple said.

"Don't say anything, but listen," Malvo said, and he started a tape that he was holding next to the phone.

"Dearest police, call me God. Do not release to the press. Five red stars. You have our terms. They are non-negotiable. If you choose option one, you will hold a press conference, stating to the media that you believe you have caught the sniper like a duck in a noose. Repeat every word exactly as you heard it. If you choose option two, be sure to remember he [*sic*] will not deviate. P.S. Your children are not safe."

"I am listening," Dalrymple replied. "I am listening."

But Malvo hung up. The call had lasted for thirty-eight seconds. It picked up perfectly from the Ponderosa note. The same code phrases. The stars. The threat to children. No kook could know those details. After two weeks of bungled trying, the snipers and their pursuers were now in clear, unmistakable contact.

Figuring out where the call was made was the job of the U.S. Marshals Service. The marshals had been in on the case since the beginning. Their mission was the same as it had been since the Old West—finding fugitives—only these days, they used, among other things, telephone records and sophisticated electronic surveillance. For example, they had the technology to identify all the cell phones that were on in an area at the time of an incident, and had done it numerous times during the sniper shootings. Many of the cell phone numbers that turned up, however, belonged to investigators.

At 8:03, six minutes after Malvo made his call, Marshal Inspector Tim Hein, stationed outside the negotiators' room in the command center, heard about the call from Dalrymple. To Hein, those six minutes seemed like six hours. With these kinds of calls, every second counts. The slight delay in giving the number to Hein was just the first miscue that morning that would turn opportunity into fiasco.

Armed with the number from caller ID and aided by a local phone company, Hein tracked the call to a pay phone outside the Exxon station at Parham Road and West Broad Street within minutes. The gas station was located about a block from where the sheriff's deputy had run the Caprice's tag sixteen hours earlier and about four miles from where the snipers had made their futile Ponderosa call the day before.

At 8:07, Hein told top FBI and ATF officials in the JOC where the phone call came from. They, in turn, telephoned an FBI command post in Richmond, where federal agents and local police commanders had pay phones throughout the area under surveillance and were standing by. Henrico County police chief Henry W. Stanley gave the order for his officers to get to the Exxon station. Stanley—and the other officials in the Richmond command post—had no idea that the sniper had hung up ten minutes before. Their understanding was that he was still on the phone.

Hein had also called Lenny DePaul, a New York–based inspector for the marshals who had been brought in on the sniper case for his expertise with fugitives. DePaul was in his car, driving toward Richmond. "Go in soft," DePaul told Kevin Engel, another marshal who was nearing the Exxon station. "Don't heat it up." DePaul knew that their best chance of catching the sniper was to ease in and not risk scaring him with lights and sirens. DePaul didn't know that the Henrico police were on the way.

At 8:08, Henrico County police officer Roger Condrey spotted a man in a white van on a pay phone—García. Condrey radioed in what he saw, and the on-scene commander gave the order for the officers to move in. They closed down the streets and secured the gas station. The response was anything but soft. At 8:30—thirty-three minutes after the sniper had called the Rockville task force—Henrico SWAT officers swept across the parking lot, hauled García out of his Plymouth at gunpoint, and scooped up Morales for good measure. The pay phones would be seized later, too.

When he got to the gas station, Engel called DePaul back. "Uh, Lenny," Engel said, "I thought you wanted to go in soft. It looks like a fucking circus over here." García and Morales were on the ground. A helicopter thundered overhead.

At the Richmond command post, they thought they had their men. But DePaul knew otherwise. He got a call from William J. Sorukas Jr., a senior inspector with the marshals' Technical Operations Group, who had been trying to get a better fix on the phone line. Sorukas had found that García's call had started before the call to Dalrymple and had gone on long after the other call ended. It turned out there were two phones on opposite ends of the Exxon station. The hammer had come down on the wrong one.

"The two people they got are not the right guys," Sorukas told DePaul. "I know from the phone calls they're not the right guys."

"You've got to be kidding me," DePaul said.

At the Exxon station, Engel had no doubt there had been a mistake. A guy who had been getting away with the crimes of the century wasn't going to be on the pay phone for half an hour, he thought. Somebody just fucked up.

Chief Stanley was miffed when he later heard that an official in Rockville called the takedown a "rookie move." He had just acted on delayed information from the FBI, he would say later.

The next day, FBI director Robert Mueller was taking a tour of the JOC when he stopped at Hein's desk and shook his hand.

"I understand there was some time delay in getting the location of that number to Virginia," Hein would remember him saying.

"I did it as fast as I could, sir," Hein replied. He knew—but didn't say—that the delay had nothing to do with the U.S. Marshals Service.

García and Morales were just unlucky. Neither spoke much English or knew the other. They were released in a few hours. But their problems were just beginning. Within a few months, both would be back in their home countries, technically not deported but "repatriated."

DePaul knew how stupid it was. They'd gone in too fast and botched it. What he didn't know was that the tunnel vision the investigators had vowed to avoid had sabotaged them again. They had artfully lured their prey, only to be crossed up by the vision of a white van.

Not until later would they learn how close they had come. Malvo would tell his interrogators that he was among the bystanders who had watched the raid as it went down. "I saw the Mexicans get stopped," he said. "I watched it, but I wasn't in the car."

He didn't hang around for long. Two hours later, the Caprice was photographed by a traffic camera going through a red light at Broad and Birch Streets in Falls Church, Virginia, about one hundred miles from the Exxon station and about two miles from where Linda Franklin was killed.

In the command center, Forsythe had followed the Virginia events on the bank of TVs that were set up behind his desk. Something about it didn't feel right. "Whole world going to respond to take a hard look," he wrote in his logbook. As the hours passed and there was no word from Virginia, it became clear that these were not the right guys. If they were, someone would have called. Forsythe understood how dynamic the situation was. He knew that even with technology it was extremely hard to get a call, track it, deploy police, and grab a jittery caller before he hung up. No one was really to blame.

Cavanaugh agreed. It was hard to knock the Henrico police for jumping the white van. Under the circumstances, they'd have been crazy if they hadn't. In a case like this you had to be out there doing stuff, shaking things up. You could not sit back and wait for the action to come to you.

The authorities may have realized almost immediately what had happened at the Exxon station, but the media didn't. The networks broke into their regular morning programming, strongly implying that this might be it. At 10:09 A.M., Moose emerged from police headquarters in Rockville. He knew that the wrong people had most likely been detained, and he wanted to reach out again to the sniper. He again asked for the media's indulgence and said: "We are going to respond to a message that we have received. We will respond later. We are preparing our response at this time."

What did that mean? If the case was nearly solved, why was Moose still issuing mysterious statements? Stuart Cook, the Hanover County sheriff, didn't clear up the confusion when he held a news conference at 1:15 P.M. After announcing that the bullet fragments from the Hopper shooting were the sniper's, he mentioned the "two males" who had been detained that morning in neighboring Henrico County. "Those two individuals are being questioned at this time," he said.

Are they suspects in the sniper shooting? someone asked.

"The two people that we have in custody are being questioned in regards to the sniper shooting," Cook replied. He would go no further.

In Rockville, Captain Nancy Demme could not get any information from the Virginia authorities about the van incident. If it turns out they caught the sniper, great, she thought. But if they didn't, the sniper is going to be very angry.

Most public and private schools in the Richmond area were closed that Monday. Over 150,000 students from Chesterfield, Goochland, Hanover, Henrico, and Powhatan Counties and the city of Richmond got the day off. It was the only time during the sniper spree that large numbers of schools closed because of the case. Outside the Richmond area, parents and educators wondered why. Did school superintendents there know something other school authorities didn't? The answer was yes.

On Sunday night, Sheriff Cook called local school officials and told them that the Ponderosa note had contained a line about children not being safe. Cook had wanted to keep the details of the letter quiet. But in talks with Rockville task force officials, he was left with the impression that the task force intended to make part of the message public. He was against it, and he said so, heatedly.

But Richmond area school officials had said publicly that the schools were safe. Cook worried that the snipers might have seen that as a challenge. If the task force was going to make some of the message public, he might as well try to help out the local school officials. The schools were closed. They would be closed Tuesday as well.

————

At 4:17, Chief Moose, flanked by the ATF's Mike Bouchard and the FBI's Gary Bald, stood under a white tent outside police headquarters in Rockville and twice read carefully from a statement to the sniper: "The person you called could not hear everything you said. The audio was unclear. And we want to get it right. Call us back so that we can clearly understand."

The call in fact had raised new questions for investigators, beginning with the reference to the duck in the noose. Investigators quickly figured out that it came from an obscure folk story about a boastful rabbit that tried to catch a duck with a noose. The duck was caught but flew away, dragging the rabbit until it finally let go and fell. Members of the task force sat around, listening to a tape of the recorded "duck in a noose" call over and over and over. One agent thought the voice was Hispanic; another guessed it might be Asian. "It sounds like a kid," one said. ATF negotiator-adviser Peter Mangan thought the voice was foreign, and the "duck in a noose" reference sounded Caribbean, maybe Jamaican. He ran the idea past a Jamaican-born ATF agent, Mark Peterkin. But Peterkin had never heard of the "duck in a noose."

"Pete, man, there are no ducks in Jamaica," Peterkin jokingly said. "No ducks in Jamaica."

The U.S. Marshals were also pondering a Jamaican connection. Late that night Lenny DePaul and a couple of colleagues from the New York regional task force were hanging out in the lobby of a hotel in Manassas, exhausted but not ready for sleep. DePaul had a copy of the letter left in Ashland. He also had a computer disk of Malvo's recorded call to the dispatcher in Rockville who interrupted him.

"I feel like choking her every time I rewind the tape," he joked.

An FBI agent from Richmond had told DePaul that he thought the voice on the tape was a Puerto Rican from New York. But De-Paul had a different theory. He sounds like a young black kid from one of the islands, he told the marshals.

"He pretty much sounds Jamaican," DePaul said.

One of the New York task force members, Vinny Senzamici, was an expert on New York City gangs; another detective knew Jamaican gangs. DePaul handed them the letter. Senzamici was fascinated with the five stars at the top of the first page. He had heard of a Ja-maican band that sang a song called "Word Is Bond." He also knew that on the street the phrase "five-star general" referred to the highest-ranking guy in a street gang.

DePaul and the others got onto the laptop and began typing in phrases from the letter.

"Word is bond" was part of the lyrics of rap songs by several recording artists, including Busta Rhymes. The hip-hop group House of Pain had a song that caught their attention. It opened with the lyrics "Word is bond. Pop pop pop pop. Grab your chest. Now ya bleedin (punk)." DePaul found a reggae group with a song called "Word Is Bond" that had recently performed in Washington.

"Holy shit, look at this," DePaul said. "Print me out everything about these groups." Later, the marshals also found an Internet site for a black British rap group that used the phrases "Mr. Police" and "Call me God," which also appeared in the Ashland letter.

––––––––

The task force had just missed their quarry at the Exxon that morn-ing. If the authorities could get the sniper to call again, the police might be more lucky. But Muhammad and Malvo knew that, too. They were already paranoid about the phone calls. They had an-other plan in mind.

Two hours later, a Montgomery County police officer spotted an old blue Chevrolet Caprice with tinted windows driving in Rockville.

It had New Jersey license plates. The officer was suspicious of the car and ran the tag number through his computer. Nothing he was concerned about came back. The officer let the car proceed.

A little after 11:00 P.M., Muhammad showed up at the Outback Steakhouse in Aspen Hill. He chatted with a customer, who later remembered that Muhammad said he was feeling sick and was seated in the hostess area as the restaurant closed. The customer watched as Muhammad drove away in a blue Chevy Caprice with tinted windows and New Jersey license plates. The next move for Malvo and Muhammad would again be in Montgomery County.

Early the next morning, October 22, a thirty-five-year-old bus driver with a wife and two children was standing on the front steps of a blue-and-white public bus operated by Montgomery County's Ride On transit system. It was still dark, and Conrad E. Johnson, the son of Jamaican immigrants, was illuminated by the inside lights as his bus was parked at a morning staging area just off Connecticut Avenue in Aspen Hill. The spot was less than a mile from where Premkumar Walekar was killed and where the Michaels store window was shot three weeks earlier. Sarah Ramos had been killed just a mile to the north. James Martin had been shot to death about two miles south. And James Buchanan and Lori Lewis Rivera had been killed about four miles south.

Johnson, known as "Cee Jay," was a popular figure at the sprawling Silver Spring, Maryland, bus depot where he had started his day. He wore a goatee and two diamond earrings. He had a shaved head and tattooed arms and had been a bus driver for ten years. His Route 34 run, from Aspen Hill to Bethesda, was about to start. His bus was parked so that the open door faced an outdoor basketball court and a patch of woods beyond. He had a female trainee on-board with him that day who was learning a new route. They had just had breakfast on the bus, and the trainee was sitting in a front seat on the right side.

Johnson kicked some trash out the front door and came back up the steps, putting down a cup of coffee on the change box. As he stood in the doorway, Johnson, who was six feet two inches tall and weighed 250 pounds, made a big target. At 5:55, a gunshot boomed from the woods. Johnson staggered back and fell in the aisle. A .223 rifle bullet had struck the right side of his upper abdomen just under his right rib cage. It tore through his liver, destroying most of it, and then his pancreas and right renal artery, shedding lead and pieces of its copper jacket as it went.

The trainee called 911, pleading for help.

"A Ride On bus driver's been shot at Aspen Hill!" she said. "Aspen Hill! Bus 705! Aspen Hill!"

"Aspen Hill and what?" the dispatcher asked.

"Right here by the post office!" the caller said. "Bel Pre!" she added, giving the name of a nearby street. "Please, he's been shot about two minutes. . . . Hurry up, please. I'm on the bus with him. . . . He's been shot. He's laying here, sir. Please, hurry up. . . . I'm scared. Hurry up."

At first, Johnson did not seem to be critically injured. Medics who arrived found him lying on his back in the bus aisle, still conscious. The medics saw a small entrance wound but no exit wound. They carried him off the bus, put him in an ambulance, and rushed him to a nearby fire station. From there, a Maryland state police helicopter rushed him to Suburban Hospital in Bethesda.

Johnson arrived conscious and sitting up. He was taken to the fifth-floor operating room, where a surgeon, Dr. Dany Westerband, began trying to repair the damage. He had been at work about an hour when Jim Robey, who had worked on Buchanan and Rivera and was in the hospital to perform some elective surgery, stopped at the OR to see if he could help.

"Dany, what's going on?" Robey said.

"Oh boy, this is really bad," Westerband replied. The patient's liver was severely damaged. There was extensive internal bleeding that was hard to control. Robey volunteered to help.

The two doctors worked another hour and a half, at one point performing a desperate procedure in which Johnson's blood was detoured around his shattered liver. The procedure worked, but the organ damage was massive. Johnson's body temperature was dropping. His blood wasn't clotting. His blood pressure fell and wouldn't come back up. Then his heart went into a fatal arrhythmia. He died on the operating table at 9:26 A.M. Westerband and Robey went to tell Johnson's family. The waiting room erupted in grief.

The news spread across the county like a shock wave. It had been nineteen days since the bloody third of October. Since then, the sniper had moved one hundred miles away, ranging over other jurisdictions and another state. The hope was that perhaps he would stay elsewhere, that Montgomery County had paid its price, that the killing might not revisit the place where it started. But now it had.

Just one glance at a distraught colleague as he walked in the command center that morning was enough to tell Barney Forsythe that there had been another killing. She explained what had happened and where. Forsythe sighed. He was not all that surprised. He figured if the killer went uncaught long enough, he'd be back. Forsythe walked to the rear of the room and spoke to the staff from the midnight shift. "Just tell the people who are coming on that I'm going down to the scene," he said. It was still dark outside, and it was cold. He did not use lights or siren in his unmarked car. He radioed ahead that "nine-Henry-ten"—the call sign for the chief of homicide—was responding.

By the time he got there, Johnson had been taken to the hospital. No other commanders had arrived yet; the rest of the task force brass was either still in bed or back at the JOC. Forsythe could hear sirens and helicopters in the distance, but it was eerily quiet inside the crime tape. The audacity of the killer made him angry. He'd been able to strike again despite the heat of the investigation, and do it where he had started, back on Forsythe's turf. This guy's out of his mind, Forsythe thought. But maybe the killer had slipped up. Maybe this time there would be a clue.

The ATF's Joe Riehl was on the Capital Beltway heading for the JOC when he got the word. Riehl raced to the scene, forcing his way through the now congested traffic in the area. Demme, the police spokeswoman, was on her way to work and got caught in the traffic gridlock. A reporter called her on her cell phone to ask what was going on.

She said she didn't know. "Why don't you do me a favor," she said in exasperation. "Why don't you tell people if they're not out already, stay home." She hung up, realizing she had probably spoken in haste. When she turned on the radio, she heard the reporter repeating her words. Oh, my God, she thought, I've shut down the federal government.

At the shooting scene, there were many familiar faces. The investigators all knew one another by now. Forsythe had already been there awhile when Riehl arrived. "Hey, Barney," Riehl said. "How you doin'?"

After three weeks of twelve-hour days, scant sleep, high stress, and junk food, Riehl was exhausted. The case had been like a sick relative you didn't want to leave because something surely would happen if you did. Riehl hadn't expected to be outside in the chill, and he rummaged in the trunk of his car for something to put on. Later, he and others would gather in a metro bus that was parked nearby just to get warm.

Forsythe's deputy, Phil Raum, was home when Forsythe called him. "Sons of bitches," Raum said. Johnson had already been taken away when Raum arrived about 7:00 A.M. As other investigators reached the scene, the day warmed, and the massive Beltway dragnet again came up empty. Judging from the fact that Johnson had been standing in the doorway, it seemed likely that the shot that killed him had come from the woods just beyond the basketball courts. It was a perfect place for an ambush and had been carefully selected. The setup was like the Brown and Hopper shootings. The woods provided cover, the basketball court a free field of fire. There was a big busy apartment complex next door, where the car could be parked for a smooth getaway. Around 1:20 P.M., Nick DeCarlo organized a team of about thirty police and federal agents equipped with rakes who went shoulder to shoulder through the underbrush, looking for clues. They found a pile of excrement. Fifteen minutes into the search and about fifty feet into the woods, an ATF agent spotted a Ziploc bag impaled on a broken tree branch. Inside that bag was another Ziploc bag. And inside the second Ziploc bag was a note. It had red stars stuck to it and writing on both sides of a piece of paper.

County police forensics specialist David McGill pulled the bag off the tree branch and placed it in an evidence envelope. An investigator called out to Raum that a note had been found. Raum told him to lower his voice, motioning toward the media gathered not far away. Bring the note and walk slowly with me to the evidence truck, Raum said.

Inside the truck, the note was handed over to federal agents for processing. But Raum had to be able to tell his bosses what it said. He got a piece of looseleaf paper, knelt on the floor, and copied it as exactly as he could.

"For you, Mr. Police," the front side began. " 'Call me God.' Do not release to the press. P.S. Your children are not safe. Can you hear us now? Do not play these childish games with us. You know our demands. Your choice. Thank you."

The other side read: "For you Mr. Police. 'Call me God.' Do not release to the press. You did not respond [to] the message. You departed from what we told you to say, and you departed from the time. Your incompetence has cost you another life. You have until 9 a.m. to deliver the money, and until eight a.m. to deliver this response, 'We have caught the sniper like a duck in a noose . . .' to let us know that you have our demands."

The note was clear and chilling. And already it was hours past both deadlines the senders had stipulated. Raum called Forsythe, but Forsythe didn't have a chance to inform Moose right away. Moose found out from someone else. Minutes later Forsythe got a page from Moose's secretary: "The chief wants to see you right now." Moose was upset. "Did you forget to tell me something?" he asked Forsythe. But he calmed down once Forsythe explained.

When he was finished copying the note, Raum hurried to police headquarters. Forsythe, Moose, and other top task force officials were gathered around the small conference table in Moose's office, and Raum, who was unaccustomed to all that brass, read them the note. Forsythe told him he had done a good job. Then a discussion began over the meaning of the note, which seemed more angry and demanding than the previous one. The sniper was saying that Johnson had been killed because of the inadequate response to the previous note, and there was another threat to hurt children. Some kind of response had to be made. But what?

———

The pressure on the task force was growing. At Moose's news conference that afternoon, he was grilled about the details of the Ponderosa note. The *Richmond Times-Dispatch* had reported that Richmond area schools remained closed because of a possible threat to schools contained in the note.

"Can you confirm it, or enlighten us?" a reporter asked Moose.

Moose tried to avoid the question by saying everyone, including children, was in danger.

"There were schoolchildren specifically mentioned in the letter? That was the question, sir," the reporter said. "That's what we want to know."

Moose responded that it would be "inappropriate" to talk about such things.

But parents would want to know if there was such a threat, the reporter said.

Moose replied that he would pass on something he felt people needed to know.

"You'd pass along a specific threat, in other words?" he was asked.

Moose again said the discussion of evidence was inappropriate, but that if he came upon information he felt was "releasable," he would provide it.

The reporters would not let it drop. Was the Richmond newspaper account inaccurate? another one asked.

"Sir, again, I was trying to say that this is the wrong forum to have any further discussions with regards to your question," Moose said. "It's very inappropriate."

"What's the right forum?" someone asked.

County Executive Douglas Duncan, who would later call this "the bad press conference," was asked the same thing. If the Richmond schools were closed, why weren't Montgomery County's?

Later, Nancy Demme got a call from her sister, Tracy, the mother of a nine-year-old daughter and three-year-old son. She said she was sure that Demme knew what was in the letter and that she wouldn't tell her, but she wanted to know one thing: If Shannon were your daughter, would you send her to school? "I would," said Demme, who is extremely close to her sister's family. "But I would take her myself. We have to go on with our lives."

———

The case was taking a toll on everyone, but Duncan was particularly worried about Moose. The chief already had been assailed by a *Washington Post* columnist who suggested that perhaps the probe should be turned over to "professionals." Duncan sensed that the media was turning on Moose. The chief had his own worries about the future. He knew some cases like this never got solved. If this one wasn't, he knew it could cost him his job. A woman from Georgia had recently e-mailed the department: "What the hell are you guys up there doing anyway? . . . all the resources at your disposal and this asshole is still on the loose."

The frictions within the task force were worsening, mainly because people felt they were not being kept in the loop. Police and agents on the street and in offices across the region were furious that information in Rockville wasn't being shared with them. Some county detectives were upset with Forsythe; federal prosecutors were upset with Gary Bald. There was bad blood between Moose and Gansler and between Gansler and some of the federal prosecutors. One Virginia prosecutor wished "a pox" on both Gansler and the feds.

Innocent people were still being slain, and the authorities seemed helpless to stop it. Reporters were getting tired of being told their questions were inappropriate. The killer had romped untouched over the region, spreading fear and grief for three weeks, and now was back where he had started. The fear, Cavanaugh would remember, hung over the area "like the damned Washington humidity."

A few nights earlier, Montgomery County prosecutor John McCarthy and his wife, Jeanette, who worked at a local high school, were awakened in their bed by a helicopter roaring over their home near Aspen Hill. For weeks, it seemed, they had been hearing the sound of the helicopters. There was a park behind their house that was always being checked. McCarthy and his wife were regulars at the shopping center where Sarah Ramos had been killed. Jeanette McCarthy had been in the Starbucks there twenty minutes before the attack. McCarthy knew all about the sniper notes. The couple were afraid to let their children go out to play and were thinking about taking them out of town for Halloween.

Now, as the clatter of the helicopter pounded through the darkness, Jeanette McCarthy screamed in fear. She began to cry. "I can't take this anymore, I can't take it," she said as her husband tried to console her.

All the while, Kevin Lewis of the FBI was worried about his dying mother. One day after Lewis returned from visiting her, Forsythe stood up in the JOC and asked everyone to "welcome Kevin back." Forsythe explained the situation and said, "Let's keep him in our prayers."

———————

Shortly after 5:00 P.M., Moose returned to the satellite trucks and reporters after a long discussion at the command center about how to handle the sniper's latest threats to children. Ramsey, the D.C. chief, had urged the release of the threat. The FBI's Gary Bald was worried about a report that two news organizations were about to claim, erroneously, that the threat referred to shooting students on school buses. Malvo would later say that he and Muhammad planned just such an attack but aborted it at the last minute because "the bus pulled in wrong."

Cavanaugh, like Ramsey, said the threat they had received should be made public. "Just release the last sentence of the letter," he said. "That's the truth. That's what he said."

Someone argued that it might upset children.

"Look," Cavanaugh said. "He's already shot a child. Let's get it out there. . . . Get the truth out to the public and let adults, parents, and school officials decide what precautions they need to take in their community."

It was agreed, so Moose now explained that he was going to provide the exact language of the sniper. "It is in the form of a post-script: 'Your children are not safe anywhere, at any time.' " He explained that he would not provide the rest of the message and did not answer any more questions.

Back inside headquarters, Moose told Demme it was the hardest thing he had ever done. "We're saying we can't do our job. We're supposed to keep people safe, and we can't."

Two hours later, he was back in front of the reporters. At 7:14 P.M., more than twelve hours past the deadline for the payment mentioned in the latest note, Moose read a statement, this time for the sniper.

"These past several days, you have attempted to communicate with us," he said. "We have researched the options you stated and found that it is not possible electronically to comply in the manner that you requested. However, we remain open and ready to talk to you about the options you have mentioned. It is important that we do this without anyone else getting hurt. Call us at the same number you used before. . . . If you would feel more comfortable, a private post office box or another secure method can be provided. You indicated that this is about more than violence. We are waiting to hear from you."

The task force was trying to put off the killer's demand for money without rejecting it. The authorities weren't about to put $10 million into the Visa card account. But the FBI had discussed setting aside $100,000 to use in the event the negotiations got to an exchange of cash. That was a lot of money for the local authorities, but not for the federal agencies. Cavanaugh had spent three times that much on undercover gun and explosives buys.

At the same time, Moose was signaling that a deal might still be struck, as long as no one else got hurt. The authorities needed time; they just weren't sure how much.

———————

The key developments that day, however, had nothing to do with the incipient negotiations.

In Tacoma, investigators finally went to interview Robert Holmes, almost a week after he had first called to voice his suspicions. Holmes told them about Muhammad and his rifle, and his sidekick, Malvo, and Muhammad's ex-wife, Mildred, and the silencer. He gave them the silencer components that had been left at his house.

And just before 7:00 A.M., Mitch Hollers, an FBI fingerprint expert in Washington, D.C., took the prints from the gun catalog brought from Montgomery, Alabama, the day before and ran them through the FBI's new Integrated Automated Fingerprint Identification System. The system, which was only three years old, was a vast computerized database containing the prints of forty-four million individuals arrested by an array of police agencies across the country.

When Hollers ran the prints, there was a match—from a Jamaican teenager who had been arrested as an illegal immigrant in Bellingham, Washington, on December 19, 2001. His name was Lee Boyd Malvo. And when his brief arrest report was pulled, it said Malvo was in the middle of some kind of custody dispute involving his mother and another man, one John "Mohammed."

The two subjects of that report had spent the afternoon working out. People later said they saw them at a YMCA in Silver Spring a

little while after the Johnson murder. The pair said they didn't have
the $3 guest fee and were allowed in for free. A trainer saw Muham-
mad in the locker room, drenched in sweat, his face in his hands.
Was anything the matter? the trainer asked. "No," said Muhammad.

At 5:59 P.M. on Tuesday, Muhammad made a phone card call
back to Washington State. He was apparently calling from a rest stop
off Route 50 in Stevensville, Maryland, east of Annapolis and just
past the eastern end of the soaring Bay Bridge over Chesapeake Bay.
It was a short call, a little over six minutes. It would be his last call on
the phone card.

11

Duck in a Noose

With two names to go on, the vast law enforcement resources at the task force's disposal swung into action. Snapshots of Malvo from his arrest with his mother by the border patrol in December were transmitted across the country and copied by the hundreds. A picture of Muhammad was found, taken when he was detained by immigration officials in Miami in 2001, but it wasn't very clear.

Billy Sorukas was in his Marshals Service office in suburban Virginia, about to put in one of the long days for which he was famous. Around 1:00 A.M. on Wednesday, October 23, after hearing that Muhammad had once lived in California and had a driver's license, he called Ralph Garofalo, an old marshal friend in San Diego, where he had once worked.

"I need a favor," he told Garofalo.

About an hour later Garofalo called back. "I got your picture," Garofalo said. It was the black-and-white shot of Muhammad, squinting and dressed in military fatigues, that was taken for his license. "How do you want it?"

Sorukas said to e-mail it as quickly as possible. What was the big hurry? Garofalo asked. "Take a good look at the picture," Sorukas said. "You're getting one of the first views of one of the snipers in D.C."

At 2:30 A.M., Sorukas contacted the FBI's Criminal Justice Information Services Division, in Clarksburg, West Virginia, to request what was called an "off-line," or specialized, law enforcement computer sweep on Muhammad and Malvo that would turn up any contact they might have had with police. He had already asked Michael P. Moran, a marshal inspector working out of the Rockville command center, to run Muhammad's name through the FBI's Rapid Start database of sniper leads. Moran called back to say there was one hit. Under the heading "Facts of Complaint," the entry briefly detailed Holmes's account of Muhammad and Malvo and the rifle. What floored Sorukas was the part about Muhammad's bitter divorce from a wife "who may reside in the Washington, D.C., area."

At 5:00 A.M., while Sorukas was trying to catch some sleep on his couch, a fax came in from Clarksburg. It was a brief reference to Muhammad's encounter with a Baltimore police officer outside a doughnut shop on October 8. Sorukas couldn't tell from the entry what had happened. Brian Sheppard, a deputy U.S. marshal in Baltimore, was asked to see what he could find out.

In Baton Rouge, authorities interviewed Muhammad's relatives. In Tacoma, FBI agents played a recording of Malvo's call to the Rockville police for Holmes and asked if it sounded like the teenager he had seen with Muhammad. Holmes said, offhandedly, that bullets from Muhammad's rifle might still be in the tree trunk out back. If the investigators could get those bullets, they could compare them to the fragments recovered from the sniper's victims, and suddenly the tree trunk outside Holmes's modest house on South Proctor Street became a potentially critical piece of evidence.

But authorities didn't want to chance searching for the slugs in Holmes's yard. They might damage them. The task force issued instructions for the whole stump to be removed and flown east for proper analysis. But it had to be done discreetly. If the media found out and reported it, the killers could find out, too. Investigators at the task force wanted the removal done by a few guys in flannel shirts who would not arouse suspicion.

The FBI, meanwhile, tracked down Malvo's mother, Una James, and interviewed her in Seattle. She was vague about how she had met Muhammad but told agents how her son had left Florida to join Muhammad, how she had gone to find him and had asked the Bellingham police to help. She said the only way she had of contacting her son was through a phone number for a nurse who lived in Tacoma and was a friend of Muhammad's. She gave the FBI the nurse's name and number, and Muhammad's old girlfriend was stunned when she was told why they were looking for him. She could not conceive of such a good and gentle man doing these things. This was not the John Muhammad she knew.

The FBI told her she must alert them if he showed up, and she knew she would have to choose between a man she loved and her obligation to the authorities. She prayed she wouldn't have to make that choice.

Another woman had once figured in Muhammad's life, his ex-wife Mildred, and when police discovered the anger he had exhibited toward her, they rushed to Quiet Brook Lane in Clinton and hustled her and her children into protective custody. She would later conclude that the whole sniper spree was a cover for her eventual murder. As in the slaying of Keenya Cook, Muhammad would not have been suspected.

———

The pieces of a once scrambled puzzle were falling into place. Word began spreading inside the JOC Wednesday morning. After weeks of dashed hopes, and dozens of people "washed" off the suspect board, Malvo and Muhammad now were at the top. About midday, Phil Raum was talking to John McCarthy from the state's attorney's office when he took a clip of money from his pocket and slammed it on a table. "These are the guys," Raum said. "What's the probability that it's not them?"

Muhammad and Malvo, however, were still invisible, still moving around. At 2:13 P.M. that day, they were in a Kmart store at

Georgia and Connecticut Avenues, in Aspen Hill, a quarter mile from where Johnson had been slain. They bought a canvas duffel bag for $22.99. The day before, police searching the Johnson scene had found a suspicious black duffel bag in the woods not far from the sniper's note. It was empty except for a pocketknife in a nylon case, a Q-tip, and a pepper shaker. They had seized it as evidence.

Task force leaders knew that whatever promising information was coming in, it had been eighteen hours since Moose's response the night before and almost thirty hours since the sniper's last deadline. The sniper could, and probably would, strike again soon if something else wasn't done.

A heated debate had been raging within the command center. Members of the task force who were experts in negotiating, led by the FBI's Gary Noesner, chief of the Bureau's Crisis Negotiation Unit, urged a quick response. The ATF's Cavanaugh agreed. The killer might be out there right now lining up his next shot. He ought to be engaged right away. Dialogue might prevent more shooting—it had at Waco. With dead and injured ATF agents outside, and wounded and hostile Davidians inside Koresh's compound, Cavanaugh had talked his way to a cease-fire that, for the time being anyway, had saved lives.

The negotiators, who helped draft Moose's painstaking replies to the sniper, felt undervalued. They believed that too much emphasis had gone into trying to compile a psychological profile of the killers. Profiling was a crap shoot, they thought. Noesner, a thirty-year FBI veteran who had also been at the Waco siege, would later wonder if more adept handling of communication with the snipers might have saved lives.

Now, Noesner argued, it was vital to respond. "The snipers are basically saying, 'You're not doing what we told you to do. Quit playing these foolish games.' They're killing people because we're not responding."

But other members of the task force believed responding would only empower the sniper, and for the moment their position prevailed.

Meanwhile, the negotiating team was not even allowed to see the latest note, infuriating Noesner. How could he craft a response if he didn't know what the note said? His people were manning the phones. What if the sniper called again? Finally, that morning, they were told the contents of the note.

By noon they had drafted a reply, which included the line "You asked us to say, 'we have caught the sniper like a duck in a noose.' " Cavanaugh favored releasing it as quickly as possible. But the profilers thought the sentence might be inflammatory. Forsythe, who knew from experience the value of good negotiators, would later seek a private meeting with Moose to urge him to hear out both sides.

Publicly, Moose was saying little. At a news conference shortly after noon, he announced that ballistics comparisons had matched the bullet that killed Johnson to the sniper. It had been agreed that he would make the duck-in-a-noose response at 2:00. "We've crafted a statement we want you to read," Cavanaugh told him. "We want to prevent a killing tonight."

The media got word that a statement would be coming shortly. But 2:00 P.M. came and went. Another hour went by, and then another, and another, with no statement. Noesner began calling FBI colleagues to find out what the holdup was. He was told that Bald was uncomfortable with the statement; that he wanted more input from the profilers; and that he had postponed its delivery. Noesner was afraid somebody else was going to get shot. "Nothing has changed," Cavanaugh said during an impromptu meeting outside Chief Moose's office. "We lost the opportunity to get the message out early, lost the punch on that. We should still put it out."

Just before 7:30 P.M., the first clue about what might be happening backstage appeared on TV. Networks broke into their normal programming to show footage of a bizarre scene. Firefighters were in the backyard of a small twin ranch house in Tacoma, Washington. They were using chain saws to remove a tree stump. The backyard of the house had been divided into lanes with police tape. Investigators with metal detectors were scouring the yard for evidence. Dozens of police were on hand, along with many reporters. News helicopters hovered overhead. The word was that it had something to do with the sniper.

Members of the task force were furious. This was supposed to be done quietly. If Muhammad was the sniper, and if he was watching TV along with the rest of country, he might take off. It was hard, however, to send police to a small house in a quiet neighborhood, search the backyard for hours, and cut down a tree stump without drawing the attention of the media. In the JOC, Forsythe sighed in frustration. Well, he thought, no way the toothpaste was going back into that tube. But Sorukas, the U.S. marshal who had been up all night, was so upset when he saw the scene in Tacoma on TV that he had to leave his office to try to settle down. When he got back, another marshal, Michael Garwood, walked in and said, "Hey, great job."

"What are you talking about?" Sorukas asked.

Garwood explained that the search of the Baltimore police radio calls, done at Sorukas's request, had been a success. Muhammad had been in a car, and the officer had radioed its make, model, and license number. The Baltimore police had checked for any records of the October 8 encounter with Muhammad and hadn't found any. But they then pulled the audiotapes of radio calls around that time. After some initial difficulty, Officer Deborah A. Kirk, of the Information Retrieval Unit, found that James Snyder, the officer who had stopped Muhammad, had mentioned his name as well as a description of his car and its license number. It was a 1990 blue Caprice with New Jersey tags.

"Wait a minute," Sorukas said. New Jersey? That didn't sound right. But when he called Brian Sheppard, the deputy marshal in Baltimore, Sheppard had no doubts. "No, no, it's the right guy." He had a Washington State driver's license. The car was registered to Muhammad and another man in New Jersey.

The license number was now quickly run through the crime computer databases. Numerous hits came back from tag checks going back three weeks, scattered across the Washington region, in stunning proximity to many of the killing sites. Word quickly reached the JOC. Moran from the Marshals Service beckoned Forsythe over. He showed him a piece of paper bearing a license number and a description of a car.

"Is that what I think it is?" Forsythe asked.

It is, Moran said.

"Go put it out," Forsythe said, but Moran hesitated.

Moran wanted Danny Kumor, an ATF agent from Boston, to tell the command center. The marshals had just come up with a vehicle and license number associated with the suspects, Kumor told the room. Now they had pictures, the make and model of the car, and a license number.

Still, they had very little evidence. Even if the task force located the car, police would need warrants to arrest the occupants, and Muhammad had not been linked to any state offenses. But some form of federal charge was possible. The combination of the old domestic order of protection, his possession of a rifle, and the rifle's out-of-state manufacture added up to a federal offense.

The only evidence they had against Malvo were his fingerprints on the catalog and the shopping bag receipt at the Alabama liquor store shooting. Cavanaugh telephoned the Montgomery police chief, John Wilson, who was an old friend. Was Wilson ready to file charges against Malvo in that case? Not yet, Wilson replied. He wanted more evidence than just fingerprints.

Cavanaugh had an idea. If the prints placed Malvo at the scene of the Alabama shooting, and the sniper calls linked the Alabama shooting to the sniper case, then Malvo was a potential sniper witness. He could be detained on a federal warrant as a "material," or crucial, witness. The warrant was drawn up.

At around 8:30 P.M., Sorukas, in his Virginia office, heard that meetings were under way at the JOC to discuss whether the New Jersey license plate number should be released. He decided he couldn't wait for those discussions to end. There was not a minute to spare. If the sniper was watching television and saw the scene in Tacoma, he would know the police were on to him. Sorukas needed to alert all police and marshals about the car and the connection it had to the sniper case. If an officer stopped the Caprice for a routine traffic violation and didn't know it was linked to the sniper, there could be a shoot-out because the sniper might assume the officer was after him.

From Sorukas's point of view, he didn't need to check with the command center. At that point, different law enforcement agencies were doing different things. Hitting the streets and finding the bad guys was what the marshals did best. By that hour, the marshals also held the arrest warrant for Malvo. Why wait?

Sorukas called the marshals' emergency operations center and asked them to get the plate and the suspects' names out as soon as possible. At 8:47 P.M., the marshals sent out a nationwide BOLO teletype on Muhammad, Malvo, and the car. It included the car's color, make, model, and license number. "Please hold the car and any occupants," the BOLO said, "and contact the U.S. Marshals Service for further instruction."

———————

As the evening went on and the footage of Holmes's backyard played over and over on television, the media hordes camped outside county police headquarters sensed something was up. Moose was supposed to appear, and then didn't. Demme explained that he was delayed because developments were taking the investigation in a new direction. At first, all the frantic reporters could learn was that the police were interested in two men, one with a military background and some kind of tie to the house in Tacoma. Gradually, more information leaked out.

At around 10:30, task force officials in the JOC, unaware of the marshals' bulletin about two hours earlier, issued a second alert for nationwide broadcast. This one was authorized by Forsythe, Cavanaugh, and the FBI's Stephen Wiley. It described Muhammad,

Malvo, and the Caprice and included the car's license number. It erroneously reported that both suspects were Jamaican. It said they were believed to be "indigent" and staying in shelters or cheap motels.

Reporters monitoring police radio could now hear the bulletins being broadcast. Shortly before 11:00, TV stations began reporting that police interest centered on Muhammad and Malvo, who were in an old Chevy Caprice with New Jersey tag number NDA-21Z. The license number flashed on TV screens across the country. The task force was incensed. Could nothing be kept from the media? They hadn't wanted the license number made public so soon.

At 11:50, Chief Moose finally appeared to announce that an arrest warrant had been issued for Muhammad, also known as John Williams, on a federal firearms charge. While the charge had nothing to do with the sniper shootings, Moose said, Muhammad may have information "material to our investigation." Moose added that Muhammad, who was probably armed, might be with an unnamed juvenile. The chief urged people to call 911 or the FBI tip line if they had any information. Police handed out photos of Muhammad. He added, in "a strong word of caution," that no one should assume from the charge that Muhammad was involved in the sniper shootings.

The second part of his message was, at last, Gary Noesner's long-awaited reply to the sniper's letter.

"You have indicated that you want us to do and say certain things. You asked us to say, 'We have caught the sniper like a duck in a noose.' We understand that hearing us say this is important to you. However, we want you to know how difficult it has been to understand what you want because you have chosen to use only notes, indirect messages, and calls to other jurisdictions." Moose urged the sniper to call again, or write, so he could be given a toll-free number. The chief gave a post office box number. "Our word is our bond," he concluded, echoing the sniper's phrase. "If we can establish communications with you, we can offer other means of addressing what you have asked for. Let's talk directly. We have an answer for you about your option. We are waiting for you to contact us."

Moose took no questions, though now there were more than ever.

Not all the investigators were sure Muhammad and Malvo were the snipers. Moose had not mentioned Malvo's name, even though marshals had already released it and the county had prepared a wanted poster for both suspects that included their names, pictures, and descriptions. Nor had he given any details about the car, even though the make, model, and license were already being reported across the country on television.

It didn't really make much difference. For the first time, task force investigators had pulled off what Cavanaugh had longed to do—they had gotten a step ahead of the killers. They had come close before, on that rainy morning at the Exxon in Virginia. But this time they had done it. After a twenty-two day rule of chaos and confusion, the ghost of the white van was dead. With it went the invisibility that had shielded Muhammad and Malvo for three weeks and allowed them to move through the mayhem they had created with such brazenness. As if a spell had been broken, they were suddenly visible.

———

Just beyond Frederick, Maryland, on Interstate 70, about a mile northwest of the hamlet of Jerusalem on the east slope of South Mountain, is a secluded rest stop with phones, bathrooms, vending machines, and picnic tables. It was a good place to stay out of sight, and Malvo and Muhammad had indicated the spot on one of their computer maps. When they arrived there Wednesday night, they backed the Caprice into a parking spot where they could watch who came and went. Muhammad lay down in the backseat and went to sleep. Malvo stayed in the front seat. He may have been told to keep a lookout. "I was suppose to cover, but I failed," he would say later. He, too, soon fell asleep.

Whitney Donahue knew about the rest stop, too. A stocky man who maintains supermarket refrigerators for a living, Donahue made repair calls all over the Washington area but lived in Greencastle, Pennsylvania, just across the Maryland line, and he liked a place to break up his trip home.

His last call that night had been at a Shoppers Food Warehouse in Manassas, Virginia, not far from where Dean Meyers was killed. Donahue was well aware of the sniper. He drove a white Ford van—the only one, he thought, that had never been stopped by the police. He was listening to *The Charlie Warren Show* on Washington's WMAL radio, waiting for Chief Moose's press conference to begin, when he heard the news about Muhammad and Malvo. He got out his pen and wrote down their names and the car's license number on the back of his time sheet. Donahue owned a blue Caprice, a 1994. It was a pretty good car, a "200,000-mile car." The chances of actually spotting the car were nil, but it would be interesting to keep a look-out, and it would help keep him awake. He had a good hour or more before he reached his wife and three daughters at home. He listened to Moose and eyeballed cars as he drove.

At about 12:30 A.M., Donahue pulled into the rest area. As he did, his headlights swept over the only two other cars there. One belonged to the overnight rest stop's custodian, Larry Blank, someone he knew. The other, which was backed into its spot, was a dark Chevy Caprice. Donahue looked at the license plate. It was New Jersey, NDA-21Z. Oh, man, Donahue said to himself. His heart started pounding. He pulled into a parking place, front first, directly across from the Caprice.

He dialed 911 and reached the police dispatchers in Washington County, Maryland, on the other side of the mountain. He could hear them, but they couldn't hear him. They hung up. He tried again, and again the connection was bad. They hung up. Donahue got out of his van and went to the rest room, but when he came back he walked to the rear of his vehicle. He pretended to be examining one of the tires but stole some glances at the Caprice. He verified the license number and through the window glare thought he saw two forms inside the car.

He got back in his van and drove to an area of the lot where tractor trailers park. He was now out of sight of the Caprice, but within better cell phone range. He dialed 911 and this time got a good connection. The Washington County dispatch center transferred him to

the Frederick County dispatchers because the rest stop was technically inside Frederick County. It was 1:00 A.M. when Emergency
Communications Specialist II Vicky Martin got Donahue's call.

"Go ahead, sir," Martin said.

Donahue said, "Ah, the 1990 blue Caprice that you-all are looking for—"

"Uh-huh," said Martin.

"—is sitting at the rest area, Route 70 westbound on South
Mountain. . . . I read the tag when I pulled in."

"What's the tag number?"

"Uh, let's see . . . NDA, 21, Z," Donahue replied.

"What state?" Martin asked.

"New Jersey," Donahue replied.

"And it's in the westbound rest area near Myersville?" Martin
asked.

"Yes, ma'am," Donahue said. "It looked like there were two people sitting in the car. . . . I didn't want to look too close, like I was
looking at it."

Donahue thought they sounded a little confused at Frederick dispatch, as if maybe they didn't know yet about Muhammad and Malvo
and the Caprice. Martin asked him if he was sure it was the right car
and if he could check it again. Donahue kept the line open, stuck his
phone in his pocket, and walked back toward the Caprice. He didn't
want to get too close, but he still couldn't see the license plate. Then
he saw another motorist coming from the rest room and beckoned the
man over. He asked the man if he would, as he drove out of the parking area, check the license plate on that Caprice. He told the man the
license number. He asked the man to just toot his horn on the way out
if the number was correct. He didn't explain why.

The man agreed. But when he drove out of the lot, he blasted
his horn. "I was ready to strangle him," Donahue would later joke.
He pulled out his phone and told Martin it was definitely the car.
She told him to go back to his van and sit tight. Although Donahue
was out of sight of the Caprice, he'd see it if it tried to leave. He
would stay on the phone for the next three hours.

At 1:09 A.M., Major Thomas Bowers, commander of criminal enforcement for the Maryland state police, got a call at home telling him the suspect car had been spotted at a rest stop on I-70, in an area of state police responsibility. Bowers was amazed. The information on Muhammad and Malvo had been out there only a few hours, and Bowers had gone to sleep thinking an arrest could take weeks. Now the potential apprehension of the suspects had dropped in their laps. He called the Frederick police barracks and asked who was in the rest stop area. He was told it was Rob Draskovich, a six-foot-five-inch, 240-pound trooper with a shaved head and the nickname "Drak."

"Have Drak ride up by there, routinely just ride through the rest area, and make sure before we go and call out the cavalry," Bowers said. Draskovich was already on the case. He had received the call about the sniper car right after Donahue reached Frederick dispatch. Draskovich had heard Moose's press conference and a news report describing the Caprice on the radio. He telephoned Frederick dispatch to see if there was an official description of the Caprice. He was read the marshals' lookout, and it matched what Donahue reported.

Draskovich headed for the rest area with trooper Chris Paschal and two other state troopers from Hagerstown to back them up. Together, they blocked the rest stop's entrance and exit. They thought about seizing the suspects then and there but they were told to wait. The troopers spoke to two truckers who were just leaving and asked them to further block the exit with their trucks. They also evacuated the rest stop on the opposite side of the interstate.

Meanwhile, Maryland state police lieutenant David Reichenbaugh, a member of the task force, happened to be driving through the area to distribute wanted posters on Malvo and Muhammad. When he radioed in, the duty sergeant told him the suspects had been sighted nearby. Reichenbaugh, the highest-ranking trooper in the area, said, "Send every trooper you've got." When he got to the rest area, Reichenbaugh ordered the interstate shut down in both directions, instructing troopers to tell motorists there had been a bad accident. He stationed German shepherd police dogs on the highway median strip. "If you see anyone on foot," he told the handlers, "let the dogs eat them."

The only escape routes not covered were through the woods. Reichenbaugh had hunted on South Mountain and knew how rugged the terrain was. If the suspects somehow fled there, they couldn't escape and would be "all busted up" when they were caught.

Reichenbaugh knew, through Frederick dispatch, that Donahue was not seeing any movement in the car. If that changed, Richenbaugh was ready to storm the car. But if the suspects were out of the car, he didn't want a gun battle. The troopers' sidearms and flak vests would have been no match for a rifle. Better to wait for the SWAT teams.

At that moment, the three leaders of the overnight SWAT units patrolling Montgomery County in search of the snipers were riding together in an unmarked car near Silver Spring. Jeff Nyce of the county police was driving, and with him were First Sergeant Keith Runk, commander of the Maryland state police SWAT unit, and Charles B. Pierce, a supervisor with the FBI's elite Hostage Rescue Team.

If there was discord elsewhere on the task force, there was none among the SWAT teams. These were the units assigned to seize the snipers or shoot it out with them if it ever came to that. Early on, SWAT members from the county police, the state police, and the FBI had been smoothly blended into teams.

At about 1:30 A.M., Nyce's car, call sign "nine-tango-thirteen," got word that someone had just called in claiming to be the sniper and was dispatched to a pay phone where the call had originated. But just as they arrived there, they were told the Caprice had been located at an interstate rest stop fifty miles away in rural Maryland. They should proceed there immediately. Minutes later, they were contacted again. The task force wanted Nyce, Runk, and Pierce to get to Richard Montgomery High School in Rockville, where a state police helicopter would pick them up to go to Myersville. The trip took sixteen minutes. It was a beautiful night, and as Nyce looked

out the window, he could see the dome lights of police cars streaming northwest toward the rest area.

When the helicopter landed, the three SWAT team leaders were
directed to the parking lot of a nearby McDonald's, where they
were briefed. A nineteen-man SWAT team had been assembled, five
from the county, five from the state police, and nine from the FBI's
Hostage Rescue Team. Nyce, Runk, and Pierce would be part of the
six-man "assault element," which would include the FBI's William T.
McCarthy, Paul T. Jaskot, and Neil Darnell. "We started this thing as
a team," Pierce later told the state and county officers. "We ended it as
a team." Runk, a fourteen-year SWAT veteran, gave them a special
advantage. As a state trooper, he knew the rest stop well. He drew up
a diagram of the layout on a piece of steno pad paper.

It was now almost 3:30 A.M. Pierce figured the two suspects, if
they were in the car, were probably resting, one in the back, one in
the front. The assault team would attack both sides of the car from
behind. Each side would have one "breacher," one "extractor," and
one cover/shooter. Runk and Nyce were the designated shooters.
But they had to be very careful. Nyce put his automatic weapon on
single-shot mode.

The plan was to pull the front-seat occupant out the left-side
door and the backseat occupant out the right-side door. Pierce cautioned the men not to turn on the powerful illumination lights attached to their weapons until the breaching started. Before they left
for the final staging area at the rest stop, they did a dry run on a police car.

Gary Bald of the FBI was the commander on the scene. Bald
had left the JOC earlier that night and headed for the hotel room he
had booked in Rockville, but the room had been given away, so he
began wandering Interstate 270 in search of some place with a va-
cancy. He had finally found one, but as he was walking into his room
he was paged about the Caprice. Bald turned around and got back
onto the highway just as the northbound SWAT teams passed by. He
fell in behind.

Whitney Donahue, meanwhile, was still waiting in his van, where he had been told to stay, with an open line to the county dispatchers. About half an hour into his vigil, he spotted the rest stop night attendant, Larry Blank, walking across the parking lot carrying his handheld police scanner, which was crackling softly with radio traffic.

Donahue rolled down his window. "Hey, buddy, where you going?" he said.

"Man, I hear all kinds of stuff going on this scanner," Blank said. "They're shutting down 70. I'm going up to see what's going on."

"Hold on a second," Donahue said. "I'll tell you what's going on. Get in the truck with me."

In the darkness, the two men listened on Donahue's cell phone and Blank's scanner as police quietly closed the net around the sleeping suspects.

The task force had gone so far as to have the airspace around the rest stop restricted to keep out intruding press helicopters. But it wasn't the press that Reichenbaugh found intrusive. It was the dozens of eager federal agents who kept trying to force their way past his state troopers to get to the scene. Reichenbaugh was already steamed at the feds. Earlier in the evening, he had been trying to telephone emerging details about Muhammad and Malvo to his troopers. But an FBI agent had stopped his call, saying it was premature. "This is ridiculous," Reichenbaugh said. "Which one of you bastards is going to pay for the state trooper's funeral?" Now, on South Mountain, he felt the federales were on state police turf.

Reichenbaugh telephoned Johnny L. Hughes, the U.S. marshal for the District of Maryland and a retired state trooper. "We've got it under control," Reichenbaugh said. "We don't need any more cops up here unless they're in uniform and I know who they are." Hughes issued a radio order instructing arriving federal agents to hold their positions and not approach.

But key task force members were let through: Montgomery County commander Drew Tracy; Major Bowers of the state police, who had raced the eighty miles from Baltimore in his silver command car. Joe Riehl of the ATF would be there later; Forsythe and Raum of the county police were on the way in Raum's car. Forsythe badly wanted to get to the rest area before the assault so the county was represented. He wanted county crime scene techs summoned, and he wanted his sergeant, Roger Thomson, to be there.

After calling Forsythe and Raum from the command center, Thomson had contacted two Montgomery detectives at police headquarters and told them to leave one at a time, one minute apart, and meet him at a local gas station. He did not want to alert the reporters still camped outside. At the gas station, Thomson told them what was going on and said they should head for Myersville in their unmarked cars. Remember, he said, "no lights and sirens until after we get out of Montgomery County."

They passed a TV news truck on the way.

Raum believed these had to be the right guys; Forsythe wasn't sure. Boy, he thought, I'd really like to find their weapon. After three weeks of false alarms, he would not let himself get excited. If there was a God, they would be the right ones, he told Raum. "You and I both know there is a God," Raum said, "so this has to be the right guys." Forsythe hoped the takedown would be "clean." He didn't want to lose a shot at talking to them.

When they arrived at the rest stop it was quiet except for the rumbling of the tractor-trailer engines. Standing there in his trench coat, Forsythe had the strange sensation that the focus of the world was on this secluded spot.

———

After their practice run, Nyce, Runk, Pierce, and the others were driven in Maryland state police cars to the entrance of the rest stop. Keeping low and near the trees lining the driveway, Runk crept up until he could see the Caprice in the bright lights of the rest stop. He came back and Pierce joined him for a look. Everything was still quiet.

Sniper teams were assigned to the woods to cover the entire area in case the suspects had any friends. When the snipers and perimeter teams were in place, the assault group entered the woods and made its way toward the car. Runk thought either Malvo or Muhammad must surely be awake and keeping watch, ready to give the alarm. Nyce, the other cover man, tried over and over to visualize the details of what he would do.

The team halted near two big oak trees just at the edge of the woods, about twenty yards from the car. The men were helmeted and heavily armed. They wore gray gloves and black uniforms. Here the woods thinned. Beyond, there was no cover. It would take only a few seconds to rush the car. The worst case would be if the vehicle went "mobile." The keys would probably be in the ignition. But they guessed it would take the suspects four seconds to react, turn the key, start the car, put it in gear, and get going. The team felt it could be on the suspects in three and a half seconds. But they still couldn't see through the tinted windows and weren't 100 percent sure the suspects were even in the car. There was a good possibility they had already been spooked by the media reports and just ditched the car here.

Pierce held up three fingers and silently counted down: three, two, one. The six men rushed the car, smashing the windows and lighting up the car with the bright lights on their automatic weapons. Pierce found the front door locked, reached in, and opened it.

FBI! Police! Hands up!

Malvo was asleep, lying on his right side and facing the rear of the car, his head by the steering wheel. Jaskot pulled him out the front door. Someone asked him his name, but Malvo refused to reply.

Inside the now brightly illuminated car, the team could see Muhammad sit up and raise his hands. McCarthy and Darnell got him out. Nyce and an FBI man now covered the trunk with their weapons, while Runk got the car keys, which were in the ignition. The men didn't know what might be inside. It could be a bomb or another person. Runk opened it carefully. "Clear!" yelled a SWAT team member.

The assault was over. It had lasted about thirty seconds. Muhammad and Malvo were handcuffed. Nyce noticed that despite the cool night air, Malvo was sweating heavily and that his hair was filled with shards of broken glass that sparkled in the lights from the parking lot. Nyce also noticed a small lateral oblong hole cut in the car's trunk just above the license plate.

The SWAT team turned Muhammad and Malvo over to the state police. Looking at the disheveled and defeated-looking suspects in handcuffs, A. J. McAndrew, a state police captain who had supervised the analysis of all the tips the task force received, couldn't help but feel surprise. He had expected the sniper to be someone tough and aggressive.

Draskovich took Muhammad, Paschal took Malvo. Both suspects were filthy. Draskovich thought they looked totally unremarkable, "just street thugs." Muhammad looked terrified. He was shaking so badly when Draskovich replaced his flexible handcuffs with metal ones that Draskovich had to hold him still. Once he'd gotten them on, Draskovich strip-searched Muhammad to check for weapons.

Forsythe thought the two looked beaten, resigned. Bowers was struck by how short they were. Muhammad, sitting with his hands cuffed behind his back, didn't look like much, Bowers thought. Malvo, similarly cuffed and only five feet five inches tall, looked like a kid.

The car was filled with trash and dirty clothes, and it was clear from the debris and the way they smelled that Muhammad and Malvo had been living in it. "Son, if you had got that ten million, I sure hope you would have bought some soap," Reichenbaugh heard a state trooper tell Malvo.

Whitney Donahue was finally released from his white van and told he could go home. Major Bowers thanked him. "Good eye," Bowers said. "You don't realize what you've done." But Donahue had an inkling: A repairman in a white van had found the snipers. He arrived home at about 5:30, went into his house, and woke up his wife, Teresa, irritating her no end.

"I have something I want to talk to you about," he told her.

His wife grumbled: "This better be good."

12

Virginia Justice

As Muhammad and Malvo sat handcuffed at the rest stop, the first question was who should take custody of them. They had been captured by the FBI, the Maryland state police, and the Montgomery County police. They were being arrested on federal warrants. And they were in a jurisdiction patrolled by the state police, who had been first on the scene. Bowers already had started arranging their shipment to the state police barracks in Frederick, which was standard procedure. Bowers thought they could be taken there while things were sorted out, but asked Forsythe what he thought.

"I'd just as soon we take them back to Montgomery County," Forsythe said. "We'd like to interview these guys, if they're amenable to it." He had a detailed interview plan in place, with designated interrogators, and an out-of-the way county family services facility where the questioning could be conducted. There were audio and video facilities to document any statements that might be made. Best of all, the media didn't know where it was.

Bowers said he had no problem with the suspects going to Montgomery County. Neither did Gary Bald of the FBI. He was aware of the interview plan, liked it, and thought it would be pointless to take the suspects elsewhere. The feeling was that it was Montgomery County's case and, for now, the suspects could go there. Bowers called for two olive-drab-and-black Maryland state police cruisers. Malvo was placed in one, Muhammad in the other. Each was joined by a state trooper and two FBI men. Malvo slept during the trip; Muhammad was awake and alert but said nothing.

The Caprice, meanwhile, its windows broken and doors still ajar, sat like an open treasure chest that the police were forbidden to touch. They were allowed a cursory check but needed a search warrant to go over it thoroughly. At 4:41 A.M., Montgomery County forensics evidence specialist McGill, who had handled the Johnson sniper note, arrived at the rest stop. Again there was a jurisdictional problem. The FBI and ATF also had crime scene technicians present. But after conferring, they agreed that McGill would take the lead in examining the Caprice for evidence. There was still no warrant to search the car, so McGill started taking photographs. Meanwhile, the paperwork requesting a warrant was drawn up, and at 5:55 A.M., the request was approved by Jillyn K. Schulze, chief magistrate judge for the U.S. District Court in Maryland.

Two and a half hours later, McGill and an ATF ballistics expert, Tim Curtis, began working their way into the car. By now, it was dawn. Riehl and Thomson stood by. In the parking lot near the driver's-side door, where Malvo had been pulled out, McGill noted a pair of gray-and-black mittens, a quarter, and a pair of Perry Ellis blue jeans with a belt. At 8:53 A.M., near the left rear door, he logged paper towels, a CD cleaner, and a green military duffel bag with a padlock. Inside were assorted items, including vitamins. Muhammad's black wallet was found on the hood of the car. During the takedown, the SWAT team had found it on the front seat and removed it to confirm his identity. The wallet contained a phone card, Muhammad's Washington State driver's license, three fake ID cards, and $32 in Canadian money.

Then they started searching the car. It had 156,311 miles on the odometer. Police would later learn the reading had been 146,975 when Muhammad bought the car in September. He had put 9,336 miles on it in forty-four days.

They still weren't sure they had the killers. "God, I hope this is them," said Thomson. What would prove it was finding the gun.

They'd already found a .223 bullet on the ground in the parking lot. If the two were the snipers, and if they hadn't ditched the rifle, the weapon should be somewhere in the vehicle. Charles Pierce, the FBI SWAT leader, noticed that it looked as if someone had tampered with the backseat, and when the technicians examined it they discovered that the vertical seat-back cushion had been altered so that it was hinged at the top.

After swinging the seat up, they found what they were looking for. Neatly held in place with a bungee cord was the Bushmaster rifle, the bipod folded under its barrel. Before anyone could touch it, pictures had to be taken. Then Curtis put on a pair of gloves, reached into the car, and undid the bungee. The rifle still had an ammo clip in its magazine well, so he released the magazine and it dropped to the floor of the car. There was also a live round in the firing chamber. Curtis cleared the rifle, and the bullet also fell to the floor. It was a .223 Remington.

Curtis took the rifle out of the car. Everybody knew what they had now: a gun like the one they had figured the sniper was using; a gun that was loaded, that could be test-fired and examined for fingerprints. It was the best piece of evidence imaginable, and it seemed like a miracle to have found it. Thomson immediately paged Forsythe, who had already returned to the JOC.

We got a rifle, he said.

Forsythe could feel the weight of three weeks of anxiety begin to lift from his shoulders. He'd felt the same way when the doctors told him the difficult delivery of his first child had gone fine and that his wife, Marcia, and baby were well. Now, he looked around for Jim Cavanaugh to share the good news. "Go ahead and let everybody know," Cavanaugh told him, pointing to the podium in the front of the room.

"Everybody, can I have your attention for a couple minutes," Forsythe said. "Got an announcement to make. I just got a call from somebody at the scene. They've recovered an automatic weapon."

An ATF agent whispered: "It's not an automatic. It's semiautomatic."

"A semiautomatic weapon," Forsythe added.

Everybody cheered.

————

Back at the rest stop, it was decided that further searching of the car ought to be conducted at an indoor county police facility. David Copperthite, the assistant U.S. attorney who was at the command center, said he wanted the Caprice searched properly, in a controlled environment. The question was how to move it. The vehicle was still loaded with potential evidence. It would later yield a set of walkie-talkies, a tape recorder, a global positioning device, thumbtacks, Zip-loc bags, an earplug, $31.01, and a copy of the *I Ching,* the ancient Confucian text. Bowers, who took responsibility for its transportation, knew that a standard or flatbed tow truck wouldn't work, so he put out the word: He wanted an enclosed trailer, like the ones that hauled race cars. It took a while to find one, and when it finally arrived, the Caprice was pushed inside. Accompanied by a police escort, the trailer headed south to Montgomery County.

Joe Riehl of the ATF was two cars behind. TV crews were stationed by the roadside to film the caravan as it whizzed by. Others filmed as they drove alongside the trailer. Riehl, too, had felt a terrific weight lift from his shoulders when the rifle was found. He called his father in Florida, who was retired from the ATF. "Hey," he said, "something good's happened today. Just pay attention to the TV and keep up." He couldn't say any more. But his father understood.

"I'm really proud of you," he replied. "You guys did a great job."

————

The suspects were put in separate rooms when they arrived in Rockville. Montgomery County detectives Terry Ryan and Jim Drewry were assigned to interview them—Ryan with Malvo and

Drewry with Muhammad, assisted by Jansen Jordan of the FBI—
but they were at a disadvantage because they had little or no information about the snipers' letters and phone calls.

Malvo was placed in a locked room and handcuffed. An ATF
agent was stationed in the hallway outside as a guard. Ryan was in a
nearby conference room with other detectives discussing how to
proceed when they heard a loud crash. They rushed into the hallway
to find the ATF agent fumbling to open the door. Malvo had slipped
one hand out of a cuff and put a chair on top of the table. He had
jumped up and pushed aside one of the tiles and was trying to climb
into the space above the ceiling when the chair fell with a crash.
Ryan and the agent pulled Malvo back, and he bounced off the table
and hit the floor with five investigators on top of him. Malvo was
covered with tile dust.

"Are you okay?" Ryan asked him. "Are you hurt?"

Malvo smiled at Ryan and said, "I'm okay."

Ryan took a photograph of Malvo to show that there were no serious injuries. Malvo had soiled himself, so Ryan went to his car and
brought back some extra clothing that he kept for emergencies. He got
a pair of coveralls and a T-shirt and took them to Malvo and went into
the bathroom with him while Malvo cleaned himself up. Four detectives waited outside just in case. Several hours later a jailer in Baltimore would spot Malvo eyeing the ceiling in his cell and tell him to
forget about it.

Ryan then moved Malvo to a more secure room where the furniture
was bolted to the floor and the door had a window in it. After offering
him something to eat or drink, which he refused, Ryan began the interview. An experienced interrogator, he tried first to establish rapport
with Malvo. Malvo refused to say anything, running his fingers across
his lips as if zipping them closed. But in a bizarre pantomime he responded by using hand signs, nodding his head, and drawing imagi-
nary shapes in the air and on the table. To the detectives watching on
the TV monitor, it seemed as if Malvo was playing a game. For the
most part he seemed cocky, as if he was enjoying himself.

Ryan asked if the shootings were all about money. Malvo rubbed a thumb, index finger, and middle finger together and shook his head. Malvo then placed one hand at about the level of his chest and raised it higher, in a gesture Ryan took to mean it was about more than money. When Ryan asked Malvo if that was so, Malvo nodded.

Ryan told Malvo that a lot of evidence had been found at the scene of the Conrad Johnson murder. Police would later say it included the duffel bag, an earplug, and clear plastic goggles. Ryan told Malvo that it looked as if something had happened that caused him to leave things behind at the scene. Malvo nodded again and his eyes filled with tears. Malvo then grasped the collar of the coveralls and began to rock in his chair.

Ryan told Malvo that police checks—presumably of the Caprice—placed him and Muhammad in the area on October 2 and 3. Malvo nodded yes. Ryan then asked Malvo if he was a Muslim and followed the teachings of the Koran. Malvo struck his chest and nodded yes. He appeared wary of Ryan, and several times he made hand gestures imitating a noose around his neck.

At 10:15 A.M., in an adjacent room, Drewry and Jordan began a conversation with Muhammad. Muhammad started by giving the investigators a bogus birth date. He mentioned his oldest son, Travis. He talked at length about his service in the military. He talked about Mildred and blamed his business and marital problems on an affair he said she once had.

He said he had moved the children to Antigua, which was true, and had an oceanfront condo, which was not. His account of meeting Malvo and bringing him to live with him and his children in Bellingham was mostly true, and he described wandering the country with him by visiting family and friends and looking for his children. He called Malvo his "son." He claimed they spent a month in California, a month in Texas, and a month in Arizona, where they visited his sister in Tucson. They also stopped to see Muhammad's family in Baton Rouge, then took a bus to New Jersey, where he said he bought the car for $800, $550 more than he really paid. Malvo, he said, had found the rifle in a dumpster in Baltimore the day before they were arrested and knew nothing about firearms. Neither of them had ever fired the rifle. When the detectives started steering toward the precise details of the case, Muhammad asked for a lawyer. It was about 1:00 P.M.

————

Forsythe had gone back to police headquarters that morning. He had slept no more than an hour in the past two days and decided to take a break. He needed a shave and some clean clothes. He would be back later. He told Moose he was going home for a nap and on the way stopped at the elementary school where his wife was a teacher's aide. For weeks, he had hardly told her anything about the case, and she had understood. Now he felt he could at least put her mind at ease. She looked surprised when he turned up at the door of her classroom. When she went out to meet him in the hallway, he hugged her.

"We got them," he whispered in her ear. "You just can't go around telling everybody."

Forsythe telephoned his parents when he got home. They had just moved back to Maryland from North Carolina and had been following the case on TV. They often joked that they always saw the chief but never Barney. He never told his parents about his cases, but this time he felt he owed it to them. Both had been ailing lately, especially his father. Forsythe would not learn for several more weeks that his father was terminally ill with cancer. He told them to keep it quiet, and they said they were proud of him.

As it gradually became known that the suspects were in custody, the entire region seemed to relax. The sniper tarps came down from gas stations. School lockdowns were ended, children were allowed to play outdoors, and drivers of white vans celebrated. Halloween and the fall elections could go forward as planned. You could take a walk again and not have to worry.

In the command center, a buzz went around the room when the Caprice arrived at the police garage. Some of the ATF people asked Cavanaugh if he wanted to come along and take a look. "What is it, a '90 Caprice?" said Cavanaugh, who fixed cars for a hobby. "I've seen plenty of them."

When they came back, Cavanaugh thought they seemed disappointed. "What did it look like?" he asked. A '90 Caprice, someone answered.

But as the morning went on, Thomas M. DiBiagio, the U.S. attorney for Maryland, began to worry. DiBiagio felt that Muhammad and Malvo were technically not supposed to be in Montgomery County. They were supposed to be in jail outside Baltimore. The task force had asked for federal arrest warrants. Federal officials had procured them. When the arrests were made with those warrants, DiBiagio expected Malvo and Muhammad to be taken to the FBI lockup in Woodlawn, Maryland. But at 8:00 A.M., Copperthite, his chief deputy, who had been on duty all night, called and reported that the suspects were in Montgomery County.

Why? DiBiagio wanted to know. There were federal charges against Muhammad and Malvo, and they were supposed to be in Baltimore before a federal judge in a few hours. Copperthite said Bald had approved the transfer and that he hadn't been consulted.

"David," DiBiagio said, "did you tell anybody about the initial appearance?" Copperthite said he had, but that he had gotten the cold shoulder at the county facility where the suspects were being held. He had been shuttled from room to room, well away from the deliberations about the suspects.

Copperthite said he thought the county was afraid he was going to seize the suspects and take them to Baltimore, which is exactly what he wanted done. Frustrated and angry, Copperthite went back to Baltimore to prepare for the court appearance.

The sniper investigation had been a career case for most of the law enforcement officers, and it promised to be the same for the prosecutors who tried Malvo and Muhammad. DiBiagio's office wanted the case, but it would have to compete to get it. Not only did a rival U.S. Attorney's Office—in Alexandria, Virginia—want it, so did Doug Gansler in Montgomery County, as well as prosecutors in all the Virginia counties where shootings had occurred.

Who prosecuted the crimes depended on whether the charges were state or federal, and implicit in any decision was the question of the death penalty, which essentially boiled down to where Muhammad and Malvo were most likely to be executed if they were convicted.

No federal murder charge existed. The so-called Hobbs Act, used in extortion cases, did have provisions for the death penalty, and the $10 million demand was extortion. But Malvo, as a juvenile, could not be executed under federal law.

The state of Maryland could file murder charges. But juveniles there couldn't be executed under Maryland law, either. In addition, Maryland currently had a moratorium on carrying out death sentences. Juveniles could be executed in Virginia, however, and the state had a reputation for vigorous use of the death penalty.

It was a complex and slightly unseemly debate. The first phase would now be played out in a struggle between state and federal prosecutors in Maryland.

Gansler, his top deputies, Katherine Winfree and John McCarthy, and some key federal agents involved in the case believed strongly that Muhammad and Malvo should stay in Montgomery County for trial. Six of the ten sniper murders had been committed there. A seventh victim, Dean Meyers, had been killed in Virginia but had lived in the county. The first murder was there as well as the last. Montgomery County was where the task force was headquartered and where the citizens had been terrorized the longest.

Gansler had grown up in the county, the son of a Defense Department official. An All-American lacrosse player at Yale and a graduate of the University of Virginia Law School, he had been a federal prosecutor in Washington, D.C., before he was elected the county state's attorney in 1998. At thirty-nine, he was loquacious, approachable, and media savvy, but he could also be blunt and opinionated.

Gansler believed the application of the Hobbs Act would be absurd. Plus, Montgomery County, for the moment, had physical custody of the suspects. "These guys aren't going anywhere," one county detective proclaimed. They were going to be charged with six counts of murder in Rockville.

Around 1:00 P.M., Gansler telephoned DiBiagio from the family services complex. He asked DiBiagio to dismiss the federal charge and suggested he would then file state murder charges. DiBiagio refused. "I'm not making that call," he said. "That decision is going to be made in Washington at the Department of Justice." He would later explain that he believed he would have looked foolish if he had called Attorney General John Ashcroft and said he had dropped his charges in deference to Gansler.

In Rockville, Gansler and his deputies, Winfree and McCarthy, were listening on a speakerphone. They heard DiBiagio invoking the White House. Winfree and Gansler were outraged. Screw them, Winfree said after the call ended. "We don't work for them. They're trying to throw their big fat federal asses around." This was a state murder case, plain and simple. This federal stuff was "bullshit," said Winfree, who once worked at the Justice Department and was still known and respected there.

The three prosecutors then put in a phone call to Moose. They told him that Nick DeCarlo had the state charges ready, but that DiBiagio wouldn't dismiss the federal charges. Moose was grateful for the federal cooperation. Winfree and Gansler would recall that Moose got angry and said he didn't want to get involved in a fight over the issue. He apparently had no problem with the suspects going to Baltimore and sorting it all out later.

DiBiagio was also angry. At noon he had telephoned Bald, whom he blamed for the suspects' being taken to Rockville.

"I need an initial appearance in Baltimore today," DiBiagio said. "They were arrested at three A.M. They will have been in custody twelve hours at three P.M."

Bald told him the two were being interviewed at that moment and he didn't want to interrupt.

"I order you to immediately bring the two defendants for their initial appearance," DiBiagio said.

"Tom," Bald repeated, "they're in the middle of being inter-viewed. I'm not going to stop it."

DiBiagio said the law called for both suspects, especially the juvenile, to be brought before a judge without delay. Otherwise there might be legal problems with whatever statements were ob-tained. It took an hour, he pointed out, to get to Baltimore from Rockville.

Bald believed DiBiagio was exaggerating. He was determined, in the interest of the investigation, not to disrupt the questioning.

"Tom," he said, "I ain't doing it."

The conversation ended in a stalemate. By midafternoon, Malvo and Muhammad were ready to be taken to Baltimore anyway. Malvo wasn't talking, and Muhammad had stopped and asked for a lawyer.

They were transported separately. McCarthy, the county prose-cutor, was a few steps behind Muhammad as he was led from the complex to the black vans lined up in a U-shaped driveway outside. He was guarded by police in riot gear. The windows of the sur-rounding three-story office buildings were jammed with observers. As Muhammad was placed in a van, the bystanders began pounding on the windows and cheering on the police.

The suspects arrived in Baltimore about 5:00 P.M. Copperthite had scrambled to make the arrangements for the hearing and would handle the first formal appearance of the sniper suspects in court. The Garmatz Federal Courthouse in downtown Baltimore was sur-rounded by Baltimore police officers in SWAT gear when the sus-pects arrived with a motorcycle escort.

Malvo appeared first. Because he was a juvenile, his hearing was held in a courtroom where the public was kept out, the windows cov-ered, and the doors locked. Malvo, in a green jumpsuit and white T-shirt, refused to identify himself, shaking his head when Judge James K. Bredar asked his name. Copperthite identified him for the judge and said that while no parent was present, he had reached Malvo's mother, Una James, early that morning in Tacoma. Copperthite asked that Malvo be held pending further investigation. The judge agreed.

Muhammad's hearing was open to the public, and the big ceremonial courtroom was jammed with spectators, reporters, and even judges as Muhammad, in handcuffs, entered wearing a short-sleeved green prison jumpsuit and blue prison-issued slippers. Copperthite thought he looked meek.

The hearing was brief. "I know where I'm at, and I know what I'm doing," Muhammad told Magistrate Beth Gesner. He was held without bail on the federal weapons charge.

When the hearing ended, Copperthite was mobbed by reporters seeking copies of the charging document that detailed the accusations against Muhammad. "Back up," he shouted when the reporters pushed him against a table. "Give me a break." He had to be helped by a U.S. marshal.

While jubilation spread across the area, Montgomery County officials assembled the families of the local sniper victims in the police training facility, just as they had on October 3.

Moose, who had not been at the first meeting, was there along with Forsythe, Bald, and Duncan. This time, Forsythe stayed in the background as Moose began by saying he thought he owed the families an apology. He said he regretted that he had not been able to catch the suspects in time to save their loved ones. He said he had failed them.

Moose had expected anger, but instead there was only gratitude that he had finally gotten the killers off the street. One relative of Conrad Johnson went up to Moose afterward and hugged him. That night when he went home, the scene would bring tears to eyes.

While Moose met with the families, Demme, his press aide, was calling key local law enforcement officials to invite them to Moose's office, in anticipation of good news from the ATF ballistics lab. By late afternoon, Bald of the FBI; Bouchard of the ATF; Ramsey of the Washington, D.C., police; Manger of the Fairfax police; Deane of the Prince William police; Colonel Dave Mitchell, head of the

Maryland state police; and others had all assembled in Moose's second-floor office.

The rifle was being analyzed in the ATF laboratory down the
road from police headquarters. The ATF's chief ballistics examiner,
Walter Dandridge, test-fired the weapon four times into a ten-foot-
long water tank, then retrieved the spent bullets. Under a microscope, he carefully measured the markings left on the test bullets and
checked them against the markings on bullets taken from the victims. He did the same with the ejected shell casings, comparing the
test casings against those recovered at the shooting scenes. When
Dandridge finished, he gave the results to Riehl, who hurried to police headquarters and Moose's office with the news.

County Executive Doug Duncan heard cheers inside the office.
The bullets test-fired from the Bushmaster matched bullets in
eleven of the fourteen shootings. Dandridge had concluded that the
rifle had fired the bullets in the cases of Walekar, Ramos, Rivera,
Charlot, Seawell, Brown, Meyers, Bridges, Franklin, Hopper, and
Johnson. Only in the cases of Martin, Buchanan, and the first
Michaels store shooting could no match be conclusively made. It
was tremendous evidence. The vaunted tree stump faded in significance. The chiefs poured out of Moose's office. Duncan and Moose
embraced. "It's over," the chief said.

At 8:00 p.m., Moose, Bald, Bouchard, and a task force entourage
emerged for a celebratory news conference. There was some jostling
for position in the tent where the officials were gathered. The local
congresswoman, Connie Morella, locked in a tight race for reelec-
tion, zipped to the front.

After a moment of silence for a Virginia state trooper, Mark
Cosslett, killed the day before in a traffic accident while responding
to a suspected sniper call, Moose introduced the assembled chiefs.
Bald stepped forward and described the arrest. Bouchard discussed
the ballistics and said the Bushmaster had been found to be "the
murder weapon."

After Duncan read the names of the sniper victims, Moose declared: "We will never forget. We'll never know their pain, and we only wish we could have stopped this to reduce the number of victims."

Then he said, "We're going to let a lot of the members of the task force, the people you see here, we're going to let them go home, hug their children, hug their spouses, and just think about the fact that we continue to live in the greatest nation. So thank you all."

There was applause as the group filed back into headquarters. Children in the crowd held THANK YOU balloons. Cards, food, and flowers were already arriving at police headquarters from grateful citizens.

Forsythe, physically and emotionally spent, had already gone home. He had put on his old trench coat and walked from the command center across the parking lot to headquarters. He wanted a brief word with the chief to say that it had been a pleasure and that he thought Moose had done a great job. But headquarters was mobbed with big shots. Forsythe couldn't get near Moose. And most people didn't pay Forsythe much mind.

He went downstairs to his office and said he was leaving for the night. He'd be back the next day at 6:00 A.M. He hadn't done any press conferences so far, and he wasn't going to hang around for this one. Hell, he thought, I can watch the press conference and be home with the family. He walked to his green Dodge and headed north on the interstate. He tuned in his favorite smooth jazz station on the radio. At home he and his wife, Marcia, settled into the couch in their family room to watch the conference on TV. When it came on, and all the VIPs were jammed before the microphones, his wife said to him, "You should have been there."

"Sweetheart," he replied, "that was for the chiefs. There was no room for a captain."

In the JOC across the parking lot from headquarters, the rest of the task force also watched the press conference on TV. For many, it was anticlimactic. The discovery of the rifle in the car had sealed it for them. Cavanaugh and others were itching to go have a beer. Someone said President Bush had tried to call from Air Force One but couldn't get through. Then White House chief of staff Andrew Card did get through to the FBI's Kevin Lewis.

"This is Kevin Lewis of the FBI," Lewis said.

"How you doin', Kevin?" Card said. "I got the president right here."

"I'll get Chief Moose," Lewis said. But Moose was across the parking lot at headquarters and Lewis told Card he would have to call him back.

When Moose arrived, the room suddenly became quiet, and a number of people stood up. Cops didn't normally hear from the president of the United States, and some of the task force members quickly called home and held their cell phones in the air to catch the president's words on the speakerphone. As Bush thanked them for lifting the "shadow of fear," many of the investigators were in tears.

Afterward, Moose signed some autographs and thanked the members of the task force. Just when he seemed done, he joked, "I'm going to tell my wife she can pump her own damn gas."

He started to walk way from the podium, paused, and came back. "And don't you tell her I said that."

The room dissolved in laughter.

The next day, when everyone was back at work, Cavanaugh and Forsythe were standing outside the chief's headquarters office and Moose came out to greet them. Cavanaugh reminded Moose that the case had been the world's biggest at the moment.

"You ought to give your chief of detectives a gold star for solving the case," Cavanaugh said. The suggestion, which would mean promoting Forsythe to assistant chief, would be a good gesture before Forsythe retired, Cavanaugh thought.

Forsythe laughed appreciatively. "I like your style."

Moose smiled. He and Forsythe knew that competition for the rank was keen and a star was awarded only upon approval of the county council. Nobody got it for doing one big case.

Forsythe would not get his star.

That night he joined Cavanaugh, Bouchard, some visiting Dutch police officers, and other ATF officials at the local Italian restaurant that had become a task force hangout. Before dinner, Cavanaugh raised his glass and offered a toast to the sniper victims. Afterward there was an awkward silence until Cavanaugh proposed another toast: "To Captain Barney Forsythe, chief of detectives of the Montgomery County police, a world-class police force, for solving the case." He then recited the old Irish blessing that ends, "May you be in heaven an hour before the devil knows you're dead," adding with a laugh that an hour was plenty of time to tip off the devil.

Forsythe then raised his glass. "To good cops," he said.

After dinner broke up, Cavanaugh lingered at the bar with some friends and then returned to his hotel. The next morning he had a flight back to Nashville, where other cases were waiting. The Atlanta Olympics bombing suspect, Eric Rudolph, was still on the loose. Cavanaugh hadn't been home in weeks. The washing machine was broken. An upstairs bathroom sink was clogged. The gutters were filled with leaves. His wife's car was on the blink. There were squirrels in the attic.

But Cavanaugh was still thinking about the sniper victims, who were, in a way, like his four dead agents at Waco. It was terrible, he thought, that investigative victory always seemed to come with personal tragedy. A lot of police work was like that. Life sort of was, too.

Gansler had scheduled a meeting that day with DiBiagio to discuss where and how the two suspects would be tried. DiBiagio had planned to attend but was summoned instead to a meeting on the same issue at the Justice Department. The meeting was held in the elegant conference room outside the office of Deputy Attorney General Larry D. Thompson. It included DiBiagio; Thompson; Paul McNulty, the U.S. attorney for the Eastern District of Virginia; Roscoe Howard, the U.S. attorney for the District of Columbia; and David Ayres, chief of staff to Attorney General John Ashcroft, who was out of the country. The group discussed the merits of federal prosecution in Virginia and Maryland, as well as state versus federal prosecution. DiBiagio argued the case for a federal trial in Mary-land; McNulty argued for a federal trial in Virginia. The consensus was that a federal prosecution would have more advantages than a state prosecution.

Thompson urged DiBiagio to reach out to Gansler and suggest a prosecution partnership. DiBiagio, who badly wanted the case for his office, assumed from Thompson's request that the case was probably coming his way.

DiBiagio called Gansler from the train station before he headed back to the office. Gansler asked if any decisions had been made on the case. DiBiagio said no and then raised the issue of a partnership prosecution. Gansler said he planned to file state murder charges the next day. DiBiagio asked him to hold off. He hoped to announce state and new federal charges together. But Gansler said he wasn't going to wait because people in Montgomery County wanted mur-der charges filed.

After hanging up, Gansler held a press conference outside the county courthouse in Rockville to announce that county police would shortly be getting a murder warrant against Muhammad and Malvo for the six homicides in Montgomery County. Gansler said he would seek the death penalty for Muhammad and that Malvo would be charged as an adult, though as a juvenile he would not be eligible for the death penalty.

Gansler said that as "the community most affected and most im-pacted by the sniper shootings," it ought to be Montgomery County that filed the first charges against the two suspects. He acknowl-edged that federal charges would preempt state charges and that federal prosecutors held "the trump card" because the suspects were in federal custody. But he expressed doubt about the grounds of a federal case. He said he believed murder was a local crime. "But we will be supportive of the decision that they make ultimately."

———

At a Baptist church in Landover, Maryland, thousands of people gathered Saturday, October 26, for the tenth and last funeral for a victim of the shootings. Duncan had been at almost all of them, but this one, for Conrad Johnson, was the most emotional. His face grew red and he began to cry as he addressed the congregation.

"When I met the Johnson family at the hospital, they said, 'Catch him,' " Duncan said. "Here we are today. I'm finally able to say this: 'We caught him.' "

The congregation stood and burst into applause.

"We caught them for you," Duncan shouted, motioning toward the congregation. "We caught them for Conrad, so they will never, ever be able to do this again!"

Gansler's press conference had further irritated DiBiagio, who was now convinced Gansler was "screwing" it for any Maryland prosecution. The Justice Department was upset, too. Thompson would later say that after all the joint effort in the sniper case, he was "disappointed" with Gansler's announcement. Anonymous federal sources were quoted in the newspapers as saying Gansler broke an agreement to hold off on his charges and that he was "exploiting" a tragedy for political purposes.

In appearances on the TV talk shows that Sunday, Gansler heatedly denied there had been any agreement. "I would love to know what they're talking about and with whom such an agreement would have been made," he said on *Meet the Press.* He called the political accusation "disingenuous." Gansler said he believed the federal government would, in the end, "do the right thing" and turn the case over to the states for prosecution.

But that Monday, October 28, Thompson's office telephoned DiBiagio and told him he would be getting the Muhammad case. "You're doing it, and you're doing it by yourself," DiBiagio would recall being told. Malvo's case would likely be going to state court in Virginia.

DiBiagio and his prosecutors went to work. The next day, the Justice Department filed twenty federal charges against Muhammad under the Hobbs Act, accusing him of committing murder during an extortion scheme. Seven of the charges carried the potential of the death penalty.

Federal officials said publicly that they still had not decided whether the case would actually be tried in federal court or in a state court in Virginia. They said they would probably not let the case go to state court in Maryland because of the state's reluctant record with the death penalty. "It's important that we have available the most serious penalties in a setting like this," Attorney General Ashcroft said.

Malvo was charged in the same manner in federal court, but the accusations against him were sealed because of his age. Gansler said he hoped the Justice Department might still send the case to Montgomery County.

But Wednesday, the federal prosecution was thrown into turmoil. *The New York Times* reported on its front page that DiBiagio's insistence that the suspects be brought to Baltimore interrupted a conversation between Muhammad and investigators that could have turned into a confession. The paper quoted an unnamed local law enforcement official as saying, "It looked like Muhammad was ready to share everything." The paper quoted unnamed state and federal officials as saying DiBiagio had invoked the White House and the Justice Department to get the suspects moved to Baltimore.

It was a serious accusation. It also sounded to DiBiagio as if it had come right from Gansler, who would later deny being the story's source. DiBiagio vehemently denied the story. He said he had not cited the White House in discussing where Muhammad and Malvo would be held or where charges would be brought. He said there was no indication that Muhammad was giving useful information and he had stopped talking before he was taken to Baltimore.

The *Times* later printed a correction on the story, saying, "The article drew a conclusion unwarranted by the reporting." The reporter who wrote the story, Jayson Blair, was later forced to resign for fabricating stories and plagiarism. But DiBiagio believed he had been "done" in *The New York Times*. He now had "baggage," as he termed it later.

Six days later, a representative from Thompson's office called DiBiagio and told him the Justice Department had thoroughly researched all the options and decided the sniper cases were going to Virginia. He instructed DiBiagio to dismiss his federal criminal complaints. It was the case of a lifetime, and now it was gone. Thompson said later the *Times* story had nothing to do with the decision.

The next morning, Paul Ebert, the commonwealth's attorney for Prince William County, Virginia, got a phone call from Paul McNulty, the U.S. attorney in eastern Virginia. McNulty asked Ebert if he could be at the Justice Department that afternoon for a press conference. The department wanted Muhammad tried in Prince William County for the murder of Dean Meyers. McNulty made a similar call to Robert Horan, the Fairfax prosecutor, and told him Malvo would be tried there for the murder of Linda Franklin. Like Ebert, Horan was surprised, but he thought the arrangement made perfect sense.

The press conference began a little before 4:00 on Thursday, November 6. Ebert and Horan appeared with Ashcroft and were joined by DiBiagio; task force members Bald, Bouchard, and Moose; Montgomery County executive Douglas Duncan; and the police chiefs of Fairfax and Prince William Counties. In Rockville, Gansler, who had not been invited, watched the press conference on TV with his staff. They were consoled by the fact that at least DiBiagio wasn't getting the case.

Ashcroft said the Justice Department had conducted a "deliberative" review of the shootings and had decided that the two Virginia counties would go first. State charges of murder had already been lodged against both suspects, by Fairfax the day before and by Prince William the week before. Both suspects faced the death penalty in Virginia.

"We believe that the first prosecutions should occur in those jurisdictions that provide the best law, the best facts, and the best range of available penalties," Ashcroft said. "Innocent victims . . . have paid the ultimate price. It is appropriate; it is imperative that the ultimate sanction be available for those who have committed these crimes."

Ebert noted Virginia's vigorous use of the death penalty. "The death penalty's reserved for the worst of the worst," he said. "And I think, from the evidence that all of you are aware of over the last month or so, these folks qualify."

Ebert's top two assistant prosecutors were a rugby player and former police detective named Richard A. Conway and James A. Willett, a gourmet cook and triathlete who had himself sent six murderers to death row. Both had children who had been terrified by the sniper saga.

Conway would later try to explain his new role in the sniper case to his eight-year-old son, Matthew. He had told the boy before about how, in other cases he had prosecuted, the "bad guys" could be executed with lethal injections. This time, his son wanted to know about the sniper.

"Will they give him the shot?"

"They might," Conway said. "They might."

In Manassas that day, Willett was watching the Ashcroft press conference on television in the county sheriff's office when the sound of sirens announced that Muhammad's prison motorcade had arrived. TV trucks were already in place and helicopters rumbled overhead. Muhammad was going into the local jail behind the courthouse, which itself then loomed into view. He had never seen anything like it in Manassas.

By that time, Malvo had already arrived at the Fairfax County Courthouse fourteen miles away, where he was met by June Boyle, a Fairfax detective, who took him to her office beside the courthouse and then to an interview room.

Boyle, the lead detective in the Linda Franklin case, was joined by Brad Garrett of the FBI. It was a little after 3:30 P.M. They asked Malvo if he wanted anything to eat. He said he wanted a veggie burger with ketchup. Okay, the investigators said, it was on the way.

Boyle and Garrett told Malvo they wanted to talk to him. Did he get to see his lawyer? he asked. Sure, Boyle said. But they wondered if they could get some background on him first.

Malvo had said nothing in his court appearance in Baltimore, but he was not so reticent with the prison guards. On the day of his arrest he had been taken to the Maryland Correctional Adjustment Center, a so-called supermax prison, where, over the next few days, he bantered with his guards, Corporal Wayne Davis and the shift supervisor, Captain Joseph Stracke.

The two men later testified in court that Malvo had asked what the media was saying about him and laughed about the attacks. He told Davis that most of the shootings had been in Montgomery County because that's where "the rich people" lived. He said he and Muhammad really thought they could extort $10 million and intended to withdraw it from ATMs in increments of $100,000 or $200,000.

Malvo said he hated white people. One reason for the shootings, he said, was that whites had tried to hurt Louis Farrakhan, the leader of the Nation of Islam, to which Muhammad had belonged. He told Stracke that he had often fasted for days before his "killing" missions. "You get more oxygen to the brain," he said. "You stay more alert."

His conversation with Boyle and Garrett was far more extensive. He talked about his life in Jamaica, and Florida, and Washington State. He'd always wanted to come to America, he said, but it was easier to visit Cuba. He talked about his father back in Jamaica, and his mother, and an unnamed person he called his "friend"—almost certainly Muhammad. He said he had found his friend in a search for knowledge. He could feel his friend's "energy" and knew when he was around. "We protect each other from harm," he said. His mother was like that, too. Garrett asked if we have the right to harm others. If they harm your family or things, Malvo replied.

Boyle and Garrett said it sounded as if he wanted to talk about the case but told him he had the right to have a lawyer present. Would he talk without a lawyer? He said he would. They asked him if he was sure. He said he was. After reading Malvo his *Miranda* rights, they asked him to sign a paper waiving his rights to see a lawyer, but he refused. Malvo said he was afraid his signature on the document would be used to incriminate him. The investigators asked whether he would be comfortable just putting an X on the waiver, and that was what he did. Was he still sure he wanted to talk without a lawyer? He was. "If I don't want to answer," he said, "I won't." In all, he had been asked four times if he wanted a lawyer and four times he said no. It was 5:55 P.M.

For the next several hours, Malvo, shifting and yawning, described his odyssey. He talked about the killings and the tactics and strategy. He said he had no friends, only "allies." He explained how they sought to shock and horrify the community, how it was psychological, like terrorism, like battle. You fail; you die. In the end he had failed, he said—"crushed" like Japan after World War II.

He said he didn't really want to talk about all the details of what they had done because then someone else could copy them. But he said the head shots were the best, because then you were "down, dead." He claimed he had never missed a shot. In the car trunk he could curl up like a tire. And the sound of firing the rifle in the car didn't bother him. He was "immune." He lamented what he said was his poor equipment. If he had a steadier barrel "they would have all been head shots." But the Bushmaster was a good rifle. "It will mess you up," he said.

"Does John tell you when to shoot?" the investigators asked.

"The shooter makes the decision," Malvo responded.

While Malvo talked at great length about his own role, he was vague about Muhammad's. He never mentioned him by name but implied that Muhammad was the one who drove; Malvo was the "navigator." He never specifically said that Muhammad had fired the rifle, but Boyle and Garrett pressed him on the question of who determined when to shoot.

"When your friend shot, it was up to him?"

Malvo said yes.

Malvo said the shootings were part of a regimen that included smooth breathing and clear thinking. He meditated, ate one meal a day, took several vitamins, and worked out at the YMCA.

Was it about money? he was asked, and this time he nodded yes. He talked about the missed communications and hinted, without explanation, that the attacks could have stopped after the sixth shooting. After the Johnson attack, he said, he thought the payoff was only a few days away. He talked about the car and the roadblocks, and about how tough, and book-read, and smart he was. He talked about the notes, and the priest, and philosophy and movies. "Watch *The Matrix*," he advised Garrett. It sounded, at times, as if he was proud of the whole thing.

"Does it bother you to shoot people?" he was asked.

"No," he replied. "Ninety-nine percent of the people couldn't do what I did. . . . What we did was unstoppable."

He said he was unaware that the police had been looking for them the night they were arrested. If they had known, he said, they would have disappeared. "You would have hated that," he told the interrogators.

At times a conscience seemed to flicker. Did the slain people have a right to live? Yes, Malvo said. But he had to follow through when he said he would do something. "Let your word be your bond," he said. Were there consequences in life for actions? Yes, Malvo replied, and punishments. Yet he scoffed at his capture. "Kill me, I don't care," he said. "Or torture me. Or if it takes bondage. Nothing bothers me. . . . You can't build a jail strong enough to hold me."

So was all this worth it? the investigators asked him. No, he said. Would he do it again? Yes. "I wouldn't change my life a bit," he said. "If I had it to do over, I'd do the exact same thing."

Garrett asked if he believed in reincarnation. Malvo said he did. What did he think he'd come back as next time? Garrett asked.

A mountain, Malvo replied, condemned to be walked on for five thousand years.

ACKNOWLEDGMENTS

This book would not have been possible without the help and support of our many colleagues at *The Washington Post*. We must first thank Donald E. Graham, chairman of the *Post;* Boisfeuillet Jones Jr., the publisher; Leonard Downie Jr., the executive editor; and Steve Coll, the managing editor, for fostering an atmosphere of freedom, dedication, and creativity in the tradition of Benjamin C. Bradlee and the late Katharine Graham.

We owe our most heartfelt thanks to Jo-Ann Armao, the newspaper's unrivaled assistant managing editor for metropolitan news, who honored us with this assignment and who directed the local staff's superb coverage of the sniper shootings.

Assistant managing editor Bill Hamilton was our teacher, counselor, and advocate during this project. He guided us along an unfamiliar road with extraordinary editorial skill, calm, and reassurance under the pressure of a looming deadline. David Maraniss, Marilyn W. Thompson, Rick Atkinson, Bob Woodward, Elsa Walsh, and Jeff Leen provided invaluable advice and encouragement.

Our incomparable researcher, Julie Tate, deserves special thanks for her wit, patience, perseverance, and reportorial skill, and for saving us from many errors. Thanks also to reporters Marcia Slacum Greene and Serge F. Kovaleski and to city editor Gabriel Escobar, who provided crucial last-minute help. Photo editor Michel E. duCille and researcher Carmen E. Chapin chose the photographs and cartographer Gene Thorp the graphics. Research editor Margot Williams and metro researcher Bobbye Pratt gave us tremendous assistance with research and data management. Josh White, of the paper's Virginia desk, and Stephen Hunter, of the Style section, enthusiastically volunteered their help. Our thanks also to Valerie Strauss, Lena Sun, and the Maryland desk's tireless sniper editor, Paul Duggan, for their friendship and inspiration.

Special thanks and admiration go to Random House vice president and editorial director Jonathan Karp, an exceptional editor, who conceived of this book and helped mold its final form. We are also grateful for the wonderful work of Random House editorial assistant Jonathan Jao, production editor Steve Messina, and copy editor Sona Vogel.

Roger Troup, of the Fairfax, Virginia, Rod and Gun Club, gave us his time and guidance on the subject of firearms. Isaac Fulwood Jr., the retired chief of the Washington, D.C., police department, provided insight and advice about the world of the police. We are also grateful to the scores of people in and out of law enforcement who explained their roles in the sniper case. Several spent long hours with us in person and fielded endless phone calls, saying they wanted to get the story right. At times their recollections were heartbreaking and terrifying. Others whom we cannot name gave us invaluable aid and information. We sincerely thank them.

Finally, and most important, we would like to thank our families for their love and understanding: Bill and Rachael Schultz, Katie Lee, and Emily, Julia, and Sean Ruane.

We are grateful for the support of our parents, Zella Horwitz and the late William Honor Horwitz, and Regina and Eugene Ruane; and to Wendy and Jay Greenwald, Heidi Horwitz, Angie Gully, Kathy Ruane, Frank and Ginger Schultz, Adrian and Marie Lee, Kathi George, Hy Hoffman, Rebeca L. Vasconez, Eugene Suplee, John, Kathy, and Caroline Schultz, Teri Ruch, David Paul,

Matt Seltzer, Roger Zuckerman, Neil Henderson, and our extended families.

We reviewed a variety of newspaper, magazine, and TV coverage of the sniper case, including that of *Time, Newsweek, U.S. News & World Report*, the Baltimore *Sun, The New York Times, The Bellingham Herald*, the Baton Rouge *Advocate, The Seattle Times*, the *Seattle Post-Intelligencer*, the *Richmond Times-Dispatch, The Oregonian*, the *Jamaica Gleaner*, the *Antigua Sun*, the Fort Myers *News-Press*, and the *Chicago Tribune*. Dave Statter of WUSA-TV gave us special help.

But this book was built on a foundation of the matchless journalism of the following reporters, editors, and researchers at *The Washington Post*, who covered the sniper attacks in October 2002:

Nurith C. Aizenman, Michael Amon, Amy Argetsinger, Michael Barbaro, Karlyn Barker, Bob Barnes, Jo Becker, Paul Bernstein, Justin Blum, Michelle Boorstein, William Booth, William Branigin, R. B. Brenner, Donna Britt, Ruben Castaneda, Sewell Chan, David Cho, D'Vera Cohn, Michael H. Cottman, Alice Crites, Christian Davenport, Patricia Davis, Claudia Deane, Jon DeNunzio, Petula Dvorak, Dan Eggen, Tarik El-Bashir, Judith Evans, Karl Evanzz, David A. Fahrenthold, David Fallis, Darryl Fears, Stephen C. Fehr, Manny Fernandez, David Finkel, Marc Fisher, Mary Pat Flaherty, Gilbert M. Gaul, Steven Ginsberg, Maria Glod, Avram Goldstein, Fred Gonzalez, Annie Gowen, Tracy Grant, Ashley Halsey, Hamil R. Harris, Keith Harriston, Christine Haughney, Dana Hedgpeth, Rosalind S. Helderman, Nelson Hernandez, Scott Higham, Alison Howard, Spencer Hsu, Stephen Hunter, Anita Huslin, Tom Jackman, Chris Jenkins, Colleen Jenkins, Darragh Johnson, Erica Johnston, Tamara Jones, Phyllis Jordan, Fredrick Kunkle, Theola Labbe, Lyndsey Layton, Madonna Lebling, Allan Lengel, Carol Leonnig, Susan Levine, Phuong Ly, and Bob Lyford.

Also, Brenna Maloney, Brooke Masters, Jay Mathews, Roland Matifas, Raymond McCaffrey, Phil McCombs, R. H. Melton, Kevin Merida, Eugene L. Meyer, Dana Milbank, Bill Miller, Courtland

Milloy, Lori Montgomery, Carol Morello, Sylvia Moreno, Richard Morin, Matthew Mosk, Ylan Q. Mui, Caryle Murphy, David Nakamura, Evelyn Nieves, Don Podesta, Donald Pohlman, Sue Anne Pressley, Dana Priest, Monte Reel, Tracey Reeves, Alice Reid, Lisa Rein, Thomas Ricks, Elaine Rivera, Bridget Roeber, Manuel Roig-Franzia, Hanna Rosin, Jacqueline L. Salmon, Bob Samsot, Christina A. Samuels, Greg Sandoval, Arthur Santana, Susan Schmidt, Brigid Schulte, Paul Schwartzman, Mike Semel, Liz Seymour, Lucy Shackelford, Ian Shapira, Katherine Shaver, Michael D. Shear, Mary Beth Sheridan, Amy Shipley, Leef Smith, Margaret Smith, David Snyder, Miranda Spivack, Jamie Stockwell, Avis Thomas-Lester, Cheryl Thompson, Bob Thomson, Craig Timberg, Nancy Trejos, Neely Tucker, Scott Vance, Barbara Vobejda, Steve Vogel, Martin Weil, Eric M. Weiss, Mary Lou White, Craig Whitlock, Peter Whoriskey, Debbi Wilgoren, Clarence Williams, Krissah Williams, Vanessa Williams, April Witt, Yolanda Woodlee, and Bruce Wright.

INDEX

ABOUT THE AUTHORS

SARI HORWITZ is an investigative reporter on the metropolitan staff of *The Washington Post*, where she has reported on crime, education, and social services for nineteen years. She has won numerous awards, including two Pulitzer Prizes, the Robert F. Kennedy Grand Prize for reporting on the disadvantaged, and the Investigative Reporters and Editors Medal. She lives in Washington, D.C., with her husband, Bill Schultz, and daughter, Rachael.

MICHAEL E. RUANE is a general assignment reporter on the Maryland desk of *The Washington Post*. He was previously a reporter for *The Philadelphia Inquirer* and served as the Pentagon correspondent in Knight-Ridder's Washington bureau. He was a 1991–92 Nieman Fellow at Harvard University. He lives in Washington, D.C., with his wife, Katie Lee, and children, Emily, Julia, and Sean.

ABOUT THE TYPE

This book was set in Ehrhardt, a typeface based on the original design of Nicholas Kis, a seventeenth-century Hungarian type designer. Ehrhardt was first released in 1937 by the Monotype Corporation of London.